D0208456

page 101 Hist

ST. GREGORY THE GREAT
PASTORAL CARE

REGULA PASTORALIS

Ancient Christian Writers

THE WORKS OF THE FATHERS IN TRANSLATION

EDITED BY

JOHANNES QUASTEN, S. T. D.
Professor of Ancient Church History
and Christian Archaeology

JOSEPH C. PLUMPE, Ph. D.
Professor of Patristic Greek
and Ecclesiastical Latin

The Catholic University of America
Washington, D. C.

No. 11

ST. GREGORY THE GREAT
PASTORAL CARE

TRANSLATED AND ANNOTATED

BY

HENRY DAVIS, S. J.

B. A. London
Professor of Moral and Pastoral Theology
Heythrop College
Chipping Norton, Oxon., England

NEWMAN PRESS

New York, N.Y./Ramsey, N.J.

Cum Licentia Superioris Ordinis:
Eduardus Helsham, S.J.
Praep. Prov. Angliae, Soc. Jesu

Nihil Obstat:
Johannes Quasten, S.T.D.
Censor Deputatus

Imprimatur:
Patricius A. O'Boyle, D.D.
Archiepiscopus Washingtonensis
die 7 Martii 1950

Library of Congress
Catalog Card Number: 78-62459

ISBN: 0-8091-0251-X

PUBLISHED BY PAULIST PRESS
Editorial Office: 1865 Broadway, New York, N.Y. 10023
Business Office: 545 Island Road, Ramsey, N.J. 07446

PRINTED AND BOUND IN THE UNITED STATES OF AMERICA

CONTENTS

ST. GREGORY THE GREAT

PASTORAL CARE

INTRODUCTION

"Who would not read with consolation a book which, if meditated on perseveringly, is a medicine for the soul, and which, by inspiring contempt for the decrepit, fluctuating, and ever changing things of this world, opens the eyes of the mind to the stability of the life eternal! Your book is a school for all virtues." [1] These are the words which Licinianus, bishop of Cartagena, wrote to St. Gregory after he had received and read the treatise which is here presented in English. Since its first translation into English in the ninth century we have continued to call this book *Pastoral Care,* a title which is most probably derived from its opening words: *Pastoralis curae me pondera.* But the author, Gregory the Great, in a letter to Leander of Seville [2] refers to it as *Liber Regulae Pastoralis,* the *Book of Pastoral Rule,* and this title corresponds more precisely to its contents.

On the death of Pope Pelagius II in the year 590, Gregory, abbot of St. Andrew's Monastery at Rome, was acclaimed his successor by the clergy and people of the Eternal City. He sought to decline the office and dignity, and in this he was utterly sincere. His own statements in the matter are too spontaneous and humble to leave any doubt about his deep-rooted disinclination for the honour. He wrote that he "undertook the burden of the dignity with a sick heart," that he was "so stricken with sorrow that he could hardly speak," that "the eyes of his

3

soul were darkened with grief." [3] John, archbishop of Ravenna, chided Gregory for his reluctance in assuming the office to which he was elevated.[4] By way of reply to John's letter, the Pope wrote the present treatise, in which he deals with the great responsibility of the episcopal office and its onerous nature. Thus, the *Pastoral Care* is, according to its purpose, an apology for the author's wish to escape the burdensome office of a bishop. Gregory of Nazianzus who fled after his father had ordained him to the priesthood, composed a similar apology, found among his *Orations* or *Discourses* (2), in which he justifies himself for wishing to shun the priestly office, by describing the responsibility involved in such a dignity. It seems that this work inspired Gregory the Great to write his *Regula Pastoralis*. Further, if we read St. John Chrysostom's work *On the Priesthood*, we see that this classic was written for the same purpose: the author wished to defend himself for his attempt to escape the office of a bishop. All these writings set forth the awesome character and difficulties of the office of the priesthood, and they purpose to show how to fulfil the duties that go with it as they should be fulfilled.

St. Gregory's work consists of four parts. The first part explains the difficulties of the pastoral office and the requirements it places on him who is called to it. The second part sets forth the inner and outer life of the good pastor. The third deals with the manner of teaching the various classes of persons whom the pastor is called upon to rule. The fourth part states briefly how the pastor should be mindful of his own infirmities.

Gregory begins his treatment of the pastoral care by

examining the qualities that are required in a ruler of men, for to rule others is the art of arts. As a qualified physician is needed for grave diseases, so, too, an expert in the guidance of souls is needed for those greater diseases, the diseases of the soul. He, therefore, who seeks the distinction of the office, cannot teach humility to his flock; he is rather a leader to perdition. Those are to be deterred from taking office who do not exhibit in their way of life what they have learned in meditation.

In ruling others the pastor must expect to meet with adversities, but should not shrink from them. He may achieve success, but he must fear it, lest his mind become conceited and proud. In the exercise of his office, the mind of the pastor is distracted and the heart divided, so that he must not be too much taken up with external affairs; otherwise, he forgets whither he is going. He should, therefore, preserve quietude of mind, yet he may not, in an exaggerated desire for that quietude, refuse to come forth from his solitude to be of service to the many. He must follow the example of Christ, who came forth from the bosom of the Father to save us. If he is enjoined to undertake this great burden, he has not genuine humility if he flees from it. It is, indeed, safer to decline the office of preacher, but it is not to be declined if God imposes it.

The pastor, therefore, who takes on the guidance of souls must be one who dies to the concupiscence of the flesh, puts aside worldly prosperity, fears no adversity, desires only what is interior, does not covet the goods of others, dispenses his own lavishly, must be inclined to be merciful, yet not sin by excess. He should have compassion on the weakness of others and grieve for their sins as though they were his own. If he would intercede with God for others, he must himself be pleasing to God. His life must be such that he is able to water the parched hearts of his subjects with the fountains of his teaching.

The second part of the *Pastoral Care* deals with the way of life of the shepherd of souls. He must be pure in thought, that he may cleanse the stains in the hearts of others, for being a vessel of the Lord, he must himself be clean, and in cleanness of heart bring other living vessels to the temple of eternity. To do so, he must meditate unceasingly on the lives of the Saints, and discriminate carefully between good and evil. He must be first in action, and since he must teach what is the highest, he must exhibit the highest perfection. He must be discreet in silence and helpful in speech, for indiscreet speech leads to error, and indiscreet silence leaves in error those who might have been instructed. Nevertheless, in his office of teaching and preaching he must not be excessive in speech, even in saying what is good, for the hearts of hearers are wearied by importunate speaking.

Again, the ruler of souls must be a neighbour to all in his sympathy, but raised above them in contemplation and the desire of things invisible, even as St. Paul, rapt to the third heaven, could compassionate the infirmity of others. Moses also entered into the Tabernacle in his desire to contemplate, and came from it to display his care for the weak. Subjects should reveal to the pastor their secrets, coming to him as a child to its mother's breast, for the comfort of his exhortation and the tears of his prayer.

The pastor must, moreover, be a friend to those who act well, and yet in his righteousness rise up against the vices of sinners. Nature has begotten all men equal, but has placed some above others. But rulers should regard, not the power of their rank, but rather the equality of human estate, and rejoice to be of service, not to be overlords. Yet rulers should be feared by subjects, so that these may fear to sin from at least a human fear, when they are not deterred by the divine judgment. But the ruler must not on this account become proud, for he must seek, not his own glory, but the righteousness of his subjects.

The spiritual ruler should not relinquish all care for what is external in his solicitude for interior things. On the other hand, some rulers are wholly taken up with external occupations and the cares of this life, and know nothing about spiritual matters, to the great harm of their subjects. These mundane things must be attended to by inferiors, while the ruler is engaged in higher matters.

Furthermore, the ruler should not aim at pleasing men, yet should attend to what ought to please them, for one who inordinately desires to be popular is attracting the love of others to himself, rather than to his Master, and to prevent their love for him growing cold, dares not correct their faults. Thus he shows that he loves truth less than the favour of men. Yet rulers must endeavour so to please their subjects as to induce them to love truth, and thus be drawn to love their Creator.

Again, the ruler must be able to distinguish virtue from its counterfeit—thrift from niggardliness, spiritual zeal from anger, generosity from prodigality. Sometimes, it is true, he must use discretion and disregard the faults of certain subjects, letting them see, however, that he is conniving at them; and even if the faults are openly acknowledged, he must sometimes put up with them. On occasion, too, he will rebuke gently, but severely at other times.

Lastly, the ruler of souls must daily ponder on the words of Sacred Writ and assiduously meditate on them.

The third part of the *Pastoral Care* is entitled: "How the ruler should teach and admonish his subjects by his holy life." In this part, by far the longest, Gregory explains at length the methods of teaching various classes of people and how the teacher should suit his words to the hearts of his hearers. The preacher must play on the hearts of his hearers as a harpist plays on the harp, gently or vigorously according to circumstances, but never in such a way as to pluck the strings to breaking point.

In this part of his work Gregory displays a remarkable acquaintance with the virtues and vices of human nature. He deals with nearly forty different classes of people, in such a way as to suggest a vast knowledge of human propensities, which he surely derived from introspection into his own heart and from a wide experience as a man of the world, a monk, a papal nuncio, experience with emperors, kings, generals, soldiers, merchants, the rich and the poor, the ambitious, the lowly, the sorrowful, the depressed, and, certainly not least, with priests and bishops and patriarchs. It is this part of the work which commends it to succeeding generations, and still serves as a source of knowledge, inspiration, and enlightenment to rulers, pastors in high office or low, preachers, and confessors.

The fourth part of the *Pastoral Care* consists of only one chapter. It is entitled: "How the preacher when he has done everything as required, should return to himself, to prevent his life or preaching from making him proud."

The preacher should never give way to pride because of the good he has done, but should recall his own infirmities and the good which he has left undone. Gregory concludes by saying that he has portrayed a fair picture with but ill-success, for he is a wretched painter, and while he has directed others to the shore of perfection, he is himself buffeted by the waves of his sins. He prays that in the shipwreck of this life he may be upheld by the prayers of his friend.

Although the occasion of the *Pastoral Care* was Gregory's reluctance to take the office of a bishop of Rome, there is sufficient evidence to show that the plan of this treatise was in the author's mind earlier, while he was still working on his *Commentary on Job*.[5] It is not unlikely that he composed parts of it while he was still at St. Andrew's Monastery, though it received its final form only after his consecration[6]—that is, early in the year 591—when the letter of John of Ravenna gave the occasion for its publication.

In order to determine what Gregory originally had in mind, one ought to consider the Latin title, *Liber Regulae Pastoralis,* carefully. The word *regula* is particularly important. This word had been used for some time to designate an order of life for a religious society. Thus St. Jerome translated the monastic rule of St. Pachomius under the title *Regula patris nostri Pachomii hominis Dei.* Caesarius of Arles composed a *Regula ad monachos* and a *Regula ad virgines.* The most famous example, however, is the *Regula Sancti Benedicti.*[7] We know how devoted Gregory was to monasticism and how reluctantly he forsook the silence of the monastery for the exacting

duties of the papacy. Fifteen or sixteen years earlier he
had renounced the world and a political career in order
to become a simple monk at St. Andrew's, the monastery
he had established in the palace inherited from his father
Gordianus. It is quite possible that Gregory from the
beginning of his monastic life followed the Rule of St.
Benedict. He must have been acquainted with this celebrated *Regula* even before the Benedictine monks of
Monte Cassino in 581 brought the Rule (the original
manuscript) of their founder from their burnt monastery
to Rome.[8] There is every reason to assume that Gregory
in conceiving the plan for the *Liber Regulae Pastoralis*
intended to provide the secular clergy with a counterpart
to this *Regula*.

At any rate, this is precisely what he did—his *Pastoral
Care* furnished a similar pattern of conduct for the secular
priests as the Rule of St. Benedict did for the monks of
the West. And from the day of its publication its success
was wide-spread. Gregory sent a copy of it to his good
friend Leander, archbishop of Seville, who introduced it
into all the churches of Spain. He also sent copies to
several other bishops and to the Irish monk and missionary, Columban, all of whom received it with great delight.
Moreover, during Gregory's lifetime it was translated into
Greek by Anastasius, patriarch of Antioch, by order of the
emperor Maurice. A son of St. Benedict, Augustine,
brought Gregory's work to England.

The esteem in which the *Pastoral Care* was held by one
of England's great sons is evident from the words which
Alcuin wrote to Eanbald, the archbishop of York, in 796:
"Wherever you go, let the pastoral book of St. Gregory
be your companion. Read and re-read it often, that in it

you may learn to know yourself and your work, that you may have before your eyes how you ought to live and teach. The book is a mirror of the life of a bishop and a medicine for all the wounds inflicted by the Devil's deception." [9] At the close of the ninth century King Alfred the Great, assisted by some of his clergy, translated the *Pastoral Care* into West Saxon. This translation is a most valuable record for the historian of Old English prose.[10] The king wished that every bishop in England be provided with a copy of the translation, and used the *Shepherd's Book*, as he called it, to initiate a reform of clergy and laity.

Even more striking than the role played by the *Pastoral Care* in the reform of King Alfred the Great, is its use in the Carolingian Church and monastic reform, in Carolingian missionary activity, and even in the political theory of the age.[11] In a series of synods held by command of Charlemagne in 813 at Mayence, Rheims, Tours, and Chalon-sur-Saône, the study of the *Pastoral Care* was made obligatory for all his bishops, and the records of all these synods contain frequent references to the *Regula Pastoralis*. As a means of realising the Carolingian ideal of the *Civitas Dei*, Gregory's treatise served the education of priests in the sacred sciences and the guidance of souls, and thus also became a potent force in the spiritual advance of the laity. Somewhat later, as Archbishop Hincmar of Rheims informs us, it became customary to give the *Pastoral Care* together with the Canons of the Church into the hands of bishops at their consecration.[12] In the words of the liturgy which accompanied this ceremony, they were admonished to observe this *Rule* in their life, their teaching, and their pastoral decisions (*in vivendo, docendo, et iudicando)*. As time went on, the influence of this little treatise remained. It is difficult to estimate the contribution it has made to the moulding of the Middle Ages and Europe. Dudden is correct when he states:

Its influence during this period can scarcely be overrated—indeed, it is felt even now in its results. The maxims of Gregory have moulded the Church. They have sensibly shaped the conduct and the policy of the Church's rulers, and, as a modern writer well expressed it, have "made the bishops who made modern nations." The ideal which Gregory upheld was for centuries the ideal of the clergy of the West, and through them the spirit of the great Pope governed the Church, long after his body had been laid to rest beneath the pavement of St. Peter's.[13]

The question arises: What sources did Gregory use in composing this treatise which exerted such influence through the centuries? In the letter addressed to Gregory by Leander, archbishop of Seville, acknowledging receipt of his copy of the *Pastoral Care,* he remarks that he found therein a "palace of all virtues" and "excellent teaching in the tradition of the holy ancient Fathers, Doctors, and Defenders of the Church—Hilary, Ambrose, Augustine, Gregory of Nazianzus." Close examination, however, reveals no evidence that he used any of these authors directly, except his namesake Gregory. As was mentioned above, Gregory of Nazianzus had composed a similar treatise under similar circumstances, which is the second among his *Orations* or *Discourses.* In this work Gregory gives the motives for his flight: his bewilderment at his sudden ordination by his father, his preference for the peace and calm of the monastic life, and his unworthiness. He felt unworthy of the sacerdotal office because he thought himself unqualified to rule and guide the souls of men. The ruler of others must be outstanding in virtue and knowledge. His task of being a spiritual leader is far more difficult than, for instance, that of a physician. He must cure souls, not bodies only; it is not the physical man he cares for, but the inner, hidden man of the heart. It should be but natural, therefore, that a man shrink from accepting ordination to the priesthood.

There are a number of passages in this discourse which show close resemblance in thought to the *Pastoral Care*, and indicate that Gregory made use of it in several instances. First, there is an express acknowledgment in the prologue to Part Three of the *Regula Pastoralis*, where Gregory states: "As long before us Gregory of Nazianzus of revered memory has taught, one and the same exhortation is not suited to all, because they are not all united in common by the same quality of character." The Pope here refers to a passage in his namesake's apology: "As it is not usual to administer the same medicine and food to men's bodies, but a difference is made depending on their condition of health or infirmity, so, too, are souls treated with varying instruction and guidance." The author then follows with an enumeration of the different types of human characters, temperaments, and moods which must be taken into consideration by the physician of souls.

Although this is the only passage in which Gregory the Great directly mentions Gregory of Nazianzus as his source, it is by no means the only resemblance of thought which we find by comparing these two treatises. It seems that Gregory the Great borrowed from his Greek predecessor in at least five more passages.[15] Thus the list of different types of souls given in *Pastoral Care* 3.1 corresponds in great part to the list given by Gregory of Nazianzus in his apology 28-29. If Gregory the Great in 1.1 calls the *regimen animarum* the *ars artium,* we find the same expression in Gregory of Nazianzus (16) who calls it τέχνη τεχνῶν. The comparison of the pastoral office with that of a physician in *Regula Pastoralis* 1.1 and 3.37 has its counterpart in Gregory of Nazianzus' apology 21 ff. Finally, the imagery in the prologue to Part Three of the *Pastoral Care* is also found in Gregory of Nazianzus (39). In both places the attentive minds of the preacher's audience are compared with the strings of a lyre, the preacher acting as the plectrum which, with varied strokes, moves these strings into a harmonious melody. It is evident, therefore, that Gregory the Great used Gregory of Nazianzus' apology as a source when he composed his *Pastoral Care.* The question remains how this was possible, since *Gregory the Great* states that he himself knew no Greek.[16] It is conceivable that he read this treatise in the translation by Rufinus [17] or in some other Latin translation. As for the similar work by John Chrysostom, there is no evident indication of the Roman's dependence on it.

＊　＊　＊

The text used for the present translation is the reprint of the Benedictine edition (Paris 1705) in Migne's *Patrologia Latina* 77 (Paris 1896) 13-128. This same text was reproduced in several special editions of the *Regula,* by Hurter, de Micheletti, and others. Very serviceable is the reprint offered by the Benedictine Ordinary of Newport, Bishop John Cuthbert Hedley, in his *Lex Levitarum, or Preparation for the Cure of Souls* (Westminster 1905) 161-349.

The following modern translations may be noted, the first and last of which have been consulted:

Barmby, J., *The Book of Pastoral Rule and Selected Epistles of St. Gregory the Great* (A Select Library of the Nicene and Post-Nicene Fathers of the Church, Second Series 12, New York-Oxford-London 1895) 1-72.

Boutet, J., *Le "Pastoral" de S. Grégoire le Grand* (Coll. Pax 29, Maredsous 1918).

Bramley, H. R., *St. Gregory on the Pastoral Charge; the Benedictine Text, with an English Translation* (Oxford-London 1874).

Funk, J., *Gregor des Grossen Buch der Pastoralregel* (Bibliothek der Kirchenväter, 2te Reihe 4, Munich 1933) 63-267.

DIVISION

16

PART THREE

PART FOUR

HOW THE PREACHER WHEN HE HAS DONE EVERYTHING
AS REQUIRED, SHOULD RETURN TO HIMSELF, TO PREVENT
HIS LIFE OR PREACHING FROM MAKING HIM PROUD..... 234

PART ONE

GREGORY TO HIS MOST REVEREND AND MOST HOLY BROTHER, JOHN, FELLOW BISHOP

Most dear brother, you reprove me with kind and humble regard for having wished to escape by concealment from the burdens of the pastoral care. Now, lest these burdens might appear light to some, I am explaining, by writing this book, how onerous I regard them, so that he who is free from them may not imprudently seek to have them, and he who has been so imprudent as to seek them may feel apprehension in having them.

The book is divided into four separate treatises, that it may bring its message to the mind of the reader in an orderly manner—as it were, step by step.

The nature of the case requires that one should carefully consider the way in which the position of supreme rule ought to be approached, and when it is duly reached, how life should be spent in it; how, in a life of rectitude, one should teach others; and, in the proper performance of his teaching office, with what vigilance one should realise each day one's weakness. All this must be ensued lest humility be wanting when office is assumed, the way of life be at variance with the office accepted, teaching divest life of rectitude, and presumption overrate teaching.

Wherefore, before all else, fear must moderate the desire of compassing authority, and when this is attained by one who did not seek it, let his way of life recommend it. Then, too, it is necessary that the rectitude which is dis-

20

played in the pastor's way of life should be propagated by the spoken word. And, finally, I have only to add that consideration of our own weakness should abase every work accomplished, lest proud conceit empty it of its worth in the eyes of the hidden Judge.

But since there are many who are as inexperienced as I am, not knowing how to assess the measure of their capacity, and who yet desire to teach what they have not learned, who appraise the burden of authority the more lightly in proportion to their ignorance of its far-reaching responsibility, let these take reproof at the beginning of this book. For while in their lack of training and restraint they seek to reach the eminence of a teacher, they must be deterred from the precipitate venture at the very threshold of this our discourse.

CHAPTER 1

No one ventures to teach any art unless he has learned it after deep thought. With what rashness, then, would the pastoral office be undertaken by the unfit, seeing that the government of souls is the art of arts! [1] For who does not realise that the wounds of the mind are more hidden than the internal wounds of the body? Yet, although those who have no knowledge of the powers of drugs shrink from giving themselves out as physicians of the flesh,[2] people who are utterly ignorant of spiritual precepts are often not afraid of professing themselves to be physicians of the heart, and though, by divine ordinance, those now in the highest positions are disposed to show a regard for religion, some there are who aspire to glory and esteem by an outward show of authority within the holy Church. They crave to appear as teachers and covet ascendancy over others, and, as the Truth attests: *They seek the first salutations in the market place, the first places at feasts, and the first chairs in the synagogues.*[3]

These persons are all the more unfitted to administer worthily what they have undertaken, the office of pastoral care, in that they have attained to the tutorship of humility by vanity alone; for, obviously, in this tutorship the tongue purveys mere jargon when one thing is learned and its contrary taught. Against such as these the Lord complains by the mouth of the Prophet: *They have reigned . . . not by me; they have been princes and I knew not.*[4] These reign by their own conceit, not by the will of the Supreme Ruler; they are sustained by no virtues, are not divinely called, but being inflamed by their cupidity, they seize rather than attain supreme rule.

Yet the Judge within both advances and ignores them, because those whom He tolerates on sufferance, He actually ignores by the sentence of His reprobation. Therefore, even to some who come to Him after having worked miracles, He says: *Depart from me, ye workers of iniquity, I know you not.*[5] This unfitness of pastors is rebuked by the voice of the Truth, through the Prophet, when it is said: *The shepherds themselves knew no understanding.*[6] Again, the Lord denounces them, saying: *And they that held the law knew me not.*[7] Therefore, the Truth complains of not being known by them, and protests that it does not know the high office of leaders who know Him not, because they who do not know the things that are the Lord's, are ignored by the Lord, as

Paul says: *But if any man know not, he shall not be known.*[8]

This unfitness of the pastors does, in truth, often accord with the deserts of their subjects, because, even if the former have not the light of knowledge through their own fault, it is due to a severe judgment that through their ignorance they, too, who follow, should stumble.

It is, therefore, for this reason that the Truth in person says in the Gospel: *If the blind lead the blind, both fall into the pit.*[9] Consequently, the Psalmist in his ministry as Prophet, but not as expressing a wish, says: *Let their eyes be darkened that they see not, and their back bend down Thou always.*[10] For those persons are "eyes" who, set in the forefront of the highest dignity, have undertaken the duty of showing the way, while those who follow on and are attached to them are termed the "back." When, then, the eyes are blinded, the back is bent, for when those who go before lose the light of knowledge, certainly those who follow are bowed down in carrying the burden of their sins.

CHAPTER 2

*Those should not take on the office of governing
who do not fulfil in their way of life
what they have learned by study.*

Further, there are some who investigate spiritual precepts with shrewd diligence, but in the life they live trample on what they have penetrated by their understanding. They hasten to teach what they have learned, not by practice, but by study, and belie in their conduct what they teach by words. Hence it is that when the pastor walks through steep places, the flock following him comes to a precipice. Therefore, the Lord complains through the Prophet of the contemptible knowledge of pastors, saying: *When you drank the clearest water, you troubled the rest with your feet. And my sheep were fed with that which you had trodden with your feet, and they drank what your feet had troubled.*[11] Evidently, the pastors drink water that is most clear, when with a right understanding they imbibe the streams of truth, whereas to foul the water with the feet is to corrupt the studies of holy meditation by an evil life. The sheep, of course, drink of the water befouled by those feet, when the subjects do not follow the instruction which they hear, but imitate only the wicked examples which they see. While they thirst for the things said, but are perverted by the things done, they imbibe mud with their draught as if they drank from polluted fountains of water. Consequently, too, it is written by the Prophet: *Bad priests are a snare of ruin to my people.*[12]

Hence again, the Lord says by the Prophet concerning the priests: *They were a stumbling block of iniquity to the house of Israel.*[13] For no one does more harm in the Church than he, who having the title or rank of holiness, acts evilly. No one presumes to take to task such a delinquent, and the offence, serving as an example, has far-reaching consequences, when the sinner is honoured out of respect paid to his rank.[14] Yet everyone who is unworthy would flee from the burden of such great guilt if with the attentive ear of the heart he pondered on that saying: *He that shall scandalise one of these little ones that believe in me, it were better for him that a millstone should be hanged about his neck, and that he should be drowned in the depth of the sea.*[15] By the millstone is symbolised the laborious round of worldly life, and by the depth of the sea final damnation is referred to. Therefore, if a man vested with the appearance of holiness destroys others by word or example, it certainly were better for him that his earthly deeds, performed in a worldly guise, should press him to death, rather than that his sacred offices should have pointed him out to others for sinful imitation; surely, the punishment of Hell would prove less severe for him if he fell alone.

CHAPTER 3

The burden of government. Every adversity is to be disregarded, and prosperity feared.

We have briefly said thus much to show how great is the burden of government, lest he who is unfit for it should profane that sacred office, and through a desire of eminence should undertake a pre-eminence that leads to perdition. For that reason, James with fatherly concern utters the prohibition, saying: *Be ye not many masters, my brethren.*[16] Wherefore, even the Mediator between God and man, who excels in knowledge and understanding even the celestial spirits and who reigns in Heaven from eternity, shrank from receiving an earthly kingdom. For it is written: *Jesus, therefore, when He knew that they would come to take Him by force and make Him king, fled again into the mountain Himself alone.*[17] And who could have exercised supreme dominion over men so blamelessly as He whose rule would have been over subjects whom He had Himself created?

But since He came in the flesh for the purpose of not only redeeming us by His Passion, but of teaching by His life, giving an example to those who follow Him, He would not be a king, but freely went to the gibbet of the Cross. He fled from the exalted glory offered Him and chose the pain of an ignominious death, that His members might learn to flee from the favours of the world, not to fear its terrors, to love adversity for the sake of truth, to shrink in fear from prosperity, for this latter thing often defiles the heart by vainglory, but the other cleanses it by sorrow. In the one, the mind becomes conceited; in the other, even if on occasion it became conceited, it abases itself. In the one, man forgets who he is; in the other, he is recalled, even unwillingly and perforce, to the recollection of what he is. In the one, even his past good works are often brought to naught; in the other, faults, even long-standing, are wiped away. It is a common experience that in the school of adversity the heart is forced to discipline itself; but when a man has achieved supreme rule, it is at once changed and puffed up by the experience of his high estate.

It was thus that Saul, realising at first his unworthiness, fled from the honour of governing, but presently assumed it, and was puffed up with pride.[18] By his desire for honour before the people, and wishing not to be blamed before them, he alienated him who had anointed him to be king.[19] So also David. Well-pleasing in almost all his actions in the judgment of Him who had chosen him, so soon as the burden of his obligations was not upon him, he broke out into festering conceit and showed himself as harsh and cruel in the murder of a man, as he had been weakly dissolute in his desire for a woman.[20] And he who had known how in pity to spare the wicked, learned afterwards without let or hesitation to pant for the death of even the good.[21] At first he had, indeed, been unwilling to strike down his captive persecutor, but afterwards, with loss to his wearied army, he killed even his loyal soldier. His guilt would, in fact, have removed him a long way from the number of the elect, had not scourgings restored him to pardon.

CHAPTER 4

Preoccupation with the governing of others dissipates the concentration of the mind.

Often it happens that when a man undertakes the cares of government, his heart is distracted with a diversity of things, and as his mind is divided among many interests and becomes confused, he finds he is unfitted for any of them. This is why a certain wise man gives a cautious warning, saying: *My son, meddle not with many matters;*[22] for, in fact, the mind cannot possibly concentrate on the pursuit of any one matter when it is divided among many. When it permits itself to be drawn abroad by concerns intruding upon it, it empties itself of its steadying regard for its inmost self. It busies itself setting external matters in order, and, ignorant only of itself, it knows how to give thought to a multitude of concerns, without knowing its own self. For when it implicates itself more than is needful with what is external, it is as though it were so preoccupied during a journey as to forget what its destination was; with the result that it is so great a stranger to the business of self-examination as not even to be aware of the harm it suffers, or to be conscious of the great faults it commits. Ezechias, for example, did not realise that he was sinning, when he showed the storehouse of his aromatic spices to the strangers who had come to him, and in consequence, he fell under the anger of the Judge, to the condemnation of his future offspring, for what he thought he had lawfully done.[23]

Often, when there are abundant resources at hand, and things can be done which subjects admire just because they are done, the mind is lifted up in thought, and provokes the complete anger of the Judge, though no overt acts are committed. For He who judges is within, what is judged is within. When, therefore, we transgress in the heart, men do not know what we are engaged upon, but the Judge is the witness of our sin. The king of Babylon, for instance, was not guilty of pride merely when he came to utter proud words, for from the mouth of the Prophet he heard the sentence of reprobation before he had given vent to his pride.[24] He had, indeed, already cleansed himself of the sin of his guilty pride, when he proclaimed to all his subject peoples the Omnipotent God whom he found he had offended.[25] After this, elated by the success of his power, pleased with his great accomplishments, he first preferred himself in his own conceit to all others, and then, swollen with pride, he said: *Is not this the great Babylon, which I have built to be the seat of the kingdom and by the strength of my power and in the glory of my excellence?* [26] This utterance was openly visited with wrathful punishment, which his hidden pride had enkindled.

For the strict Judge first sees invisibly what He afterwards reprehends by open chastisement. Wherefore, too, the Judge turned him into an irrational animal, separated him from human society, and associated him, deprived of his right mind, with the beasts of the field, so that by a manifestly strict and just sentence he who had esteemed himself great beyond all other men, lost his man's estate.

When, therefore, we adduce these examples, it is not to censure the office itself, but to fortify the weak heart against coveting it. We would have no one who is not fully qualified for it, to venture to snatch at supreme rule, and we would not have men who stumble on plain ground, to set their feet on a precipice.

CHAPTER 5

Regarding those who in the position of supreme ruling authority could benefit others by the example of their virtues, but flee from it for the sake of their own peace.

There are those who are gifted with virtues in a high degree and who are exalted by great endowments for the training of others; men who are unspotted in their zeal for chastity, strong in the vigour of their abstinence, replete with feasts of knowledge, humble in their long-suffering patience, erect in the fortitude of authority, gentle in the grace of loving-kindness, strict and unbending in justice. Such, indeed, in declining to undertake supreme rule when invited to do so, deprive themselves, for the most part, of the gifts which they have received not for their own sakes only, but for the sake of others also.

When these regard their own personal advantage, not that of others, they lose such advantages in wishing to retain them for themselves. Hence it was that the Truth said to the disciples: *A city seated on a mountain cannot be hid, neither do men light a candle and put it under a bushel, but upon a candlestick, that it may shine to all that are in the house.*[27] Wherefore, He said to Peter: *Simon, son of John, lovest thou me?*[28] And when Simon replied at once that he loved Him, he was told: *If thou lovest me, feed my sheep.*[29] If, then, the care of feeding is a testimony of love, he who, abounding in virtues, refuses to feed the flock of God, is convicted of having no love for the Supreme Shepherd. Wherefore, Paul says: *If Christ died for all, then all were dead. And if He died for all, it remaineth that they also who live, may not now live to themselves, but unto Him who died for them and rose again.*[30] Thus, Moses says that the surviving brother must take the wife of his brother who died without children, and raise up children for his brother's name; and should he refuse to take her, she shall spit in his face, and her kinsman shall take the shoe from one of his feet, and call his home the house of the unshod.[31]

Now, the deceased brother is He who, appearing after the glory of the Resurrection, said: *Go, tell my brethren;*[32] for He died, as it were, without sons, because He had not yet filled up the number of the elect. The surviving brother is ordered to take the wife, because it is fitting that the care of Holy Church should be assigned to him who is best fitted to rule it well. If he proves unwilling, the woman spits in his face, because, whosoever does not care to assist others by the favours which he has received, is reprobated by Holy Church also for the good he has, and, as it were, she casts spittle in his face, and a shoe is taken from one foot, so that his house may be called the house of the unshod, for it is written: . . . *your feet shod with the preparation of the gospel of peace.*[33]

If, therefore, we have the care of our neighbours as well as of ourselves, we protect each foot with a shoe. But a man who, thinking only of his own advantage, disregards that of his neighbours, loses with disgrace the shoe, as it were, of one foot.

So, there are those who, endowed, as we have said, with great gifts, in their eagerness for the pursuit of contemplation only, decline to be of service to the neighbour by preaching; they love to withdraw in quietude and desire to be alone for meditation. Now, if they are judged strictly on their conduct, they are certainly guilty in proportion to the public service which they were able to afford. Indeed, what disposition of mind is revealed in him, who could perform conspicuous public benefit on coming to his task, but prefers his own privacy to the benefit of others, seeing that the Only-Begotten of the Supreme Father came forth from the bosom of His Father into our midst, that He might benefit many?

CHAPTER 6

*Men who flee from the burden of ruling out of
humility, are then truly humble, when they
do not resist the divine decrees.*

There are some also who flee from this burden only
out of humility: they do not wish to be preferred to those
others to whom they think they are inferior. Their
humility is, indeed, genuine in God's eyes, provided it is
accompanied by the other virtues, and when it is not
obstinate in declining to undertake what is enjoined to be
profitably undertaken. For he is not genuinely humble,
who understands that the decision of the Supreme Will
is for him to take leadership, and yet refuses that leadership. But when the supreme rule is imposed on him, and
provided that he is already endowed with those gifts
whereby he can benefit others, he ought, in submission
to God's dispositions and removed from the vice of obstinacy, to flee from it in his heart and obey, though to
obey is contrary to his inclination.

CHAPTER 7

*As it happens, some men laudably desire the office
of preaching, and others no less laudably
are driven to it by compulsion.*

Sometimes, though, there are those who laudably desire
the office of preaching, whereas others no less laudably
are driven to it by compulsion. We clearly see this when
we consider the case of two Prophets, one of whom spon-

taneously offered himself for the mission of preaching, whereas the other protested from fear. Isaias, for instance, when the Lord asked whom He should send, offered himself of his own accord, saying: *Lo, here am I, send me.*[34] Jeremias, on the other hand, was sent, yet was humbly reluctant to be obliged to go, saying: *Ah, Ah, Ah, Lord God, behold, I cannot speak, for I am a child.*[35]

Observe how these two gave different utterances externally, which, however, did not proceed from contrary founts of love. For there are two precepts of love, namely, one based on the love of God, the other on love for the neighbour. Isaias, then, desired the active life in the office of preaching, moved thereto by the wish to benefit his neighbours. But Jeremias, zealously eager to cleave to the love of his Creator, but in a contemplative life, remonstrated against being sent. What, therefore, the one laudably desired, the other as laudably shrank from. The one feared that by preaching he should forfeit the benefit of quiet contemplation; the other, that by not preaching he might suffer harm for the lack of arduous work.

Now, we should carefully consider this in both cases: he who protested did not wholly resist, and he who wished to be sent, saw himself cleansed, in anticipation, by a coal from the altar.[36] One who has not been cleansed, must not dare to undertake sacred ministries; and one who has been cleansed by supernal graces, must not proudly resist under the guise of humility.

Since, therefore, it is very difficult to recognise that one is cleansed, it is safest to decline the office of preaching, yet it may not, as we have said, be pertinaciously refused, when the Supernal Will that it should be undertaken is perceived. Both obligations were admirably fulfilled by

Moses, who, though unwilling to accept the supreme rule of a great multitude, yet obeyed. For he might have been proud had he undertaken the leadership of a numberless people without fear, and again, he would have been proud, had he refused to obey the command of the Creator. Hence, in both respects he was humble, and in both obedient, namely, in his unwillingness to be set over the people when he regarded himself only, and when he consented, relying on the power of Him who gave the command.

Therefore, from such examples let the rash understand how great their guilt is if, instigated by personal desires, they do not shrink from precedence over others, and seeing that holy men fear to accept this leadership of people when God Himself commands. Moses trembled, though God urged him forward; and yet a man who is weak yearns after the burden of office, and one who is extremely likely to fall under his own burden, is willing to be overwhelmed by putting his shoulders beneath the burdens of others! He cannot bear his own deeds, and increases the burden which he bears!

CHAPTER 8

Regarding those who covet pre-eminence and appropriate a statement of the Apostle to serve their own cupidity.

Now, as often happens, those who covet pre-eminence, seeking support for their own cupidity, take advantage of the Apostle's statement when he says: *If a man desire the office of a bishop, he desireth a good work.*[37] Yet, while praising the desire, the Apostle forthwith qualifies his praise by adding a reason for fear, promptly adding, as he does: *But it behoveth a bishop to be blameless.*[38] When he proceeds with an enumeration of the necessary virtues, he explains what this blamelessness is. He, therefore, approves the desire, but warns these people by his precept, as though he plainly said: "I praise what you seek, but acquaint yourselves first with what you are seeking, lest by neglecting to take the measure of your own fitness, you become the more blameworthy and detestable, in that you hasten to be seen by all on the pinnacle of honour." The great master in the art of ruling urges subjects on by approving of their desire, but deters them by fear, in order that he may restrain his hearers from pride, and by praising the office sought, may dispose them for the kind of life that is required.

We must, however, observe that this was said at a time when whosoever was set over the people was the first to be led to the tortures of martyrdom. So, indeed, it was praiseworthy to seek the episcopate, when, in consequence of holding the office, there was no doubt that its holder would meet with the most severe sufferings. For this reason the office of a bishop is termed a good work when it is said: *If a man desire the office of a bishop, he desireth a good work.* Wherefore, that man gives testimony against himself that he is not desiring the office of a bishop, if he seeks the glory of that honour, but not the ministry of a good work. For a man not only fails completely to love the office, but he is ignorant of it, if, yearning for supreme rule, he feasts on the subjection of others in the hidden reveries of his thought, is glad to hear his own praises, feels his heart surge with honour, and rejoices in the abundance of his affluence. It is, therefore, worldly gain that he seeks under the guise of that kind of honour, whereby worldly gain should have been destroyed, and when the mind thinks to grasp the highest state of humility in order to cherish its own pride, it changes the intrinsic nature of what was exteriorly desired.

CHAPTER 9

The mind of those who crave for pre-eminence, for the most part flatters itself with imaginary promises of performing good works.

Generally those who aspire to pastoral ruling are also proposing to themselves some good works as well, and though they have such aspirations from the motive of pride, busy themselves thinking that they will do great things. Hence it is that the motive hidden within is one thing, and what is taking place on the surface of their conscious mind is another. For the mind often lies to itself about itself, and makes believe that it loves the good work, when actually it does not, and that it does not wish for mundane glory, when, in fact, it does. Being eager for a position of leadership, it is fearful in the quest of it, but audacious once it has been obtained.

In seeking office, the mind is in trepidation lest office will not ensue, but when office has arrived suddenly, the mind thinks that what it has achieved is rightly its due. Then, when the mind has begun to enjoy, in a worldly fashion, the office of superiority which it has got, it readily forgets all the spiritual thoughts it had. When, therefore, thought has been straying inordinately, it must

be promptly directed back to its activities in the past; and
if the person considers what he did when subject to
authority, he at once knows whether, as superior, he can
do what he proposed to do, for a man is quite incapable
of learning humility in a position of superiority, if he
did not refrain from acting proudly when he was in a
position of subjection. He does not know how to flee
from praise when it abounds, if he yearned for it when
it was absent. He certainly cannot conquer his cupidity
when he is advanced to the sustaining of many, if his own
resources did not suffice to sustain himself alone. Therefore, let everyone discover from his past life what manner
of man he is, lest the phantasy of his thoughts deceive
him when he craves for superiority.

Very frequently, when the office of rule is undertaken,
the practice of good deeds is relinquished, though it had
been maintained when life was undisturbed, for even the
unskilled seaman can guide a ship on an even keel in a
tranquil sea, but in a sea that is tossed with tempestuous
waves, even a skilled seaman is greatly troubled. And,
indeed, what else is power in the post of superiority but
a tempest of the mind, wherein the ship of the heart is
ever shaken by hurricanes of thought, is ceaselessly driven
to and fro, until, by sudden excesses of words and deeds,
it founders on confronting rocks? How, then, can any
course be taken in the midst of these perils, and how can
a course be held, unless the superior who comes to the
office of governing by compulsion abounds in virtue, and
one deficient in virtue declines to come to it even under
compulsion? If the former declines altogether, let him
take heed that he is not wrapping up in his handkerchief
the talents which he has received, and lest he be judged

for hiding them.[39] To wrap up talents in a handkerchief is, of course, to hide, in idle and persistent inaction, gifts that have been received. In the case, however, of one who desires to govern, though unfit to do so, let him take heed lest, by the example of his wicked act, be become like the Pharisees, namely, a hindrance to those who strive to enter the Kingdom. Such people, according to the words of the Master,[40] do not themselves enter, nor permit others to enter. He should also consider that when as chosen superior he espouses the cause of the people, he is coming, as it were, like a physician to a sick person. If, then, in his practice ailments still thrive in him, with what presumption does he hasten to heal the afflicted while he carries a sore on his own face?

CHAPTER 10

The character required of a man who comes to rule.

He, therefore—indeed, he precisely—must devote himself entirely to setting an ideal of living. He must die to all passions of the flesh and by now lead a spiritual life. He must have put aside worldly prosperity; he must fear no adversity, desire only what is interior. He must be a man whose aims are not thwarted by a body out of perfect accord through frailty, nor by any contumacy of the spirit. He is not led to covet the goods of others, but is bounteous in giving of his own. He is quickly moved by a compassionate heart to forgive, yet never so diverted from perfect rectitude as to forgive beyond what is proper. He does no unlawful act himself while deploring those of others, as if they were his own. In the affection of his own heart he sympathizes with the frailties of others, and so rejoices in the good done by his neighbour, as though the progress made were his own. In all that he does he sets an example so inspiring to all others, that in their regard he has no cause to be ashamed of his past. He so studies to live as to be able to water the dry hearts of others with the streams of instruction imparted. By his practice and experience of prayer he has learned already that he can obtain from the Lord what he asks for, as though it were already said to him, in particular, by the voice of experience: *When thou art yet speaking, I will say, "Here I am."* [41]

praxis

If, for instance, someone were to come to induce us to intercede for him with a great man incensed against him, but unknown to us, we should at once reply that we could not intercede since we had no knowledge of, or acquaintance with, the man. If, therefore, a man is too embarrassed to intercede with another on whom he has no claim, with what assurance can one take on the role of interceding for the people with God, without the knowledge of being in His favor by reason of the merits of one's life? Or how is one to ask pardon for others, when he does not know whether he himself is reconciled with Him?

In this matter there is yet another reason for anxious fear, namely, whether one who is credited with being able to appease His anger, may not himself provoke it, owing to his own guilt. For we all know full well that when a person is out of favour and is sent to intercede, the mind of the incensed person is moved to greater anger. Wherefore, let the man who is still fettered with worldly desires take heed lest, by arousing the anger of the strict Judge for taking complacency in his position of glory, he become the author of ruin to his subjects.

CHAPTER 11

The type of man who ought not to come to rule.

Therefore, everyone should wisely assess himself, lest he dare to take on the role of government, while vice still reigns in him to his condemnation; a man who is debased by his own guilt must not intercede for the faults of others.[42]

Wherefore, the voice from on high said to Moses: *Say to Aaron: Whosoever of thy seed throughout their families hath a blemish, he shall not offer bread to the Lord his God. Neither shall he approach to minister to Him.* It is immediately added: *If he be blind, if he be lame, if he has a little, or a great and crooked nose, if his foot or if his hand be broken, if he be crookbacked, or bleareyed, or have a pearl in his eye, or a continual scab, or a dry scurf in his body, or a rupture.*[43]

Now, that man is blind who is ignorant of the light of heavenly contemplation; who, oppressed by the darkness of the present life, does not behold the light to come as he does not love it, and, therefore, does not know whither to direct the steps of his conduct. Hence, the Prophetess Anna said: *He will keep the feet of His Saints, and the wicked shall be silent in darkness.*[44]

A man is lame who does, indeed, see the way he should go, but through infirmity of purpose is unable to follow persistently the way of life which he sees. Because his unstable habit cannot rise to the estate of virtue, he is not strong enough to make his conduct follow in the direction of his desires. Consequently, St. Paul says: *Lift*

up the hands which hang down, and the feeble knees,
and make straight steps with your feet, that no one halt-
ing, may go out of the way, but rather be healed.[45]

A man with a little nose is one who is incapable of
discernment, for by the nose we discern sweet odours
from stench. Rightly, then, the nose symbolises discernment, whereby we elect virtue and reject sin. Therefore,
too, it is said in praise of the bride: *Thy nose is as the*
tower which is in Libanus.[46] For, certainly, Holy Church
perceives by her discernment what temptations proceed
from various causes, and, as from an eminence, detects
the oncoming wars of vice.

But there are some who, disliking to be considered dull,
often busy themselves with a variety of inquisitions, more
than is needful, and fall into error by their excessive
subtlety. Therefore, here the addition: *A great and*
crooked nose. Evidently, a great and crooked nose is immoderate subtlety in making distinctions; when this develops inordinately, it distorts the correctness of its own
functioning.

Again, a man has a fractured foot or hand, when he is
wholly unable to walk in the way of God and is entirely
bereft of all share in good deeds. In this he is not like
the lame person who can share in good deeds, at least
with difficulty; he is bereft of them altogether.

The crookbacked is one who is weighed down by the
burden of earthly cares, so that he never looks up to the
things that are above, but is wholly intent on what is
underfoot in the lowest sphere. If at any time he hears
something good about the heavenly fatherland, he is so
weighed down by the burden of evil habit, that he does
not raise up the face of his heart; he just cannot lift up

the cast of his thought, being kept bowed down by his habitual earthly solicitude. This is the kind of man of whom the Psalmist says: *I have been bowed down and humbled exceedingly.*[47] Their fault is also reprobated by the Truth in person, saying: *And that seed which fell among thorns, are they who have heard the Word, and going their way, are choked with the cares and riches and pleasures of this life, and yield no fruit.*[48]

The blear-eyed is he whose natural disposition does, indeed, shine forth unto the knowledge of truth, but is obscured by carnal works. For in the blear-eyed the pupils are sound, but owing to a flux of serous matter the eyelids become weak and swollen, and are often worn away by the flow, so that the keenness of the pupils is impaired. And there are those whose perception is weakened by the works of a carnal life—men who were capable of a nice discrimination of what was right, which, however, is obscured by the habit of evil deeds.

The blear-eyed is, then, one whose sense was naturally keen, but whose depraved way of life has confounded it. To such it was well said through the Angel: *Anoint thy eye with eyesalve, that thou mayest see.*[49] For we anoint our eyes with salve for seeing, when we assist the eye of our understanding with the medicaments of good works, so that we may perceive the brightness of the true light.

But that man has a white film over his eyes, who is prevented from perceiving the light of truth owing to blindness, induced by the arrogant assumption of wisdom or righteousness. For the pupil of the eye, if black, can see, but if it has a white film, it sees nothing; and, obviously, when a man understands that he is foolish and a sinner, his faculty of thought grasps the knowledge of the interior light. But if he attributes to himself the radiance of righteousness or wisdom, he shuts himself off from the light of supernal knowledge; and in proportion to his arrogant self-exaltation, he futilely endeavours to penetrate the bright light of Truth—as is said of some: *For professing themselves to be wise, they became fools.*[50]

A man is "permanently scabrous," when he is constantly dominated by wantonness of the flesh. For in a case of scabies the internal heat is drawn to the skin, a condition that rightly symbolises lechery. Thus, when the temptation in the heart issues forth into action, then it can be said that the interior heat issues forth as scabies on the skin; and to the visible injury of the body corresponds the fact that as pleasure is not repressed in the thought, it gains the mastery in act. Hence, Paul was anxious to cleanse, as it were, this itch of the skin, when he said: *Let no temptation take hold on you, but such as is human*[51]—as though he wished to make plain: "It is, indeed, human to suffer temptation in the heart, but it is diabolical, when in the struggle with temptation one is overcome and does its bidding."

Further, a man has pustular disease of the skin, if his mind is ravaged by avarice, which, if not restrained in small matters, grows immeasurably. The pustular disease itself invades the body without causing pain, and spreads in the infected without resulting in annoyance, while disfiguring the comeliness of the members. So, too, avarice, while affording the mind of its victim apparent delight, ulcerates it. While filling its thoughts with the acquisition of one thing after another, it kindles enmities, but gives no pain with the wounds it inflicts, because it promises to the fevered mind abundance as the wages of sin. And the comeliness of the members is lost, because this sin results also in the marring of other fair virtues. Indeed, the whole body, as it were, is befouled, since the mind is overthrown by all vices, as St. Paul testified in saying: *Covetousness is the root of all evil.*[52]

The ruptured man is he who, though not actually given to baseness, is yet weighed down by it beyond measure by the constant thought of it; though he is not carried away by evil deeds, his mind is ravished with the pleasure of lechery, without any stings of repugnance. As to the blemish of rupture, it is due to the descent of the internal fluids to the genitals, which in consequence produces a troublesome and unseemly swelling. A person, then, is ruptured when he allows all his thoughts to run on lascivious matters, and thus carries in his heart a load of turpitude; and though he does not actually engage in deeds of shame, his mind cannot disengage itself from them. At the same time he lacks the strength to raise himself to the overt exercise of good deeds, because a shameful hidden burden weighs him down.

Whosoever, then, is subject to any of the aforesaid defects, is forbidden to offer loaves of bread to the Lord. The reason is obvious: a man who is still ravaged by his own sins, cannot expiate the sins of others.

And now, since we have briefly shown how one who is worthy should undertake pastoral ruling, and how the unworthy should fear to undertake it, we shall explain how he who has worthily undertaken the office ought to live in the exercise of it.

PART TWO

THE LIFE OF THE PASTOR

CHAPTER 1

*The conduct required of one who has in due
order reached the position of ruler.*

The conduct of a prelate should so far surpass the conduct of the people, as the life of a pastor sets him apart
from his flock. For one who is so regarded that the people
are called his flock, must carefully consider how necessary
it is for him to maintain a life of rectitude. It is necessary,
therefore, that he should be pure in thought, exemplary in
conduct, discreet in keeping silence, profitable in speech,
in sympathy a near neighbour to everyone, in contemplation exalted above all others, a humble companion to those
who lead good lives, erect in his zeal for righteousness
against the vices of sinners. He must not be remiss in his
care for the inner life by preoccupation with the external;
nor must he in his solicitude for what is internal, fail to
give attention to the external.

Let us now take up the things which we have touched
upon in this brief enumeration, and treat them at somewhat greater length.

CHAPTER 2

The ruler should be pure in thought.

The ruler should ever be pure in thought. No impurity should stain one who has undertaken the duty of cleansing the stains of defilement from the hearts of others as well as from his own. For it is necessary that the hand that aims at cleansing filth should itself be clean, lest, sordid with clinging dirt, it fouls for the worse everything it touches. Wherefore, it is said by the Prophet: *Be ye clean, you that carry the vessels of the Lord.*[1] Those who carry the vessels of the Lord are those who undertake, in reliance on their way of living, to draw the souls of their neighbours to the everlasting holy places.

Let these, therefore, realise in their hearts how purified those ought to be, who carry in the bosom of their own personal responsibility living vessels to the eternal temple. For this reason the voice of God enjoined that on the breast of Aaron the breastplate of judgment[2] should be set, bound with fillets. The import of this was that the heart of the priest should in no way harbour dissolute thoughts, but only right reason should rule and restrain it, nor should he entertain any indiscreet or unprofitable thought. One who is set up for a model to others should ever, by the strictness of his way of life, display what a wealth of reason he carries in his breast.

It was also strictly enjoined that on the breastplate the names of the twelve Patriarchs should be inscribed. To bear the names of the fathers registered on the breast, is to meditate unceasingly on the lives of those elders. The priest then walks blamelessly, when he is ever contemplating the examples of the fathers who preceded him, when without interruption he regards the footsteps of the Saints, and when he checks forbidden thoughts, lest, as he goes forward, he set his steps beyond the bounds of right order. Further, the breastplate of judgment is fittingly so styled, because the ruler should always discern good from evil, and carefully consider and scrutinise what is suitable in itself, for whom, when, and how, it is suitable; and because he is not to seek anything for himself, but to regard the good of his neighbours as his own advantage. Therefore, it is written in that place: *And thou shalt put on the rational of judgment, doctrine and truth, which shall be on Aaron's breast, when he shall go in before the Lord; and he shall bear the judgment of the children of Israel on his breast in the sight of the Lord always.*[3] The priest bearing the judgment of the children of Israel on his breast in the sight of the Lord, means that he examines the causes of his subjects in accordance only with the mind of the Judge within, so that he allows no admixture of human reason in what he dispenses in the place of God, lest personal displeasure embitter him in his zeal for correction. Whilst showing himself zealous against the transgressions of others, he should punish his own, lest his latent ill will stain the calmness of his judgment, or hasty anger distort it.

And when he considers the dread inspired by Him who rules all things, that is, the Judge within, it is not without great trepidation that he will rule his subjects. This dread, while keeping the mind of the ruler humble, purifies it also, lest it be either lifted up by spiritual presumption, or tainted with the delight of the flesh, or obscured by the importunity of unclean thought through cupidity for earthly things. These things cannot, however, fail to smite the mind of the ruler, but he must hasten to overcome them by repulsing them. He must prevent the sin which tempts him, from overcoming him by its voluptuous delight and from inflicting a fatal blow because of his too tardy rejection of it.

CHAPTER 3

The ruler should always be exemplary in conduct.

The ruler should be exemplary in his conduct, that by his manner of life he may show the way of life to his subjects, and that the flock, following the teaching and conduct of its shepherd, may proceed the better through example rather than words. For one who by the exigency of his position must propose the highest ideals, is bound by that same exigency to give a demonstration of those ideals. His voice penetrates the hearts of his hearers the more readily, if his way of life commends what he says. What he enjoins in words, he will help to execution by example. Wherefore, it is said by the Prophet: *Get thee up upon a high mountain, thou that bringest good tidings to Sion;* [4] that is to say, he who employs heavenly preaching must already have abandoned the low levels of earthly deeds, and he must be seen standing on an eminence. He will the more readily draw his subjects to better things, as by his meritorious way of life his voice calls from the supernal heights.

Wherefore, by divine ordinance the priest receives a shoulder for sacrifice, and that, too, the right one and separate.[5] His conduct should be not only profitable, but out-standing. He should not only do what is upright in the midst of the wicked, but also surpass the well-doers among his subjects, and as he surpasses them in the dignity of his rank, so should he in the virtue of his conduct.

Again, the breast of the victim together with the shoulder are assigned to him for eating,[6] so that he may learn to immolate to the Giver of all things, those parts of himself which correspond to the parts of the sacrifice which he is ordered to take. Not only in his heart must he have right thoughts, but he must invite those who behold him, by the shoulder [7] of his deeds to sublime heights. He may not covet the good things of this present life, nor fear any adversity. He must despise the blandishments of the world by heeding the fear they inspire in his conscience, yet despise all fears in view of the sweet delights which his conscience holds out to him.

And for this reason, too, by command of the supernal voice the priest is bound with the humeral veil on each shoulder,[8] that he may be ever guarded by the adornment of virtue against both adversity and prosperity; that is to say, according to the words of Paul: walking *by the armour of justice on the right hand and on the left*,[9] striving after those things only which are interior, he should not be deflected on either side to base pleasure. Let him not be elated by prosperity, nor disconcerted by adversity. Let not the smooth enervate his will, nor the rough cast him down to despair; and thus, not lowering the determination of his mind in passions, he will display the great beauty of the humeral veil covering both his shoulders.

Further, it is rightly enjoined that the humeral veil be made of gold, hyacinth, purple, scarlet twice-dyed, and fine

twisted linen,[10] so that it may be evident with what variety
of virtues the priest should be conspicuous. Thus, in the
vesture of the priest the gold is resplendent beyond all else;
so should he especially shine beyond all others in the understanding of wisdom. Hyacinth is added, brilliant with
the colour of the skies, that by every matter which he penetrates with his understanding, he may not stoop to the base
favours of earth, but rise up to the love of heavenly things.
He must beware of being incautiously snared by praise,
thus despoiling himself of even the appreciation of truth.

With the gold and blue of the vesture there is also a
mingling of purple. That is to say, the heart of the
priest, while hoping for those high matters about which
he preaches, should repress in itself the remotest suggestions of vice. He should, as it were, with kingly power
reject them, ever setting his gaze on the nobility of his interior regeneration and safeguarding by his way of living
his right to the heavenly kingdom. It is this nobility of
spirit that Peter mentions: *But you are a chosen genera-
tion, a kingly priesthood.*[11] In regard also to the power
with which we subdue vices, we are fortified by the words
of John, who says: *But as many as have received Him, He
gave them power to be made the sons of God.*[12] This dignity of fortitude the Psalmist has in view when he says:
*But to me Thy friends, O God, are made exceedingly hon-
ourable, their principality is exceedingly strengthened;*[13]
for, indeed, the mind of the Saints is exalted to princely
eminence, when in the eyes of the world they suffer
abasement.

Now, to gold, blue, and purple is added twice-dyed scarlet, to signify that in the eyes of the Judge of the heart all
that is good in virtues must be adorned with charity, and

that everything that is resplendent in human eyes must in the sight of the Judge within be lit up with the flame of love coming from the heart. Moreover, because this charity embraces both God and neighbour, its radiance is, as it were, of a double hue. He, therefore, that sighs for the beauty of his Maker, but neglects the care of his neighbour, or who so compasses the care of the neighbour as to grow listless in divine love, in neglecting either of these, does not know what it means to have twice-dyed scarlet in the adornment of the humeral.

But while the mind is intent on the precepts of charity, it remains, beyond doubt, that the flesh must be mortified by abstinence. Consequently, fine-twisted linen is joined with the twice-dyed scarlet. Now, fine linen comes from the earth with radiant hue. And what else is designated by linen but chastity, radiant in the comeliness of bodily cleanness? The twisted linen is also woven into the beauty of the humeral, for then chastity issues into the perfect radiance of purity, when the flesh is spent with abstinence; and while thus, in company with the other virtues, the merit of mortified flesh is revealed, as it were, the twisted linen is resplendent in the variegated beauty of the humeral.

CHAPTER 4

*The ruler should be discreet in keeping silence
and profitable in speech.*

The ruler should be discreet in keeping silence and profitable in speech, lest he utter what should be kept secret, or keep secret what should be uttered. For just as incautious speech leads men into error, so, too, unseasonable silence leaves in error those who might have been instructed. Often, indeed, incautious rulers, being afraid of losing human favour, fear to speak freely of what is right, and, in the words of the Truth, do not exercise the zeal of shepherds caring for the flock, but serve the role of mercenaries; [14] for when the wolf appears, they flee and hide themselves in silence. Wherefore, the Lord reproves them through the Prophet, saying: *They are dumb dogs, not able to bark.*[15]

Again, He complains of them, saying: *You have not gone up to face the enemy, nor have you set up a wall for the house of Israel, to stand in battle in the day of the Lord.*[16] Now, to rise up against the enemy is to oppose worldly powers with candid speech in defence of the flock. To stand in battle in the day of the Lord is to resist from love of justice evil men who contend against us. For if a shepherd feared to say what is right, what else is that but to have turned his back by not speaking? But when one places himself in front of the flock to defend them, he obviously is opposing a wall for the house of Israel against the enemy.

Hence again, it is said to the sinful people: *Thy Prophets have seen false and foolish things for thee, and they have not laid open thy iniquity to excite thee to penance.*[17] Now, teachers are sometimes called Prophets in Sacred Scripture, in that they point out the fleeting nature of the present and disclose the future. Here they are accused by the divine utterance of seeing what is false, because, by fearing to reprove faults, they vainly flatter evil-doers by promising them immunity. They fail to disclose the wickedness of sinners by refraining from words of reproof.

Indeed, the word of reproof is the key of detection, since

reproof discloses the sin of which frequently even the doer is unaware. Wherefore, Paul says: . . . *that he may be able to exhort in sound doctrine and to convince the gainsayers.*[18] So, by Malachias it is said: *The lips of the priest keep knowledge, and they shall seek the law at his mouth, because he is the Angel of the Lord of Hosts.*[19]

Wherefore, through Isaias the Lord admonishes, saying: *Cry, cease not, lift up thy voice like a trumpet.*[20] He who enters on the priesthood undertakes the office of a herald, so that he cries out and precedes the coming of the Judge, who follows with terrible mien. If, then, the priest does not know how to preach, what vocal sound is this mute herald likely to give?

For this reason, then, the Holy Spirit settled on the first Pastors in the form of tongues; [21] for to those whom He fills, He instantly gives His own eloquence. Therefore, Moses is enjoined to see that when the priest enters the Tabernacle, he should be encompassed with little bells,[22] a sign that he must be endowed with utterance for preaching, lest by silence he provoke the judgment of Him who sees from on high. For it is written: . . . *that the sound may be heard when he goeth in and cometh out of the sanctuary in the sight of the Lord, and that he may not die.*[23] The priest going in or coming out dies if no sound is heard from him: that is to say, he arouses the wrath of the hidden Judge against him if he goes without the utterance of preaching.

The little bells are fittingly described as fixed to the vesture; and indeed, what else is to be understood by the priest's vestments but his righteous works? The Prophet witnesses to this when he says: *Let thy priests be clothed with justice.*[24] Therefore, little bells are fixed to the ves-

ture, that even the works of the priest should loudly proclaim his way of life in the sound of his speech.

But when the ruler prepares to speak, he must bear in
mind to exercise a studious caution in his speech, for if
his discourse, hastily given, be ill-ordered, the hearts of his
hearers may be stricken with the wound of error, and when,
perhaps, he wishes to appear wise, he will by his lack of
wisdom sever the bond of unity. For this reason the Truth
says: *Have salt in you, and have peace among you.*[25] By
salt the wisdom of speech is indicated. He, then, who
strives to speak wisely, should greatly fear lest by his words
the unity of his hearers be confounded. Wherefore, Paul
says: *Not to be more wise than it behoveth to be wise, but
to be wise unto sobriety.*[26]

Hence in the vesture of the priest, in accordance with
the divine word, pomegranates are added to the little
bells.[27] What else is symbolised by pomegranates but the
unity of faith? For as in the pomegranate many seeds
within are protected by one outer rind, so, unity in faith
comprehends numberless people of Holy Church, who,
though varying in merits, are retained within her. Therefore, lest the ruler rush into careless speech, what we have
said is proclaimed by the Truth to His disciples: *Have salt
in you, and have peace among you*—as though He should
say in employing the symbol of the vesture of the priest:
"Join pomegranates to the little bells, so that in all that
you say you may guardedly and cautiously maintain the
unity of the faith."

Rulers must also see to it with careful concern that not
only should nothing evil proceed from their lips, but that
not even what is proper be said in excess or in a slovenly
manner. Often the force of what is said is wasted, when it

is enfeebled in the hearts of the hearers by a careless and
offensive torrent of words. Indeed, this sort of loquacity
defiles the speaker himself, inasmuch as it takes no notice
of the practical needs of the audience. Wherefore, Moses
aptly said: *The man that hath an issue of seed shall be
unclean.*[28] For in the mind of the hearers the seed of their
subsequent thought depends on the nature of what they
have heard, since with the reception of speech through the
medium of hearing the thought is begotten in the mind.
Hence the great preacher was called by the philosophers of
this world a "word-sower." [29] He, then, who suffers an
issue of seed is said to be unclean, because, given as he is
to much speaking, he defiles himself by the fact that if he
had been orderly in his speech, he could have produced a
progeny of righteous thought in the hearts of his hearers;
as it is, by spreading himself out in immoderate wordiness,
he has an issue of seed not for the purpose of progeny, but
to serve defilement.

Wherefore, Paul also, admonishing his disciple to be
instant in preaching, said: *I charge thee before God and
Jesus Christ, who shall judge the living and the dead, by
His coming and His Kingdom: preach the word, be instant
in season, out of season.*[30] When he was about to say "out
of season," he premised "in season," for if being in season
is not combined with being out of season, the preaching destroys itself in the mind of the hearer by its worthlessness.

CHAPTER 5

*The ruler should be a neighbour in compassion to
everyone and exalted above all in thought.*

Let the ruler be neighbour in compassion to everyone
and exalted above all in thought, so that by the love of his
heart he may transfer to himself the infirmities of others,
and by the loftiness of his contemplation transcend even
himself in his aspirations for the invisible things. Otherwise, while he has lofty aspirations, he will be disregarding
the infirmities of his neighbours, or in accommodating
himself to the weak, will cease to seek that which is above.
Thus it was that Paul was led into paradise and searched
into the secrets of the third heaven,[31] and yet, though
raised aloft in that contemplation of invisible things, he
recalled his mind's vision to the bed of carnal men, and
set up norms for their secret relations, saying: *For fear of
fornication, let every man have his own wife and let every
woman have her own husband. Let the husband render
the debt to his wife and the wife also in like manner to
her husband.*[32] And a little farther on: *Defraud not one
another, except perhaps, by consent for a time, that you
may give yourselves to prayer, and return together again,
lest Satan tempt you.*[33]

Note that he is already introduced to the secrets of
Heaven, yet by condescending love he gives thought to the
bed of carnal men; and though he raises the vision of his
heart to invisible things, being himself elevated, yet he
turns in compassion to the secrets of those who are weak.
He reaches the heavens in contemplation, yet in his solici-

tude he does not ignore the couch of the carnal, for being
united by the bond of charity to the highest and the lowest
alike, though in person mightily caught up to the high
places by the power of the Spirit, he is content in his loving-
kindness to be weak with others in their weakness. Therefore, he said: *Who is weak, and I am not weak? Who
is scandalised, and I am not on fire?* [34]

Hence, too, he says: *And I became to the Jews, a Jew.* [35]
He did this, not by abandoning his faith, but by extending
his loving-kindness. Thus, by transfiguring the person of
the unbeliever into himself, he purposed to learn personally how he ought to compassionate others, how he should
bestow on them what he would rightly wish them to bestow on himself, if their places were interchanged. Therefore, he says again: *Whether we be transported in mind,
it is to God, or whether we be sober, it is for you.* [36] For he
knew how to transcend himself by contemplation and how
to employ restraint by his condescension for his hearers.

Thus Jacob, as the Lord leaned on the ladder above and
the anointed stone was below, saw angels ascending and
descending,[37] which was a sign that true preachers do not
only aspire by contemplation to the Holy Head of the
Church above, namely, the Lord, but also descend to its
members in pity for them.

Thus Moses frequently goes in and out of the Tabernacle; and while within he is caught up in contemplation,
outside he devotes himself to the affairs of the weak. Inwardly he considers the hidden things of God, outwardly
he bears the burdens of carnal men. In doubtful matters,
too, he always returns to the Tabernacle to consult the
Lord in front of the Ark of the Covenant. He thus, no
doubt, sets an example to rulers, that when they are un-

certain what dispositions to make in secular matters, they
should always return to reflection, as though to the Tabernacle, and there, as it were, standing before the Ark of the
Covenant, should consult the Lord, whether they should
seek a solution of their problems in the pages of the Sacred Word.

Thus the Truth Itself, manifested to us by assuming our
human nature, engaged in prayer on the mountain and
worked miracles in the towns.[38] He thus showed the way
to be followed by good rulers, who, though they strive after
the highest things by contemplation, should nevertheless
by their compassion share in the needs of the weak. Then,
indeed, charity rises to sublime heights, when in pity it is
drawn by the lowly things of the neighbour, and the more
kindly it stoops to infirmity, the mightier is its reach to
the highest.

But those who rule others should show themselves such
that their subjects are unafraid to reveal their hidden
secrets to them.[38a] Thus, when these little ones are endur-
ing the waves of temptation, they will have recourse to the
pastor's understanding as to a mother's bosom; and in the
solace of his comforting words and in their prayerful tears
they will cleanse themselves when they see themselves
defiled by the sin that buffets them.

Hence also it is that in front of the doors of the Temple
there is a sea of brass for washing the hands of those who
enter the Temple, that is to say, a laver, supported by
twelve oxen, whose faces are plainly visible, but whose
hinder parts are not visible.[39] What else is symbolised by
the twelve oxen but the whole order of pastors? Of these
the Law says, as Paul reports: *Thou shalt not muzzle the
mouth of the ox that treadeth out the corn.*[40] We see the

work they do openly, but do not see the rest that later awaits them in the secret requital of the strict Judge. Those, however, who make ready in their patient condescension to cleanse the confessed sins of the neighbour, support the laver, as it were, in front of the door of the Temple. Whosoever, then, is striving to enter the gate of eternity, may reveal his temptations to the mind of the pastor, and cleanse the hands of thought or deed, as it were, in the laver of the oxen.

Now, it happens frequently that, while the ruler's mind in his condescension learns of the trials of others, he also is assailed by the temptations which he gives ear to; for in the case of the laver, too, that was mentioned as serving the cleansing of the multitude, it is certainly defiled. In receiving the filth of those who wash in it, it loses its limpid clearness. But the pastor need not fear these things at all, for when God weighs all things exactly, the pastor is the more easily delivered from temptation, as he is the more compassionately afflicted by the temptations of others.

CHAPTER 6

The ruler should in humility be the comrade of
those who live the good life; but in his zeal
for righteousness he should be stern
with the vices of evil-doers.

The ruler should in humility be the comrade of those who lead good lives, but stern with the vices of evil-doers. He must not set himself over the good in any way, and when the sins of the wicked demand it, he must assert the power of his supremacy at once. Thus, waiving aside his rank, he regards himself the equal of his subjects who lead good lives, but does not shrink from exercising the laws of rectitude against the perverse. For, as I remember to have said in the *Books of Morals*,[41] it is clear that nature brought forth all men in equality, while guilt has placed some below others, in accordance with the order of their varying demerits. This diversity, which results from vice, is a dispensation of the divine judgment, much as one man must be ruled by another, since all men cannot be on an equal footing.

Wherefore, all who are superiors should not regard in themselves the power of their rank, but the equality of their nature; and they should find their joy not in ruling over men, but in helping them.[42] For our ancient fathers are recorded to have been not kings of men, but shepherds of flocks. And when the Lord said to Noe and his sons: *Increase and multiply and fill the earth,* He at once added: *And let the fear and dread of you be upon all the beasts of the earth.*[43] Fear and dread were prescribed for all the beasts of the earth, but forbidden to be exercised over men. By nature a man is made superior to the beasts, but not to other men; it is, therefore, said to him that he is to be feared by beasts, but not by men. Evidently, to wish to be feared by an equal is to lord it over others, contrary to the natural order.

Yet it is necessary that rulers should be feared by subjects, when they see that the latter do not fear God. Lacking fear of God's judgments, these must at least fear sin out of human respect. It is not at all a case of exhibiting pride when superiors seek to inspire fear, whereby they do not seek personal glory, but the righteousness of their subjects. In fact, in inspiring fear in those who lead evil lives, superiors lord it, as it were, over beasts, not over men, because, in so far as their subjects are beasts, they ought also to be subjugated by fear.

Often, however, a ruler by the very fact of his preeminence over others becomes conceited; and because everything is at his service, because his orders are quickly executed to suit his wishes, because all his subjects praise him for what he has done well, but have no authority to criticise what he has done amiss and because they usually praise even what they ought to blame, his mind, led astray by those below him, is lifted above itself. While he is outwardly surrounded by abounding favours, the truth within him is made void. Forgetful of what he is, he is diverted by the commendations of others, and believes himself to be such as he hears himself outwardly proclaimed to be, not such as he should inwardly judge himself. He despises his subjects and does not acknowledge them to be his equals in the order of nature; and those whom he has excelled by the fortuity of power, he believes he has also surpassed by the merits of his life. He esteems himself to be wiser than any of those whom he sees he exceeds in power. For he puts himself on an eminence in his own estimation, and though he has his own limitations by reason of the equality of nature with others, he disdains to regard others as being on his level. He thus brings himself to be the like of him of whom Scripture says: *He beholdeth every high thing, and he is king over all the children of pride.*[44] He who aspired to singular eminence and disdained life in common with the angels, said: *I will place my seat in the North, I will be like the Most High.*[45] By a wonderful decree, therefore, he finds within himself the pit of his downfall, while outwardly exalting himself

on the pinnacle of power. Man is made like the apostate
angel when he disdains, though a man, to be like other
men.

In this way Saul, after having distinguished himself for
his humility, was swollen with pride in the eminence of
his power; by his humility he was advanced, by his pride,
rejected, as the Lord attested, saying: *When thou wast
a little one in thy own eyes, did I not make thee the head
of the tribes of Israel?* [46] He had previously seen himself
a little one in his own eyes, but relying on temporal power,
he no longer saw himself to be a little one. Preferring
himself to others, he regarded himself great above all
others, because he had greater power than they. And in
a wonderful way, while a little one in his own esteem, he
was great with God, but when he thought himself to be
great, he was little with God.

Usually, then, when the mind of a man is inflated with
a multitude of subjects under him, he becomes corrupted
and moved to pride by the eminence of his power which
panders to the mind. But such power is truly well-
controlled by one who knows how both to assert and
oppose it. He controls it well who knows how through it
to obtain the mastery over sin, and knows how with it to
associate with others on terms of equality. For the human
mind is prone to pride even when not supported by power;
how much more, then, does it exalt itself when it has that
support! But he disposes his power aright, who knows
how, with great care, both to derive from it what is profitable, and to subdue the temptations which it creates, and
how, though in possession of it, to realise his equality with
others, and at the same time set himself above sinners in
his zeal for retribution.

This is a distinction which will be more fully understood when we consider the examples given by the first
Pastor. Peter, who held from God the primacy in Holy
Church, refused to accept excessive veneration from Cor-
nelius though he acted rightly in humbly prostrating himself; but Peter acknowledged in him his equal, when he
said: *Arise, do not act so; I myself also am a man.*[47] But
when the guilt of Ananias and Sapphira were discovered
by him, he at once showed with what great authority he
had been made pre-eminent over others.[48] By his word
he smote their life when he laid it bare by his penetrating
spirit. He recalled to his mind that in the question of
opposition to sin he was supreme in the Church, but such
distinction was not present to his mind when among upright brethren honour was eagerly exhibited to him. In
the one instance holy conduct was met by the assertion
of common equality; in the other, zeal for retributive
justice revealed the right of authority.

Paul showed no consciousness of his pre-eminence over
his deserving brethren when he said: *Not because we
exercise dominion over your faith, but we are helpers of
your joy;* and he presently added: *For in faith you stand,*[49]
as if to explain what he had said, namely: "We do not lord
it over your faith, for in faith you stand, and we are equals
with you wherein we know you stand." It was as if he
was not aware of his pre-eminence over his brethren, when
he said: *We became little ones in the midst of you;* [50]
and again: . . . *and ourselves your servants through
Christ.*[51] But when he discovered a fault which required
correction, he at once remembered that he was master,
saying: *What will you? Shall I come to you with a rod?* [52]

Supreme rank is, therefore, well-administered, when the

superior lords it over vices rather than over brethren. When rulers correct their delinquent subjects, it is incumbent on them to observe carefully that, while they smite faults with due discipline in virtue of their authority, they acknowledge, by observing humility, that they are only the equals of the brethren whom they correct. But we should as a regular practice in thoughtful silence prefer to ourselves those whom we correct, for it is through us that their vices are smitten with rigorous discipline, whereas in the case of our own vices we are not chastised even by verbal censure of anyone. Therefore, we are the more bounden before the Lord, inasmuch as we sin with impunity before men. On the other hand, our discipline renders our subjects the more exempt from the divine judgment, as it does not exempt them here from punishment for their faults.

Consequently, humility must be preserved in the heart, and discipline in action. Between these two, we must diligently beware not to relax the rights of government by immoderate adherence to the virtue of humility, for if the superior depreciates himself unduly, he may be unable to restrain the lives of subjects under the bond of discipline. Let rulers, therefore, uphold externally what they undertake for the service of others, and internally retain their fear in their estimate of themselves. Nevertheless, let the subjects themselves perceive, by signs becomingly manifested, that their rulers are humble in their own estimation. They should thus apprehend both what they ought to fear from authority, and what to imitate in the sphere of humility.

Superiors, then, should ceaselessly take care that the greater the external manifestation of power, the more is it to be kept in subjection internally. It must not subdue their thought, it must not so carry the mind away as to captivate it for itself; otherwise the mind will be unable to control that to which it subjects itself in its lust for domination. That the mind of the ruler may not be carried away and elated in the enjoyment of power, it is rightly said by a man of wisdom: *Have they made thee a ruler? Be not lifted up, but be among them as one of them.*[53] So, too, Peter says: . . . *not as lording it over the clergy, but being made a pattern of the flock.*[54] So, the Truth in person, inviting us to the more sublime merits of virtue, says: *You know that the princes of the Gentiles lord it over them, and they that are the greater exercise power upon them. It shall not be so among you, but whosoever will be the greater among you, let him be your minister; and he that will be first among you, shall be your servant. Even as the Son of man is not come to be ministered unto, but to minister.*[55]

Wherefore it is that He indicates the punishment in store for the servant who becomes proud on his assumption of rule, saying: *But if that evil servant shall say in his heart: My lord is long a-coming, and shall begin to strike his fellow servants, and shall eat and drink with drunkards, the lord of that servant shall come in a day that he hopeth not, and at an hour that he knoweth not; and shall separate him, and appoint his portion with the hypocrites.*[56] That man is rightly accounted a hypocrite, who diverts the ministry of government to purposes of domination.

Sometimes, though, greater evil ensues when in the case of wicked persons a policy of equality is adhered to rather than of discipline. Heli, for example, overcome by misguided affection, and unwilling to chastise his delinquent sons, struck both himself and his sons before the strict Judge with a cruel sentence, for the divine utterance was: *Thou hast honoured thy sons rather than me.*[57] So, too, he chides the shepherds by the Prophet, saying: *That which was broken you have not bound up, and that which was driven away you have not brought back.*[58] One who has been cast away is brought back when, after having fallen into sin, he is recalled to the state of righteousness by the influence of pastoral care; and the ligature binds a fracture when discipline subdues sin, lest the wound's continued flow lead to death if a tight compress does not bind it up. Often, however, the fracture is made worse by an unskilful ligature, so that the lesion causes even greater pain from being bound up too tightly.

Wherefore, it is necessary that when the wound of sin in the subject is repressed by correction, even the restraint must be most carefully moderated, lest the feeling of kindness be extinguished by the manner in which the principles of discipline are exercised against the sinner. For care must be taken that loving-kindness, like that of a mother, be displayed by the ruler towards his subjects, and correction given as by a father. In all such cases treatment must be bestowed with care and circumspection, lest discipline be too rigid, or loving-kindness too lax.

We have said in the *Books on Morals* that either discipline or compassion is greatly wanting, if one is exercised independently of the other.[59] But rulers in their relations with subjcets should be animated by compassion duly considerate and by discipline affectionately severe.[60] This is what the Truth teaches [61] concerning the man who was half-dead and was taken to an inn by the care of a Samaritan, wine and oil being applied to his wounds, the wine to cauterize them, and the oil to soothe them. Thus it is necessary that he who sees to the healing of wounds should apply in wine biting pain and in oil soothing tenderness, for wine cleanses suppuration and oil promotes the course of healing. In other words, gentleness is to be mingled with severity; a compound is to be made of both, so that subjects may not be exasperated by too great harshness, nor enervated by excessive tenderness.

This, as St. Paul says,[62] is well symbolised by that Ark of the Tabernacle, in which, together with the Tables, were the rod and the manna; because if with the knowledge of the Sacred Scriptures in the breast of the good ruler there is the restraining rod, there should also be the manna of sweetness. Wherefore, David says: *Thy rod and Thy staff, they have comforted me.*[63] It is with a rod that we are smitten, but we are supported by a staff. If, then, there is the correction of the rod in striking, let there be the comfort of the staff in supporting.

There should, then, be love that does not enervate, vigour that does not exasperate, zeal not too immoderate and uncontrolled, loving-kindness that spares, yet not more than is befitting. Thus, while justice and clemency are blended in supreme rule, the ruler will soothe the hearts of his subjects even when he inspires fear, and yet in soothing them, hold them to reverential awe for him.

CHAPTER 7

In his preoccupation with external matters the ruler should not relax his care for the inner life, nor should his solicitude for the inner life cause neglect of the external.

Let the ruler not relax the care of the inner life by preoccupying himself with external matters, nor should his solicitude for the inner life bring neglect of the external, lest, being engrossed with what is external, he be ruined inwardly, or being preoccupied with what concerns only his inner self, he does not bestow on his neighbours the necessary external care. For often some persons, forgetting that they are superiors of their brethren for the sake of their souls, devote themselves with all concentration of heart to secular cares. These they gladly attend to when the occasion offers, but when the occasion is not present, hanker after them day and night with the surge of a disordered mind. When they find a respite from these occupations, because the occasion for them has gone by, they are the more wearied by the respite itself. For they take it as a pleasure to be weighed down by such activities, and regard it laborious not to be labouring in earthly concerns. And so it happens that, while they rejoice in being weighed down with tumultuous worldly business, they disregard those interior matters which they ought to be teaching others. Consequently, the life of their subjects undoubtedly grows languid, because, though these wish to make spiritual progress, they are confronted with the stumbling-block, as it were, of the example of their superior.

For when the head languishes, the members have no vigour. It is in vain that an army, seeking contact with the enemy, hurries behind its leader, if he has lost the way. No exhortation then uplifts the minds of subjects, no reproof castigates their faults, for when one who is a spiritual guardian fulfils the office of a judge of the world, the shepherd's care of the flock is lacking; and subjects cannot see the light of the truth, for when earthly cares occupy the pastor's mind, dust, driven by the winds of temptation, blinds the eyes of the Church.

When to counteract this state of things, the Redeemer of the human race, wishing to restrain us from gluttony, appositely said: *But take heed to yourselves, lest perhaps your hearts be overcharged with surfeiting and drunkenness,* He promptly added: *or the cares of this life.* On the same occasion He designedly added the element of fear, for He said: *Lest perchance that day come upon you suddenly.* The character of that day, too, He proclaimed, saying: *For as a snare shall it come upon all that sit upon the face of the whole earth.*[64] For the same reason He says again: *No one can serve two masters.*[65]

Wherefore, Paul withdraws the minds of religious persons from consorting with the world, by summoning, nay, rather by enlisting them, when he says: *No man, being a soldier to God, entangleth himself with secular businesses, that he may please him to whom he hath engaged himself.*[66] He, therefore, orders the rulers of the Church to aim at being free from these things, and by his counsel points to the remedy, saying: *If, therefore, you have judgments of things pertaining to this world, set them to judge who are the most despised in the Church,*[67] that is, those persons should engage in earthly affairs who are not adorned with spiritual gifts. Speaking more plainly, he might say: "Since these are incapable of penetrating interior matters, let them at least busy themselves with the necessary external things." Hence Moses, who speaks with God, is judged by the reproof of Jethro, a man of alien race, on the ground that he devotes himself by his ill-advised labour to the earthly affairs of the people.[68] At the same time counsel is given him to appoint others in his stead for the composing of strifes, so that he himself may be more free to learn the secrets of spiritual matters for teaching the people.

Subjects, then, are to transact inferior matters, rulers to attend to the highest, so that the eye, which is set above for guiding the steps, may not be dimmed by annoying dust. For all rulers are the heads of their subjects, and surely the head ought to look forward from above, that the feet may be able to go onward on a straight path. Otherwise, if the body's upright posture becomes bent and if the head stoops toward the earth, the feet will drag in the way of progress. But with what conscience can the ruler of souls use his pastoral rank among others, if he himself is engaged in those earthly occupations which he should reprehend in others? This is, indeed, what the Lord in the anger of His just retribution threatened through the Prophet when He said: *And there shall be like people like priest.*[69] Priest is, indeed, like people, when a man performing a spiritual office does what they do who are still adjudged in terms of carnal pursuits. This is contemplated and deplored by the Prophet Jeremias in the great grief of his charity, under the symbol of the destruction of the Temple, when he says: *How is the gold become dim, the finest colour is changed, the stones of the sanctuary are scattered in the top of every street!* [70] And indeed, what is meant by gold which surpasses all other metals, but surpassing holiness? What is meant by the finest colour, but the reverence paid to religion, beloved by all men? What, by the stones of the sanctuary, but persons in Sacred Orders? What is signified by the term streets, but the expanse of this life? Since in the Greek language width is expressed by *platos,*[71] obviously streets *(plateae)* are so termed for their expanse. The Truth Himself says: *Wide and broad is the way that leadeth to destruction.*[72]

Now, gold is dimmed when a holy life is corrupted by earthly deeds. The finest colour is changed when the former esteem of those who were credited with living religiously is diminished. For when anyone resigns himself to earthly activities after a life of constant holiness, reverence for him is ignored and grows dim, as though his lustre had faded in the eyes of men.

Further, the stones of the sanctuary are scattered in the streets when those who should have occupied themselves in the interior mysteries for the adornment of the Church, as it were in the secrets of the Tabernacle, wander outside in the broad ways of secular affairs. Evidently, they were made the stones of the sanctuary, that they might appear in the vesture of the High Priest within the Holy of Holies. But when the ministers of religion do not demand the Redeemer's honour from their subjects by their meritorious way of living, the stones of the sanctuary are not in the vesture of the High Priest. Indeed, the stones of the sanctuary lie scattered through the streets, when persons in Sacred Orders, given over to the laxity of their pleasures, cling to earthly affairs.

We should observe, too, that these are said to be scattered, not merely through the streets, but at the top of the streets; that is to say, even when they are engaged in earthly matters, they wish to appear at the top, so as to both occupy the broad ways in the enjoyment of their delights, and yet to be at the top of the street in the external repute of holiness.

Furthermore, we are not prevented from understanding these stones to be the stones from which the sanctuary had been constructed. They lie scattered at the top of the streets, when men in Sacred Orders, in whose office of holiness the glory of sanctity was previously seen to exist, devote themselves to the preference of earthly affairs. Secular employments, then, are sometimes to be sympathetically put up with, but never sought after out of affection for them. Otherwise, when they oppress the mind of him who is attached to them, he becomes submerged by the weight and sinks down from the concerns of Heaven even to the very depths.

Some, on the contrary, undertake the charge of the flock, but wish to be so free for spiritual occupations, as not to give any time at all to external matters. Now, when such people wholly neglect to attend to what pertains to the body, they afford no help to their subjects. It is no wonder that their preaching is disregarded for the most part, for while chiding the deeds of sinners, and not giving them the necessities of the present life, their words certainly do not find sympathetic listeners. Doctrine taught does not penetrate the minds of the needy, if a compassionate heart does not commend it to the hearts of hearers; but the seed of the word does germinate promptly, when the kindness of a preacher waters it in the hearer's heart.

Therefore, that the ruler may be able to plant within, he must also, with irreproachable intention, make provision for what is external. Let pastors, then, give their entire devotion to the inner life of their subjects, yet not neglect to provide for the exterior life also.

As I have said, the mind of the flock is, as it were, justified in being averse to accepting the words of the preacher, if the pastor neglects the duty of affording external help. Wherefore, too, the first Pastor gave this earnest admonition, saying: *The ancients that are among you, I beseech, who am myself also an ancient, and a witness of the sufferings of Christ, as also a partaker of that glory which is to be revealed in time to come, feed the flock of God which is among you.*[73] In this place he makes it clear whether it was the feeding of the heart or of the body that he was urging, when he presently added: *taking care of it, not by constraint, but willingly, according to God, not for filthy lucre's sake, but voluntarily.*[74]

In these words obviously a kindly forewarning is given to pastors lest, while they satisfy the needs of those under them, they slay themselves with the dagger of ambition, and when the neighbours are refreshed with succour given to the body, the pastors themselves remain bereft of the bread of righteousness. Paul excites that pastoral solicitude when he says: *He who has not care of his own, and especially of those of his house, he hath denied the faith, and is worse than an infidel.*[75] In these matters, therefore, they must always fear and watchfully take heed lest, while engaged in external cares, they be weaned away entirely from aspirations of their inner selves. For it commonly happens, as I have said, that when the hearts or rulers are incautiously occupied with temporal cares, their interior love grows cold, and immersed in external affairs, they do not fear forgetting that they have undertaken the guidance of souls. Consequently, the care that is expended externally on their subjects is to be kept within defined limits.

For that reason, it was well said by Ezechiel: *The priests shall not shave their heads, nor wear long hair, but they shall only poll their heads.*[76] For they are rightly called priests, who preside over the faithful to afford them guidance in sacred matters.[77] The hairs on the head are the thoughts about exterior matters. When these grow insensibly above the brain, they denote the cares of this life, which, sometimes arising unseasonably for lack of advertence, issue forth, as it were, while we are unconscious of them. Since, then, all who are placed over others should, indeed, have a care of external matters, but without being excessively occupied with them, priests are rightly forbidden to shave the head, or let the hair grow long, that so they may not wholly discard all consideration for the flesh on behalf of the lives of their subjects, nor again, allow it to engross them too much. Wherefore, it is well said: *They shall only poll their heads,* that is, care for temporal concerns must be displayed as much as need be, yet promptly reduced, lest it increase beyond measure. While, then, bodily life is safeguarded by employing provident care for what is external, and again, is not impeded through a moderate vigilance of the heart, hairs on the head of the priest are kept to cover the skin, but are cut away, so as not to veil the eyes.

CHAPTER 8

The ruler should not be zealous to please men, yet should give heed to what ought to please them.

At the same time it is also necessary that a ruler should be studiously vigilant that he be not actuated by the desire of pleasing men; that, while seriously penetrating the inner life, and with provident care supplying the things that are external, he does not seek to be loved by his subjects more than he seeks truth; or that while relying on his good actions and giving himself the appearance of a stranger to the world, his self-love does not render him a stranger to his Maker.

For that man is an enemy to his Redeemer who on the strength of the good works he performs, desires to be loved by the Church, rather than by Him. Indeed, a servant is guilty of adulterous thought, if he craves to please the eyes of the bride when the bridegroom sends gifts to her by him. In truth, when this self-love captures a ruler's mind, it sometimes rushes him into inordinate laxity, sometimes into asperity. For from love of himself, the ruler's mind is diverted into laxity, when he sees his subjects sinning and does not dare to correct them, lest their love of him grow weak; indeed, sometimes when he should have reproved their faults, he glosses them over with adulation. Wherefore, it is well said by the Prophet: *Woe to them that sew cushions under every elbow, and make pillows for the heads of persons of every age, to catch souls.*[78] To put cushions under every elbow is to cherish with smooth flattery souls that are falling away from rectitude and are reclining in the pleasures of this world. It is as if a person reclined with a cushion under the elbow, or a pillow under his head, when severe reproof is withheld from him when he sins, and enervating favouritism is bestowed on him, that he may recline at ease in his error, the while no asperity of reproof assails him.

This attitude the rulers show to those, of course, from whom they fear they can be retarded in the pursuit of temporal glory. Indeed, persons who in their estimation can do nothing against them, they constantly hound with bitter and harsh reproof. They never admonish them gently, but, forgetful of pastoral meekness, terrify them in the exercise of their right to govern. The divine word rightly reproves such rulers by the Prophet, saying: *But you ruled over them with rigour and with a high hand.*[79] These love themselves more than their Maker, and brag as they take measures against their subjects. They have no thought for what they should do, but only for the power that is theirs. They do not fear the judgment to come. They glory impiously in their temporal power, it pleases them to do freely what is wrong, and without any opposition from their subjects.

He, therefore, who sets himself to act evilly and yet wishes others to be silent, is a witness against himself, for he wishes himself to be loved more than the truth, which he does not wish to be defended against himself. There is, of course, no man who so lives as not sometimes to sin; but he wishes truth to be loved more than himself, who wills to be spared by no one against the truth. Wherefore, Peter willingly accepted the rebuke of Paul; [80] David willingly hearkened to the reproof of a subject.[81] For good rulers who pay no regard to self-love, take as a homage to their humility the free and sincere words of subjects. But in this regard the office of ruling must be tempered with such great art of moderation, that the minds of subjects, when demonstrating themselves capable of taking right views in some matters, are given freedom of expression, but freedom that does not issue into pride; otherwise, when liberty of speech is granted too generously, the humility of their own lives will be lost.

It is also to be observed that good rulers should wish to please men, but so as to draw their neighbours to the love of truth by the fair esteem they have of their rulers, not that these long to be loved themselves, but wish that this love should be a road, as it were, whereby they lead the hearts of the hearers to the love of the Creator. It is difficult for one who is not loved, however well he preaches, to find a sympathetic hearing. Wherefore, he who rules ought to aim at being loved, that he may be listened to, and yet not seek to be loved on his own account, lest he be discovered to rebel in the tyranny of his thought against Him whom he ostensibly serves in his office.

This is well suggested by Paul, when he reveals to us the secrets of his endeavour, saying: . . . *as I also in all things please all men;* [82] though again he says: *If I yet pleased men, I should not be the servant of Christ.* [83] Thus Paul pleases and does not please, because, in wishing to please he sought not to please men, but that through him truth might please men.

CHAPTER 9

*The ruler should realise well that vices often
masquerade as virtues.*

The ruler should also understand that vices commonly masquerade as virtues. Often, for instance, a niggard passes himself off as frugal, while one who is prodigal conceals his character when he calls himself open-handed. Often inordinate laxity is believed to be kindness, and unbridled anger passes as the virtue of spiritual zeal. Precipitancy is frequently taken as efficient promptitude, and dilatoriness as grave deliberation.

Wherefore, it is necessary that the ruler of souls discern with care and vigilance virtues from vices, lest niggardliness take possession of his heart while he exults in appearing frugal in his outlays, or when prodigally wasteful, he boast of his liberality as if it were compassion, or by passing over what should be castigated, he drag his subjects to eternal punishment, or when he mercilessly smites offences, he himself offend more grievously, or when his action could have been performed with rectitude and gravity, it become spoiled by unseasonable anticipation, or by deferring a good and meritorious act, it become changed into an evil one.

CHAPTER 10

*The prudence required of the ruler in applying cor-
rection and connivance, rigour and gentleness.*

It should also be observed that at times the faults of
subjects must be prudently overlooked, but they should
be given to understand that they are being overlooked.
Sometimes even what is openly known should be judiciously tolerated, while in other cases even hidden faults
must be subjected to a close scrutiny; and, as the case may
be, they should be either gently reproved or sharply censured.

Some things are, as we have said, to be prudently connived at, but the connivance indicated, so that when the
delinquent sees that he has been discovered and tolerated,
he may be ashamed to augment the faults which he realises are tolerated in silence, and may punish himself in
being his own judge, when the patience of the ruler mercifully excuses him. It was with such connivance that the
Lord fitly reproved Judea, when He said through the
Prophet: *Thou hast lied, and hast not been mindful of
me, nor thought on me in thy heart. For I am silent and
as one that seeth not.*[84] He, therefore, both connived at
her faults and let her know that He was doing so. He said
nothing against the sinner, and yet declared the fact that
He had held His peace. For some things, even openly
known, are to be judiciously tolerated, when, that is, the
occasion is not suitable for public reprehension. For
wounds are more inflamed by untimely incisions, and if

medicaments do not suit the occasion, it is certain that they do not serve their purpose of healing.

But while an opportunity is being sought for the correction of subjects, the patience of the ruler is tried under the burden of their faults, and so it is well said by the Psalmist: *The wicked have wrought upon my back;* [85] for it is on the back that we carry burdens. He complains, therefore, that sinners had wrought upon his back, as though he meant to say in plain words: "Those whom I cannot correct, I carry as a burden."

Some secret matters should, however, be closely investigated, so that from certain symptoms breaking out, the ruler may discover all that lurks hidden in the minds of his subjects, and by timely reproof come to know from insignificant things what is more serious. Hence it is rightly said to Ezechiel: *Son of man, dig in the wall;* and presently the same Prophet adds: *And when I had digged in the wall, behold, a door. And He said to me: Go in, and see the wicked abominations which they commit here. And I went in and saw, and behold, every form of creeping things, and the abomination of living creatures, and all the idols of the house of Israel were painted on the wall.* [86]

By Ezechiel is symbolised the persons of those in authority; by the wall, the obduracy of their subjects. And what else is it to dig in the wall, but to open out the obduracy of the heart by thoroughgoing questioning? And when he had dug into it, a door was discovered: that is to say, when the obduracy of the heart is penetrated by either searching inquisitions or judicious reproofs, a door, as it were, is revealed, through which every interior thought is seen. Wherefore, fitting words follow: *Go in,*

and see the wicked abominations which they commit here.
He goes in, as it were, to see the abominations, and by
examining certain external symptoms, he sees into the
hearts of his subjects, so that all the evil thoughts therein
are disclosed to him.

Wherefore, the Prophet adds: *And I went in and saw,
and behold, every form of creeping things and the abomination of living things.* By creeping things thoughts that
are wholly earthly are symbolised, whereas living things
stand for thoughts which are, indeed, slightly lifted above
the earth, but such as still look for the reward of earthly
recompense. For creeping things cling with the whole
body to the earth, while living things have their bodies to
a great extent lifted above the earth, but are ever bent
towards it with their gluttonous appetite. Wherefore,
there are creeping things within the wall, when thoughts
are revolved in the mind that never rise above earthly
desires.

There are also living things within the wall, when,
though some thoughts are right and good, yet they are
subservient to the desire for temporal gains and honours,
and though in themselves, as it were lifted above the earth,
yet through their craving to ingratiate themselves—by
their gluttonous desires, so to speak—they debase themselves to the lowest. Wherefore, the apposite addition:
*And all the idols of the house of Israel were painted on
the wall.* For it is written: . . . *and covetousness, which is
the service of idols.*[87] Rightly, then, after the living things
idols are adduced: some though lifting themselves, as it
were, above the earth by upright deeds, yet lower themselves to earth by unrighteous ambition. It is also well
said that they were painted, because, when the images of

external things are drawn into consciousness, what is revolved in the mind by thinking in pictured imagery, is, as it were, portrayed on the heart. It is, therefore, to be observed that an opening in the wall is first perceived, then a door, and only then is the hidden abomination revealed; for the signs of every sin first appear outwardly, then a door for the disclosure of open iniquity is shown, and then, at last, every evil that lurks within is manifested.

Some things are, however, to be reproved gently. Thus, when sin is committed, not through malice, but through sheer ignorance or frailty, it is then, indeed, necessary to temper reproof of the sin with great forbearance. For, in truth, all of us are subject to the frailties of our corrupt nature so long as we remain in this mortal flesh. Each one, therefore, ought to infer from his own case to what degree he should have mercy on the weakness of others, lest he seem forgetful of his own estate when he violently rushes into reproof of the frailty of his neighbour. Wherefore, Paul admonishes us, saying: *If a man be overtaken in any fault, you who are spiritual, instruct such a one in the spirit of meekness, considering thyself, lest thou also be tempted.*[88] It is as though he meant to say in so many words, that when the sight of another's infirmity is displeasing, reflect on what you are, that the spirit may moderate itself in its zeal for reproving, in fearing in its own case that which it reproves.

Nevertheless, there are some things which are to be reproved severely, so that when a fault is not recognised by the one committing it, he may appreciate its gravity by the verbal reproof, or when he glosses over to himself the evil he has done, he may have serious apprehension for himself owing to the asperity of the reproof given. It is, surely, the duty of the ruler to reveal the glory of our homeland in Heaven by preaching, to show what great temptations of the ancient Enemy are lurking in this life's journey, and to correct with severe and zealous asperity those evils in his subjects which cannot be treated with forbearance, lest, being too little incensed against such faults, he himself be held guilty of all.

Wherefore, it is well said to Ezechiel: *Take thee a tile, and lay it before thee, and draw upon it the plan of the city of Jerusalem;* and it is immediately added: ... *And lay siege against it, and build forts, and cast up a mound, and set a camp against it and place battering-rams round about it.* For his own defence, it is at once added: *And take unto thee an iron pan, and set it for a wall of iron between thee and the city.*[89]

Now, of what is Ezechiel a type but of teachers when it is said to him: *Take thee a tile, and lay it before thee, and draw upon it the plan of the city of Jerusalem?* Holy teachers take to themselves a tile, when they undertake to teach the earthly heart of their hearers; and this tile they lay before themselves, in that they guard it with their entire devotion. They are also ordered to draw upon it a plan of the city of Jerusalem: that is, by preaching they are at great pains to reveal to mundane hearts the vision of supernal peace. But since the glory of the heavenly country is recognised to no purpose unless it is also learned what great temptations of the crafty Enemy rush upon us here, it is appositely added: *And lay siege against it, and build forts.* Holy preachers lay siege about the tile on which the city of Jerusalem is portrayed, when a mind that is mundane but already a seeker of the supernal country, is shown how violent is the attack of opposing vices in this life. For when it is shown how every single sin lays siege to those who are making progress, it is as if the words of the preacher were describing a siege of Jerusalem.

But because it should be known not only how vices assail us, but how virtues which are cherished lend us strength, it is rightly added: *and build forts.* The holy preacher builds forts, when he shows us what virtues are to be opposed to the several vices. And since, as virtue grows strong, the wars of temptations commonly increase, it is again rightly added: *and cast up a mound, and set a camp against it, and place battering-rams round about it.* The preacher casts up a mound, when he discourses of the mass of increasing temptation; he sets up a camp against Jerusalem, when he forewarns those hearers who are rightly disposed, of the stealthy and almost incredible ambushes of the crafty Enemy; and he stations battering-rams all round, when he makes known the darts of temptations that encompass us on all sides in this life, and how they pierce through the walls of our virtues.

But, however minutely the ruler indicates these matters, he is not discharging his responsibility for eternity, unless his fervent spirit glows with zeal in opposing the delinquencies of each individual. Wherefore, again, it is rightly added: *And take unto thee an iron pan, and set it for a wall of iron between thee and the city.* For by the pan is symbolised a scorching of the mind, and by iron, the hardness of reproof; and what scorches and excruciates the mind of the teacher more than burning zeal for God? Wherefore, Paul was burnt by the frying pan when he said: *Who is weak, and I am not weak? Who is scandalised, and I am not on fire?* [90] And since the man who is inflamed with zeal for God is fortified by a strong, permanent defence, lest he be condemned for negligence, it is rightly said: *Set it for a wall of iron between thee and the city.* The iron pan is set as an iron wall between the Prophet and the city, when rulers in their office display a vigorous zeal and this zeal serves them as a strong fortification between themselves and their hearers; thus they do not become bereft of the power of punishing, which would be the case if they were remiss in administering reproof.

But in regard to all these matters, we must bear in mind that when the mind of the teacher is incited to reprove, it is very difficult not to break forth sometimes into expressions that should have been avoided. It commonly happens that when the fault of a subject is corrected with harsh invective, the master is driven to excess in words; and when reproof blazes forth immoderately, the hearts of the sinners fall into dejection and despair. Wherefore, it is necessary that an exasperated ruler, on reflecting that he has smitten the mind of subjects more than he should have done, must take stock of himself and perform penance, to obtain pardon in the sight of the Truth by his sorrow, and for the reason, too, that it was through the ardour of his zeal that he sinned.

This is what the Lord enjoins on Moses in a figure, saying: *If a man go guilelessly with his friend to the wood to hew timber, and the wood of the axe slipped out of his hand and the iron, slipping from the handle, struck his friend and killed him: he shall flee to one of the cities aforesaid and live, lest perhaps the next kinsman of him whose blood was shed, being under the impulse of his grief, should pursue and apprehend him . . . and take away his life.*[91] Now, we go into a wood with a friend as often as we turn our attention to the sins of subjects; and guilelessly we hew wood when we cut away the faults of sinners with loving intention. But the axe flies from the hand when reproof oversteps itself and degenerates into asperity; and the iron flies from the handle, when the words of reproof are excessively harsh and the friend is struck and killed; that is to say, a contumelious utterance kills the spirit of love in the hearer.

The mind of one reproved breaks out suddenly into hatred, if reproof given taxes it more than is befitting. But he who so carelessly hews wood as to kill his neighbour, must needs flee to the three cities, that in one of them he may live protected; for if he betakes himself to penitential grief and hides himself under hope and charity in the unity of the Sacrament, he is not accounted guilty of the homicide which he perpetrated. And the next kinsman, even on finding him does not kill him; for when the strict Judge comes, He who has made Himself one of us by sharing our nature, He undoubtedly does not prefer a charge of guilt against one who is screened by faith, hope, and charity under the shelter of His forgiveness.

CHAPTER 11

The ruler's devotion to meditating on the Sacred Law.

Now, all this is duly fulfilled by the ruler if, being inspired by the supernal spirit of fear and love, he meditates diligently and every day on the precepts of the Sacred Word. The words of divine admonition should restore in him the sense of responsibility and a provident circumspection in regard to the celestial life, which habitual intercourse with men constantly destroys. One who protracts length of years in secular society should, by aspiring after compunction, ever renew himself in the love of his spiritual homeland. Actually the heart greatly deteriorates in the midst of human converse, and since it is undoubtedly manifest that, driven by the tumults of exterior occupations, it goes to ruin, it should ceaselessly make it its aim to rise again by the pursuit of instruction. Hence it is that Paul admonishes the disciple who was appointed over the flock, saying: *Till I come, attend unto reading.*[92] Hence David says: *Oh, how have I loved Thy law, O Lord! It is my meditation all the day.*[93] It was for this reason that the Lord commanded Moses concerning the carrying of the Ark, saying: *Thou shalt make four golden rings which thou shalt put at the four corners of the Ark . . . . Thou shalt make bars also of setim wood, and shalt overlay them with gold. And thou shalt put them in through the rings that are in the sides of the Ark, that it may be carried on them. And they shall always be in the rings, neither shall they at any time be drawn out of them.*[94]

What is symbolised by the Ark but Holy Church? The orders are that it is to be provided with four rings of gold in the four corners—obviously because, being extended to the four parts of the world, it is declared to be equipped with the four books of the Holy Gospels. And staves of setim wood are made and inserted into these rings for carrying, because strong and persevering teachers, like incorruptible timbers, are to be sought out, who, always adhering to the instructions of the sacred volumes, proclaim the unity of Holy Church, and, as it were, carry the Ark, by their being let into the rings. Indeed, to carry the Ark with staves is to bring Holy Church through preaching to the untutored minds of unbelievers. Furthermore, they are ordered to be overlaid with gold, that when the sound of their preaching goes forth to others, they may themselves shine in the splendour of their way of life. Regarding them it is well added: *And they shall always be in the rings, neither shall they at any time be out of them;* for it is evidently necessary that they who devote themselves to the office of preaching should never depart from the occupation of sacred reading. It is to this purpose that the staves are ordered to be always in the rings, that when occasion demands the carrying of the Ark, there should be no delay in inserting them— that is to say, when subjects consult the pastor in any spiritual matter, it is most disgraceful if he should then seek to learn at a time when he ought to solve their problem. Let the staves remain in the rings: let the teachers, ever meditating in their hearts on the Sacred Word, at once raise the Ark of the Testament, let them teach forthwith when the occasion demands it.

Wherefore, the first Pastor of the Church well admonishes all other pastors, saying: *Being ready always to satisfy every one that asketh you a reason of that hope which is in you,*[95] as if he plainly said: "Let the staves never be withdrawn from the circles, so that no delay may hinder the carrying of the Ark."

PART THREE

How the Ruler Should Teach and Admonish His Subjects By His Holy Life

We have shown, then, what the character of the pastor should be: let us now set forth his manner of teaching. Well, as long before us Gregory of Nazianzus of revered memory has taught,[1] one and the same exhortation is not suited to all, because they are not compassed by the same quality of character. Often, for instance, what is profitable to some, harms others. Thus, too, herbs which nourish some animals, kill others; gentle hissing that calms horses, excites young puppies; medicine that alleviates one disease, aggravates another; and bread such as strengthens the life of robust men, destroys that of little children.

Wherefore, the discourse of a teacher should be adapted to the character of the hearers, so as to be suited to the individual in his respective needs, and yet never deviate from the art of general edification. For what else are the minds of attentive hearers but, if I may say so, the taut strings of a harp, which the skilful harpist plays with a variety of strokes, that he may not produce a discordant melody? And it is for this reason that the strings give forth a harmonious melody, because they are not plucked with the same kind of stroke, though plucked

89

with the one plectrum. Hence, too, every teacher, in order to edify all in the one virtue of charity, must touch the hearts of his hearers by using one and the same doctrine, but not by giving to all one and the same exhortation.

CHAPTER 1

Variety in the art of preaching.

In giving admonition we must distinguish between:
men and women;
the young and the old;
the poor and the rich;
the joyful and the sad;
subjects and superiors;
slaves and masters;
the wise of this world and the dull;
the impudent and the timid;
the insolent and the fainthearted;
the impatient and the patient;
the kindly and the envious;
the sincere and the insincere;
the hale and the sick;
those who fear afflictions and, therefore, live innocently, and those so hardened in evil as to be impervious to the correction of affliction;
the taciturn and the loquacious;
the slothful and the hasty;
the meek and the choleric;
the humble and the haughty;
the obstinate and the fickle;

the gluttonous and the abstemious;

those who mercifully give of their own, and those addicted to thieving;

those who do not steal yet do not give of their own, and those who give of their own yet do not desist from despoiling others;

those living in discord and those living in peace;

sowers of discord and peacemakers;

those who do not understand correctly the words of the Holy Law and those who do, but utter them without humility;

those who, though capable of preaching worthily, yet are afraid to do so from excessive humility, and those whose unfitness or age debars them from preaching, yet who are impelled thereto by their hastiness;

those who prosper in their pursuit of temporal things, and those who desire, indeed, the things of the world yet are wearied out by suffering and adversity;

those who are bound in wedlock and those who are free from the ties of wedlock;

those who have had carnal intercourse and those who have had no such experience;

those who grieve for sins of deed and those who grieve for sins of thought only;

those who grieve for their sins yet do not abandon them, and those who abandon their sins yet do not grieve for them;

those who even approve of their misdeeds and those who confess their sins yet do not shun them;

those who are overcome by sudden concupiscence, and those who deliberately put on the fetters of sin;

those who commit only small sins but commit them

frequently, and those who guard themselves against small sins yet sometimes sink into grave ones;

those who do not even begin to do good, and those who begin but do not finish;

those who do evil secretly and good openly, and those who hide the good they do, yet allow themselves to be thought ill of because of some things they do in public.

But what is the use of running through all these groups and cataloguing them, if we do not also explain the several methods of giving admonitions to each with what brevity we can?

Admonition 1. Wherefore, men are to be admonished in one way, women in another, for graver obligations must be imposed on the former, that they may perform great things, and lighter obligations on the others, that they may be converted by gentle treatment.

Admonition 2. Young people are to be admonished in one way, old people in another, because the former are for the most part guided to make progress by severe admonition, while the latter are disposed to better deeds by gentle remonstrance, for it is written: *An ancient man rebuke not, but entreat him as a father.*[2]

CHAPTER 2

How to admonish the poor and the rich.

Admonition 3. The poor are to be admonished in one way, the rich in another, for we should offer to the former the solace of encouragement against tribulation, whereas the latter should be inspired with the fear of being proud. It is to the poor that the Lord says by the Prophet: *Fear not, for thou shalt not be confounded;* [3] and shortly after He says soothingly: *O poor little one, tossed with tempest.* [4] And again, He comforts this one saying: *I have chosen thee in the furnace of poverty.* [5]

On the other hand, Paul says to his disciple concerning the rich: *Charge the rich of this world not to be high-minded, nor to trust in the uncertainty of their riches.* [6] We must here note carefully that the teacher of humility, when mentioning the rich, does not say: "Ask," but, "Charge," because, though loving-kindness is to be bestowed on the indigent, honour is not a debt to the proud. For such, therefore, what is rightly said is the more rightly commanded as they are puffed up in the pride of their thoughts about earthly things. Of them the Lord says in the Gospel: *But woe to you that are rich, for you have your consolation.* [7] Because they do not know the eternal joys, they derive their consolation from the abundance of this life. Therefore, those are to be comforted who are refined in the furnace of poverty, whereas fear is to be inspired in the rich who are elated by the consolations of temporal glory. The former are to learn that they do possess riches, though they do not see them; and the latter must realise that they certainly cannot retain the wealth which they behold.

But frequently the moral character of people affects their personal attitude, so that a rich man may be humble and a poor man proud. Wherefore the words of a preacher should be quickly adapted to the life led by his hearer, so that he may smite the pride of a poor man the more vigorously, when he is not rendered humble even by the poverty that afflicts him, and the more gently encourage the humility of the rich, if they are not made haughty in spite of the abundance of their resources. Sometimes, however, even a rich man who is proud must be dealt with by gentle exhortation; for often, too, it happens that indurated wounds are softened by gentle fomentations, and a raging madman is often restored to sanity by a physician who humours him, and the courtesy shown so captivates him as to mitigate his affliction of insanity.

Indeed, we should not disregard the fact that whenever the evil spirit possessed Saul, David took his harp and soothed his madness.[8] What is symbolised by Saul but the pride of the mighty and what by David but the lowly life of the Saints? As often, therefore, as Saul was possessed by the unclean spirit, his madness was soothed by David's singing. So, too, whenever the disposition of men in power is turned to raving anger by pride, it is proper that we should recall them to a healthy frame of mind by gentle words, sweet tones of the harp, as it were. But at times, in taking to task the powerful of this world, they are first to be dealt with by drawing divers comparisons in a case ostensibly concerning someone else. Then, when they give a right judgment on what apparently is another's case, they are to be taken to task regarding their own guilt by a suitable procedure. Thus a mind puffed up with temporal power cannot possibly lift itself up against the reprover, for by its own judgment it has trodden on the neck of pride; and it cannot argue to defend itself, as it stands convicted by the sentence out of its own mouth.

Thus it was that Nathan the Prophet, come to chide the king, to all appearance asked his judgment in the case of a poor man against a rich man.[9] The king first was to deliver judgment and then to hear that he was the culprit. Thus he was completely unable to gainsay the just sentence which he had personally delivered against himself. Therefore, the holy man, considering both the sinner and the king, aimed in that wonderful manner at convicting a bold culprit first by his own admission, and then cut him by his rebuke. For a short while he concealed the person whom he was aiming at, and then at once struck him when he had convicted him. His stroke would, perhaps, have had less force, if he had chosen to castigate the sin directly the moment he began to speak; but by beginning with a similitude, he sharpened the rebuke which he was concealing. He came like a physician to a sick man, saw that his wound had to be incised, but was in doubt about the endurance of the patient. He, therefore, concealed the surgeon's knife under his coat, but drawing it out suddenly, pierced the wound, that the sick man might feel the knife before he saw it, for if he had first seen it, he might have refused to feel it.

CHAPTER 3

How to admonish the joyful and the sad.

Admonition 4. The joyful are to be admonished in one way, the sad in another. Thus, to the joyful are to be displayed the sad things that accompany punishment, but to the sad, the glad promises of the Kingdom. The joyful should learn by severe warnings what to fear, the sad should be told of the rewards to which they may look forward. It is to the former that it is said: *Woe to you that now laugh, for you shall weep;* [10] but the sad should be told the same Master's teaching: *I will see you again, and your heart shall rejoice, and your joy no man shall take from you.* [11]

Some men, however, become gay or sad, not owing to circumstances but to temperament. These are to be told that certain defects are connected with certain temperaments, that the gay are not far from lechery and the sad not far from anger. Hence each one must consider not only what he supports as part of his temperament, but also what worse things tend to press on him close at hand; otherwise, by not fighting against what he has to put up with, he may yield to the evil from which he thinks he is immune.

CHAPTER 4

How to admonish subjects and superiors.

Admonition 5. Subjects are to be admonished in one way, superiors in another, but the former in such a way that subjection may not crush them; the latter, that their exalted position may not lift them up; the former, that they should not do less than is ordered; the latter, that they should not command more than is just; the former, that they submit with humility; the latter, that they be moderate in the exercise of their superiority. For it is said to the former, and this can be understood figuratively: *Children, obey your parents in the Lord.* But on superiors it is enjoined: *Fathers, provoke not your children to anger.* [12] Let the former learn to keep in order their interior dispositions before the eyes of the hidden Judge; the others, how to set outwardly the example of a good life also to those committed to them. For superiors should know that if ever they do what is wrong, they deserve as many deaths as were the examples of perdition given to their subjects.[13] Wherefore, it is necessary that they should guard themselves the more cautiously against a fault, as by their misdeeds they not only perish themselves, but are responsible for the souls of those whom they ruin by their evil example.

Subjects, therefore, are to be admonished, lest they be more severely punished, should they be unable to stand acquitted at least on their own account; the others, lest they be judged guilty of the errors of their subjects, even though they no longer find reason for concern on their own account.

Subjects are to be admonished to live in the greater anxiety about themselves, the less they are involved in the care of others; and the latter, to fulfil their charge over others in such wise, as not to fail to accomplish the charge over themselves, and to be ardently solicitous on their own account in such wise, as not to grow slack in watching over those entrusted to them.

To the one who is at leisure to look after his own affairs, it is said: *Go to the ant, O sluggard, and consider her ways and learn wisdom.*[14] But the other receives a fearful warning, when it is said: *My son, if thou be surety for thy friend, thou has engaged fast thy hand to a stranger, and thou art ensnared with the words of thy mouth, and caught with thy own words.*[15] Obviously, to be surety for a friend is to take charge of the soul of another on the guarantee of one's own conduct. And so the hand is engaged fast to a stranger, because the mind is involved in the charge of a responsibility which did not exist before; and a man is ensnared with the words of his mouth, and caught with his own words, because, while he is obliged to speak what is good to those under his charge, he must first observe the matters of which he speaks. He is, therefore, ensnared with the words of his mouth, in that he is constrained by the exigency of right reason not to allow his way of life to be relaxed in a way that does not accord with his teaching. In other words, in the presence of the strict Judge he is constrained to accomplish in his own conduct what he clearly prescribes in words to others.

Consequently, to the words cited above, the exhortation is at once well added: *Do, therefore, my son, what I say, and deliver thyself, because thou art fallen into the hands of thy neighbour. Run about, make haste, stir up thy friend. Give not sleep to thy eyes, neither let thy eyelids slumber.*[16] For whosoever is put over others for an example of living, is admonished to be watchful not only over himself, but also to arouse his friend. Indeed, it is not sufficient for him to keep watch by a good life, if he does not remove from the torpor of sin the person over whom he is set, for it is well said: *Give not sleep to thy eyes, neither let thy eyelids slumber.* To give sleep to the eyes is to cease from care, and thus to neglect altogether the charge of subjects. The eyelids slumber, when our thoughts, weighed down by sloth, connive at what we know should be reproved. To be in deep sleep is neither to know, nor to correct, the actions of those committed to us. To slumber but not to sleep is to be well aware of what should be reprehended, but not to amend it with proper reproof, owing to mental sloth. Yet by slumbering, the eye is induced to sleep profoundly, because commonly the superior

who does not eradicate the evil which he observes, comes
to that state which his negligence deserves, namely, not
even to recognise the sins of his subjects.

Wherefore, they who are superiors must be warned to be
earnestly on the watch, to have vigilant eyes within and
round about, and to strive to become living creatures of
Heaven. For the living creatures of Heaven are described
as full of eyes round about and within.[17] Surely, it is fitting
that all who are set above others should have eyes within
and round about, inasmuch as they aim at pleasing the
Judge within, and while giving outwardly examples of
living, should detect what is to be corrected in others.

Subjects are to be warned not to judge rashly the way
of life of their superiors if, by chance, they observe anything reprehensible; otherwise, their just criticism of what
is wrong may plunge them by pride into lower depths
themselves. They must be warned that in observing faults
in their superiors, they do not become too disrespectful
to them. On the contrary, should the faults be of very
serious nature, their private judgment should be such that
constrained by the fear of God they still do not refuse to
bear the yoke of reverence in subjection to them.

We shall establish this the better by proposing what
David did.[18] When Saul, his persecutor, had gone into a
cave for the purpose of evacuation, David, who for a long
time had been abused by him, chanced to be there together
with his men. When his men urged him to smite Saul,
he opposed their suggestion with the reply, that he ought
not to lay hands on the Lord's anointed. Nevertheless, he
arose unseen by Saul, and cut off the hem of his robe.
Now, what is symbolised by Saul but bad rulers, and
what by David, but good subjects? The natural relieving

of himself by Saul signifies bad rulers extending the wickedness conceived in the heart to deeds of foul stench, and
displaying the evil of their thoughts in outward acts. Yet
David shrank from smiting him, because subjects with a
dutiful conscience keep themselves completely free from
the plague of disparagement, and do not attack with the
sword of the tongue the way of life of superiors, even when
they find fault with their imperfections. When they cannot refrain through frailty from speaking out, however
humbly, of some excessively evil outward act of superiors,
they, as it were, quietly cut the hem of the garment; because, when harmlessly and unobserved they depreciate
the dignity of a superior, it is as though they deface the
vesture of a king set over them. Yet they reflect and most
severely take themselves to task for even the slightest defa-
mation in words. Wherefore, too, the apposite words in
that place: *After which David's heart struck him because
he had cut off the hem of Saul's robe.*[19] Indeed, the deeds
of superiors are not to be smitten with the sword of the
mouth, even when they are rightly thought to be deserving
of reproof.

And if sometimes the tongue in criticism of them slips
in the least degree, the heart must be overwhelmed with
penitential grief. It should reflect upon itself; and when
it has offended the power set over it, it should dread the
judgment passed against it by Him who appointed superiors. For when we offend those set over us, we oppose
the ordinance of Him who set them above us. For this
reason Moses, too, when he recognised that the people
were complaining against him and Aaron, said: *For what
are we? Your murmuring is not against us, but against
the Lord.*[20]

CHAPTER 5

How to admonish slaves and masters.

Admonition 6. Slaves are to be admonished in one way, masters in another, that is, slaves are to be admonished to consider always the lowliness of their condition, masters, ever to bear in mind their own nature, namely, that they have been created equal to their slaves.

Slaves are to admonished not to despise their masters, lest they offend God by their proud opposition to His ordinance. Masters are also to be admonished that they offend God by priding themselves on His gift to them, and not realising that they who are held in subjection by reason of their state of life, are their equals in virtue of their common nature. The former are to be admonished to bear in mind that they are servants of masters; the latter, that they are to acknowledge themselves to be fellow servants of servants. To the former it is said: *Servants, obey . . . your masters according to the flesh;* [21] and again: *Whosoever are servants under the yoke, let them count their masters worthy of all honour;* [22] and to the latter it is said: *And you, masters, do the same things to them, forbearing threatenings, knowing that the Lord both of them and of you is in Heaven.* [23]

CHAPTER 6

How to admonish the wise and the dull.

Admonition 7. The wise of this world are to be admonished in one way, the dull in another. For the wise are to be admonished to stop knowing what they know; [24] and the dull are to be admonished to seek to know what they do not know. In the former, the first thing to be got rid of is the persuasion that they are wise. In the latter, whatever heavenly wisdom they know, is to be built up, because, as they are not proud, their hearts are prepared to undertake the building. In the case of the former, we should aim at making them more wisely foolish, to make them abandon their foolish wisdom, and to make them learn the wise foolishness of God. The latter are to be instructed that from what is accounted foolishness, they should advance in, and attain more closely to, true wisdom. To the wise it is said: *If any man among you seem to be wise in this world, let him become a fool, that he may be wise.*[25] To the dull it is said: *There are not many wise according to the flesh,*[26] and again: *But the foolish things of the world God hath chosen that He may confound the wise.*[27]

The former are usually more readily converted by arguments from reason; the latter are often converted better by examples. To the former it is profitable to fall vanquished by their own allegations, but for the dull it is sometimes sufficient to learn of the praiseworthy deeds of others. Wherefore, the great teacher, *a debtor to the wise and to the unwise,*[28] when admonishing some of the Hebrews who were wise, and others also who were somewhat slow of apprehension, and speaking to them of the fulfilment of the Old Testament, routed the wisdom of the former by argument, saying: *For that which decayeth and groweth old, is near its end.*[29] But when he observed that some were to be led only by examples, he added in the same epistle: *Saints had trials of mockeries and stripes, moreover also of bands and prisons. They were stoned, they were cut asunder, they were tempted, they were put to death by the sword.*[30] And again: *Remember your prelates who have spoken the word of God to you, whose faith follow, considering the end of their conversation.*[31] Thus victorious reasoning should subdue the one, but the gentle force of example influence the other to rise to higher things.

CHAPTER 7

How to admonish the impudent and the timid.

Admonition 8. The impudent are to be admonished in one way, the timid in another. The former can be restrained from the vice of impudence only by harsh reproof, but the latter are generally better disposed by gentle exhortation. The former do not know that they are in fault unless reproved by many. For effecting a change in the latter, it commonly suffices that the teacher remind them gently of their evil deeds.

The impudent are better corrected by direct reproof, but in the case of the timid it is more profitable if what is reprehended in them is touched upon, as it were, incidentally. Indeed, the Lord openly upbraided the impudent Jewish people, saying: *Thou hadst a harlot's forehead, thou wouldst not blush.*[32] Again, He consoles the timid, saying: *Thou shalt forget the shame of thy youth, and shalt remember no more the reproach of thy widowhood, for He that made thee shall rule over thee.*[33] Paul, too, openly rebukes the Galatians because of their impudent sins, saying: *O senseless Galatians, who hath bewitched you?* And again: *Are you so foolish, that, whereas you began in the*

Spirit, you would now be made perfect by the flesh? [34] But the faults of the timid he reproves as if compassionating them, saying: *I rejoice in the Lord exceedingly, that now at length your thought for me hath flourished again, as you did also think, but you were busied.* [35] Thus, harsh invective was to disclose the faults of the one, and gentle words to cloak the negligence of the other.

CHAPTER 8

How to admonish the insolent and the fainthearted.

Admonition 9. The insolent are to be admonished in one way, the fainthearted in another. The former, greatly relying on themselves, scorn reproofs from all others, but the latter, too conscious of their weakness, commonly fall into despondency. The former esteem everything they do to be singularly excellent, the fainthearted think what they do is extremely despicable, and, therefore, their spirit is broken in dejection.

And so the deeds of the insolent are to be subtly demolished by him who reproves, so that what they are complacent about may be shown to be displeasing to God. Now, we best reprove the insolent, when we show them that what they believe they have done well has been ill-done, so that a wholesome confusion may ensue from what they believe won glory for them. For sometimes, when they do not in the least perceive that they have committed the vice of insolence, they are the more quickly corrected when they are confounded by the charge of some more obvious guilt incidentally brought up. Thus, from the fact that they cannot defend it, they will realise that they wrongly uphold what they, in fact, defend.

Wherefore, when Paul saw that the Corinthians were insolent and arrogant, one against the other, in saying that one was of Paul, another of Apollo, another of Cephas, another of Christ,[36] he openly challenged them with the crime of incest committed among them, and not corrected, saying: *It is heard that there is fornication among you, and such fornication as the like is not among the heathens, that one should have his father's wife. And you are puffed up, and have not rather mourned, that he might be taken away from among you that hath done the deed.*[37] This is as if he said in so many words: "Why in your insolence do you say you are of this one and of that one, seeing that by your dissolute lawlessness you show that you are of none of them?"

But the opposite course holds for the fainthearted. We are more apt to bring them back to the path of well-doing, if by way of indirect approach we refer to some of their good points. Thus, by reproving and correcting some things, and approving and praising others, their sensitiveness is palliated by the praise they hear, though it is chastised by the rebuking of their fault. Generally we make more profitable progress with these people, if we also speak of their good deeds. And if they have done some deeds out of order, we do not then reprove this as something actually done, but utter a prohibition against it as something not to be done. Thus the favour shown them will encourage their zeal for the things which we approve, and the gentle exhortation will be the more effectual with the fainthearted against what we reprove in them.

Wherefore, the same Paul, on learning that the Thessalonians remained steadfast in accordance with the preaching which they had received, and were not a little dismayed at the prospect of an approaching end of the world, first praised them for those things in which they displayed courage, and afterwards, with prudent admonition, strengthened them in that matter wherein they were weak. This is what he says: *We are bound to give thanks always to God for you, brethren, as it is fitting, because your faith groweth exceedingly, and the charity of every one of you towards each other aboundeth, so that we ourselves also glory in you in the churches of God for your patience and faith.*[38] But when he had premised these soothing commendations for their way of living, he presently added: *But we beseech you, brethren, by the coming of our Lord Jesus Christ, and of our gathering together unto Him, that you be not easily moved from your sense, nor be terrified, neither by spirit, nor by word, nor by epistle, as sent from us, as if the day of the Lord were at hand.*[39]

True teacher that he was, he conducted matters so that they were first to recall something for which they were praised, and afterwards follow his admonition. The words of praise were to fortify their minds against feeling disturbed over the admonition. And whilst he knew their distress at the expectation of the end being near, he did not reprove them for being distressed, but, as though he knew nothing of their past attitude, he urged them not to be disquieted. Thus, while they believed their preacher to be unaware of their groundless distress, they were to fear making themselves reprehensible as much as they feared being known by him to be distressed.

CHAPTER 9

How to admonish the impatient and the patient.

Admonition 10. The impatient are to be admonished in one way, the patient in another. We should say to the impatient that when they neglect to curb their spirit, they are borne precipitately into many wrongs, even such as they do not intend, because, obviously, impetuosity drives the mind whither it does not wish. In its agitated state it acts as if it did not know what it was doing, only to feel regret when later it realises what it has done. Morever, the impatient should be told that when they are precipitate under the impulse of their emotions, they sometimes act as if they were other than they are, and hardly recognise the evil they have done. When they do not resist their turbulence, they upset the good they may have done when the mind was tranquil, and by their sudden impulse they undo what with protracted labour they have built up. Even the virtue of charity, mother and guardian of all the other virtues, is lost through the fault of impatience. For it is written: *Charity is patient.*[40] Therefore, when patience is wanting, there is no charity. Also, it is because of the fault of impatience that teaching, the nurse of virtues, is lost, for Scripture says: *The learning of a man is known by patience.*[41] The less patient a man proves to be, the less instructed does he show himself to be; and he cannot truly impart by instruction what is good, if in his own way of life he does not know how to bear with equanimity the evils that others do.

Furthermore, it is by the fault of impatience that the sin

of arrogance commonly pierces the mind, because, when a
man does not put up with being disregarded in this world,
he tries to display what good points he may have; and so
impatience leads him on to arrogance, and being unable
to tolerate contempt, he ostentatiously boasts in advertis-
ing himself. Wherefore, it is written: *Better is the patient
man than the presumptuous.*[42] Indeed, the patient man
suffers any evil rather than that his hidden good qualities
become known through the evil of ostentation. On the
contrary, the arrogant man prefers that good should be attributed to him even falsely, rather than that he should
suffer the slightest evil. Since, then, when patience is
abandoned, all the good already done is ruined, it was
proper that Ezechiel should be enjoined to have a trench
made in the altar of God,[43] that the whole burnt offerings
laid upon it might be preserved. For if there were no
trench in the altar, the rising breeze would scatter every
sacrifice laid on it. Now, what else do we understand the
altar of God to be but the soul of the just man, which lays
on itself, before His eyes, as a sacrifice all the good deeds
he has performed? What else is the trench of the altar but
the patience of good men, which, in bowing down the
mind to endure adversity, shows that it is cast in lowliness
after the manner of a trench? A trench, therefore, must
be made in the altar, lest the breeze scatter the sacrifice
laid on it: that is, the mind of the elect must maintain
patience, lest, being stirred by the wind of impatience, it
lose in addition all the good they have performed.

Rightly, too, is this trench designed to be one cubit in
breadth: [44] that is to say, if patience is not lacking, the rule
of unity is preserved. Wherefore, too, Paul says: *Bear ye
one another's burdens, and so you shall fulfil the law of*

Christic.[45] For the law of Christ is charity in unity, which they alone compass who do not fall away from it even when oppressed.

Let the impatient hear the Scripture saying: *The patient man is better than the valiant, and he that ruleth his spirit, than he that taketh cities.*[46] For victory over cities is of less account, because what is subdued is external, but to conquer by patience is a deed of far greater moment, because the mind conquers and subjects itself by itself, when patience compels it to curb itself interiorly.

Let the impatient be told what the Truth says to His elect: *In your patience you shall possess your souls.*[47] Truly, we are so wonderfully created, that reason possesses the soul, and the soul possesses the body. But the soul is dispossessed of its right over the body, if it is not first possessed by reason. Therefore, the Lord has pointed out that patience is the guardian of our estate, for He taught us to possess ourselves in it. We, therefore, realise how great is the fault of impatience, seeing that by it we lose even the possession of what we are.

Let the impatient be told what is also said by Solomon: *A fool uttereth all his mind, a wise man deferreth and keepeth it till afterwards.*[48] Under the impulse of impatience the whole spirit exposes itself, and its turbulence drives it out the more speedily, in that there is no interior discipline of wisdom to keep it in. The wise man, on the other hand, keeps back and lets the future take care of matters. When he is wronged, he does not wish to avenge himself at once, because in his forbearance he wishes others to be spared; though he is not ignorant of the fact that all things are punished justly at the Last Judgment.

On the other hand, those who are patient are to be admonished not to grieve in their hearts over what they suffer outwardly. A sacrifice of such great worth which they outwardly offer unimpaired, must not be spoilt by the infection of interior malice. Besides, while their sin of grieving is not observed by man, it is visible under the divine scrutiny, and will become the worse, in proportion as they claim a show of virtue in the sight of men.

The patient must, therefore, be told to aim diligently at loving those whom they needs must put up with, lest, if love does not wait on patience, the virtue that appears outwardly may be turned into a worse fault of hatred. Wherefore, when Paul said that *charity is patient,* he presently added that it *is kind,*[49] surely showing that those whom it puts up with patiently, it also loves with unceasing kindness. Hence, when the same great teacher, urging patience on his disciples, says: *Let all bitterness, and anger, and indignation, and clamour, and blasphemy, be put away from you,* as though this put all outward matters in order, he turns to that which is interior when he adds: *with all malice.*[50] For, indeed, it is in vain that indignation, clamour, blasphemy are put away outwardly, if interior malice, which is the mother of vices, reigns. In vain is wickedness cut away from the outward branches, if it is retained in the root within, to shoot up in more ways than ever before.

Wherefore, the Truth in person says: *Love your enemies, do good to them that hate you, and pray for them that persecute and calumniate you.*[51] Among men, therefore, it is virtuous to put up with enemies; but before God it is virtue to love them. God accepts only that sacrifice which, in His eyes, is enkindled by the flame of charity on the altar of good works. That is why He says to some who were patient but did not love: *Why seest thou the mote that is in thy brother's eye, and seest not the beam that is in thy own eye?* [52] The turbulence of impatience is the mote, but malice in the heart is the beam in the eye. The former is moved to and fro by the breath of temptation, but consummated iniquity bears along the beam almost beyond removal. Rightly, then, it is added in that place: *Thou hypocrite, cast out first the beam out of thy own eye, and then shalt thou see to cast out the mote out of thy brother's eye* [53]—as if it were said to a wicked mind inwardly grieving, while displaying its holiness by outward patience: "Throw first from yourself the beam of malice, and then reprove others for their mere impatience. Otherwise, if you do not aim at conquering your pretences, it will become worse for you to put up with the evil deeds of others."

It is a common experience even among patient people that at the moment when they suffer adversity or are made to hear contumely, they are not affected by any vexation, and in addition to showing patience they do not fail in safeguarding the innocence of their heart. But when after a time they recall what they have suffered, they become inflamed with resentment and seek out reasons for revenge, and by withdrawing the meekness displayed in their endurance, they turn it into malice. They are the sooner succoured by the preacher, if the reason of this change is disclosed.

Here, in fact, the crafty Enemy wages war against two persons, namely, he inflames one to be the first to offer insults, he provokes the other to requite insult by insult.

But often while he is the conqueror of him who is moved to inflict the insult, he is conquered by the one who bears the insult with equanimity. Wherefore, the one who is victorious over him whom he overcomes by incensing him, rises up with all his might against him, and is pained at the firm and victorious resistance offered; and, therefore, because he has been unable to incense the other by bandying insults, he ceases for the time being from open conflict. But by harassing his thought by secret suggestions, he seeks a fitting occasion for deceiving him. Because he has lost his case in open conflict, he is all on fire to lay hidden snares. At some peaceful moment he returns to the mind of the conqueror, and recalls either the temporal harm done or the darts of insult suffered, and by grossly exaggerating all that has been done to him, represents it as insufferable. He thus disturbs the mind of the other with such great vexation, that frequently the man of patience led captive after his victory, blushes for having borne the evil with equanimity and grieves for not having requited insult for insult. He seeks to pay back the other by something worse, if the opportunity offers. To whom, then, are these like, but to those whom bravery leaves victors in the field, but who, owing to negligence, are later on captured within the gates of the city? To whom are they like but to those whom a serious illness attacks, but does not deprive of life, yet who die from a relapse of fever stealing on them imperceptibly?

The patient are, therefore, to be admonished to fortify their heart after victory, to be on the lookout for the Enemy who was overcome in open conflict, but who is laying snares against the outworks of their minds, and to be the more afraid of the sickness creeping back again, lest the crafty Enemy, by a subsequent ruse, rejoice the more exultingly, in that he treads on the neck of the conqueror who for a long time had been inflexible against him.

CHAPTER 10

How to admonish the kindly and the envious.

Admonition 11. The kindly-disposed are to be admonished in one way, the envious in another. The kindly are to be admonished so to rejoice in the good in others as to wish to have the like themselves. They should so commend with affection the deeds of others as even to multiply them by imitation. Otherwise, if in the arena of this life they assist at the encounter of others as keen abettors, but inactive spectators, they will remain without a prize after the contest, inasmuch as they did not labour in it, and will then look regretfully at the palms of victory of those, in the midst of whose exertions they were idle. For, indeed, we sin greatly if we do not regard with affection the good deeds of others, and we get no reward if we do not imitate to the best of our ability the things which we love.

The kindly-disposed must, therefore, be told that if they do not bestir themselves to imitate what they approve and praise, the holiness of virtue pleases them in the same manner that the vain art of public performers pleases foolish spectators; for these extol with favours the performance of charioteers and actors, yet do not wish to be like those whom they applaud. They admire people for the pleasing exhibition they give, but decline to please others in like manner. The kindly-disposed are to be told that when they behold the deeds of neighbours, they should examine their own heart, and not presume on the actions of others, nor praise what is good, while declining to do likewise. They stand to be smitten the more severely with punishment at the end of time, forasmuch as they would not imitate what pleased them.

The envious are to be admonished to ponder well on the blindness of those who become disheartened by another's progress and pine away at the jubilation of others. What unhappiness is that of people whose state deteriorates by the progress of their neighbour, and in beholding the increase of another's prosperity, are themselves bitterly afflicted with inward grief and die of the plague of their own heart! What can be more unfortunate than such people who are grieved by the sight of happiness and become the more wretched by the torment they suffer?

Yet the good things of others which these people cannot have, they would be making their own if they but loved them. For, indeed, all are knit together in faith, just as the various members of one body, though having their different functions, are yet constituted one by mutual concord. Hence it is that the foot sees by the help of the eye, and the eyes go forward by the help of the foot, the hearing of the ear serves the mouth, and the tongue co-operates in the function of the ears, the stomach supports the hands, and the hands work for the stomach. Therefore, in the very arrangement of the body we observe what we ought to fulfil in our actions. It is, then, wholly shameful not to imitate what we are ourselves. In fact, those things are ours which we love in others, even if we cannot imitate them, and what is loved in ourselves becomes the posses-

sion of those who love it. Wherefore, let the envious consider how efficacious is charity, which renders the works of
another's labour our own, without any labour on our part.

And so the envious must be told that by not guarding
themselves from envy, they are sinking down into the
state of the ancient wickedness of the crafty Enemy, for
of him it is written: *But by the envy of the Devil, death
came into the world.*[54] For as he lost Heaven, he begrudges
it to created man, and in his own ruin he stores up more
damnation for himself by ruining others.[55]

The envious are to be admonished how liable they are
to the great pitfalls of ruin yawning beneath them.
because, by not casting envy from their hearts, they are
on the way to openly wicked deeds. If Cain, for example,
had not envied the pleasing sacrifice of his brother, he
certainly would not have reached the point of murdering
him. Wherefore, Scripture says: *And the Lord had respect to Abel and to his offerings, but to Cain and his
offerings He had no respect, and Cain was exceedingly
angry, and his countenance fell.*[56] Thus envy of another's
sacrifice was the seed plot of fratricide, for he wholly cut
off from life him whom he was grieved to see better than
himself. The envious are to be told that when they permit
themselves to be consumed with that inward plague, they
destroy whatever good they may have of their own.
Wherefore, it is written: *Soundness of heart is the life of
the flesh, but envy is the rottenness of the bones.*[57] Indeed,
what else is symbolised by flesh, but acts that are weak
and frail, and what else by bones, but acts that are valiant?
And it commonly happens that some people, possessed of
innocence of heart, appear weak in some of their actions,
while others, though performing acts that are valiant in

the eyes of men, yet pine away inwardly with the plague of envy of the good deeds of others. It is well said, therefore, that *soundness of the heart is the life of the flesh*, because if innocence of the mind is maintained, even those things that are outwardly frail are sometimes strengthened; and it is rightly added: *but envy is rottenness of the bones*, because by the vice of envy even those things which in the eyes of men appear efficacious, are nullified in God's eyes. For the rotting of the bones through envy means that certain things, even if efficacious, completely come to naught.

CHAPTER 11

How to admonish the sincere and the insincere.

Admonition 12. The sincere are to be admonished in one way, the insincere in another. The sincere are to be commended for their intention of never saying anything false, but they should be warned that they should know how to withhold the truth on occasion. For, just as falsehood always harms him who utters it, so the hearing of the truth has sometimes done harm. Wherefore, the Lord, tempering speech with silence in presence of His disciples, says: *I have yet many things to say to you, but you cannot bear them now.*[58]

The sincere are, therefore, to be admonished that, as the avoidance of deceit is always profitable to them, so they should utter the truth always profitably. They are to be admonished to unite prudence with the virtue of sincerity, that they may thus have that security which comes of sincerity, without forfeiting the safeguard of prudence. Wherefore, the statement by the teacher of the Gentiles: *But I would have you to be wise in good, and simple in evil.*[59] So, the Truth Himself admonishes His elect, saying: *Be ye wise as serpents and simple as doves.*[60] For, in truth, in the hearts of the elect the wisdom of the serpent should sharpen the simplicity of the dove, and the simplicity of the dove temper the wisdom of the serpent, so that they be not seduced by their prudence to be crafty, nor grow slack by their simplicity in the exercise of the understanding.

On the other hand, the insincere are to be admonished to realise how burdensome is the business of duplicity which they guiltily bear. For in the fear of discovery they ever try to defend themselves even dishonourably, and are ever agitated with fear and apprehension. Now, nothing is more safely defended than sincerity, nothing easier to speak than the truth. But when a man is forced to defend his deceit, his heart is wearied with the toilsome labour of doing so. Wherefore, it is written: *The labour of their lips shall overwhelm them.*[61] For what fills them now, envelops them afterwards, as by it the mind that is now elevated with a soothing disquietude, is then oppressed with bitter retribution. Wherefore, it is said by Jeremias: *For they have taught their tongue to speak lies, they have laboured to commit iniquity;*[62] in other words, they who could have been the friends of truth without labour, labour to sin, and as they decline to live in sincerity, they are at pains to perish laboriously.

For commonly, though they are discovered in their fault, they shrink from being known for what they are, and they screen themselves under a veil of deceit, and the fault

which is quite obvious they try to excuse. The result is
that often one who aims at reproving them, led astray by
the mists of disseminated falsehood, finds that he has all
but lost the certain conviction he had been holding concerning them. Hence it is rightly said by the Prophet,
under the similitude of Judea, against the soul that sins
and excuses itself: *There hath the hedgehog had its hole.*[63]
Here the term hedgehog symbolises the duplicity of the
insincere mind that craftily defends itself. For when the
hedgehog is discovered, its head is seen, its feet are obvious,
its whole body revealed; but the moment it is captured,
it gathers itself up into a ball, draws in its feet, hides its
head, and the thing disappears in the hands of him who
holds it, whereas before all the parts were visible.

Such, indeed, is the case of insincere minds when de-
tected in their transgressions. The head of the hedgehog
is seen in that one perceives from what beginnings the
sinner approaches his crime. The feet of the hedgehog
are visible, because one sees by what steps the evil was
done, and yet by advancing excuses suddenly, the insincere mind gathers up its feet, inasmuch as every vestige
of the evil is concealed. It withdraws its head, because
by strange pleas a proof is offered that evil was not even
initiated. The thing remains, as it were, in the hand of
him who holds it, like a ball, for he who reproves the evil,
suddenly loses sight of all that he had learnt, and holds
the sinner enfolded in his own consciousness; and the
other who had seen the whole at the moment of capture,
loses all knowledge of the sinner, being deluded by the
subterfuges of his wicked pleas. Therefore, the hedgehog
has its nest in the wicked, that is, the duplicity of a mali-

cious mind by withdrawing within itself conceals itself in the obscurity of its self-defence.

Let the insincere be told what Scripture says: *He that walketh sincerely, walketh confidently;* [64] for sincerity of conduct is an assurance of great security. Let them be told what is said by the mouth of the wise men: *The holy spirit of discipline will flee from the deceitful.* [65] Let them be told what is again attested by Scripture: *His communication is with the simple.* [66] Now, God's communication is the revelation of secrets to human minds by the illumination of His presence. He is, therefore, said to communicate with the simple, because in the case of supernal mysteries He illumines with the ray of His visitation the mind of those whom no shadow of duplicity obscures. But it is the particular evil of the double-minded that, while they deceive others by their perverse and double-dealing conduct, they glory as though they were singularly prudent beyond others; and because they disregard a severe retribution, they, poor fools, take delight in what is to their own harm.

Let them be told how the Prophet Sophonias holds out over them the stroke of divine reproof, when he says: *Behold, the day of the Lord is coming, great and horrible . . . . That day is a day of wrath, a day of darkness and obscurity, a day of clouds and whirlwinds, a day of the trumpet and alarm against all the fenced cities and against all the high corners.* [67] What else is expressed by fenced cities but minds suspicious and ever surrounding themselves with the defence of deceit, minds which, as often as their sin is reproved, do not allow the darts of truth to approach them? And what is symbolised by high corners (a wall being always double at its corners) but insincere hearts which, in shunning the simplicity of truth, are, as it were, doubled back on themselves by their perverse duplicity? And, what is worse, by the very fault of insincerity they uplift themselves in their thinking with the proud assumption of prudence. Therefore, the day of the Lord comes, full of vengeance and rebuke, on fenced cities and lofty corners: the wrath of the Last Judgment destroys human hearts that have been closed against the truth by bulwarks, and destroys what had been enveloped in duplicity. Then these fenced cities fall, because souls which showed themselves impervious to God shall be lost. Then the lofty corners fall down, because hearts that lifted themselves up in the prudence of insincerity, are stricken down by a just sentence.

CHAPTER 12

How to admonish the hale and the sick.

Admonition 13. The hale are to be admonished in one way, the sick in another. The hale are to be admonished to employ bodily health in behalf of mental health. Otherwise, if they divert the favour granted them of their good condition to the doing of evil and thus become the worse for the gift, they will merit punishment, which will be the graver in proportion as they do not shrink from putting to an evil use the bountiful gifts of God.

The hale are to admonished not to set aside the opportunity of winning eternal salvation, for it is written: *Behold, now is the acceptable time, behold, now is the day of salvation.*[68] They are to be admonished that if they are unwilling to please God when they can, they may not be

able to please Him when, too late, they decide to do so.
Wherefore it is that Wisdom afterwards deserts those who
disregard her call too long, for she says: *I called and you
refused, I stretched out my hand, and there was none that
regarded. You have despised all my counsel and have neglected my reprehensions. I also will laugh in your destruction and will mock when that shall come to you which you
feared.*[69] And again: *Then shall they call upon me and I
will not hear, they shall rise in the morning and shall not
find me.*[70] Therefore, when the gift of bodily health for
the doing of good is disregarded, the loss of the gift brings
realisation of its value. In vain is it sought at last, if the
gift has not been profitably employed in due season.

Wherefore, it is again well said by Solomon: *Give not
thy honour to strangers, and thy years to the cruel, lest
strangers be filled with thy strength, and thy labours be
in another man's house, and thou mourn at the last, when
thou shalt have spent thy flesh and thy body.*[71] And who
are strangers to us but the evil spirits, separated from the
lot of the heavenly fatherland? What else is our honour
but to have been created in the image and likeness of our
Creator, though we are made in bodies of slime? And who
else is cruel but that rebel angel who through pride smote
himself with the punishment of death and who, though
himself lost, has not forborne from bringing death on the
race of man? He, therefore, gives his honour away to
strangers, who, being created in the image and likeness of
God, devotes the span of his life to the behests of the
malignant spirits. He, too, gives his years to the cruel,
who expends the span of the life which he has received,
according to the will of an adversary who dominates him
for evil.

In the same place it is well added: *lest strangers be filled with thy strength, and thy labours be in another man's house.* For whosoever does not labour in the exercise of virtues by employing the gift of bodily health or his mind's endowment of wisdom, but perpetrates evil, increases the resources, not of his own house, but of the house of strangers; that is to say, he multiplies the deeds of the unclean spirits by his wantonness or pride, so as to augment the number of the lost by the addition of himself. So, it is well added: *and thou mourn at the last when thou shalt have spent thy flesh and thy body.* Commonly the gift of health is spent by vices; and when it is suddenly withdrawn, when the flesh is worn out with afflictions, when the soul is on the point of being forced to go forth from the body, then the health, enjoyed for long in evil, is sought once more on the plea of living a good life. Men then moan for having refused to serve God, when it is utterly impossible for them to serve Him and thus repair the losses due to their neglect. Wherefore, in another place it is said: *When He slew them, then they sought Him.*[72]

On the other hand, the sick are to be admonished to realise that they are sons of God by the very fact that the scourge of discipline chastises them. For unless it were in His plan to give them an inheritance after their chastisements, He would not trouble to school them in affliction. For this reason the Lord says by the angel to John: *Such as I love, I rebuke and chastise.*[73] It is for the same reason that Scripture says: *My son, neglect not the discipline of the Lord, neither be thou wearied whilst thou art rebuked by Him. For whom the Lord loveth He chastiseth, and He scourgeth every son whom He receiveth.*[74] So, the Psalmist says: *Many are the afflictions of the just, but out of them all will the Lord deliver them.*[75] So, too, holy Job, crying out in his sorrow says: *If I be just, I shall not lift up my head, being filled with affliction and misery.*[76]

The sick should be told that if they believe that the heavenly country is for them, they must needs endure labours in this country, as if it were an alien one. Hence it is that the stones for building the Temple of God were hammered outside, that they might be set in the building without the sound of hammer; [77] so we are now smitten with scourges outside, that afterwards we may be set into the Temple of God without the stroke of discipline, and that the strokes may now cut away whatever is inordinate in us, and that then only the concord of charity may bind us together in the building.

The sick should be admonished to consider how severe are the scourges of discipline, whereby our sons after the flesh are chastised for the attaining of earthy inheritances. What pains, then, of divine correction are hard, if by them an inheritance is received that is never to be lost, and eternal punishments avoided? Wherefore, Paul says: *We have had fathers of our flesh for instructors, and we reverenced them. Shall we not much more obey the Father of spirits and live? And they, indeed, for a few days according to their own pleasure instructed us, but He for our profit, that we might receive His santification.*[78]

The sick are to be admonished to consider what great health of the heart is bestowed by bodily affliction, for it recalls the mind to a knowledge of itself and renews the memory of our infirmity, which health commonly disregards. Thus the spirit which is carried out of itself to pride, is made to remember the condition to which it is subject, owing to the ills of the flesh which it bears. This was rightly indicated through Balaam (if only he had been willing to follow obediently the voice of God!) in that his journey was retarded.[79] For we see Balaam on the way to attain his purpose, but the beast under him thwarts his intention. The ass, stopped by a command, perceives an angel not seen by the mind of the man; for commonly the flesh, retarded by affliction, manifests to the mind, owing to the scourgings it receives, the God whom the mind itself did not see, though it dominates the flesh. Thus the eager spirit, though wishing to advance in this world as if proceeding on a journey, is retarded by an invisible obstacle to its progress, which is afterwards manifested to it.

Wherefore, too, the apposite remark by Peter: *There checked him in his madness the dumb beast used to the yoke, which speaking with man's voice, forbade the folly of the Prophet.*[80] A man is, indeed, rebuked for madness by a dumb beast of burden, when a proud mind is recalled by the afflicted flesh to the virtue of that humility which it ought to maintain. But Balaam did not take the gift of this reproof, because, proceeding to curse, he changed his speech but not his mind.

The sick are to be admonished to consider how great a gift is bodily affliction, in that it both cleanses sins committed and restrains such as could be committed, and that a troubled mind suffers the wounds of penitence inflicted by outward stripes. Hence Scripture says: *The blueness of a wound cleanses evils, and stripes in the more inward parts of the belly.*[81] The blueness of a wound cleanses evil, that is, the pain of chastisements cleanses wickedness, whether meditated or perpetrated. The mind is commonly signified by the term "belly" because, as the belly consumes food, so the mind assimilates cares by brooding over

them. We are taught that the mind is called the belly by
that sentence in which it is written: *The spirit of a man
is the lamp of the Lord, which searcheth all the hidden
things of the bowels.*[82] This is as if it had been said that
the illumination of divine inspiration, entering the mind
of man, shows the mind to itself by enlightening it, for
before the coming of the Holy Spirit it could, indeed, entertain evil things, but did not know how to weigh them.

So, *the blueness of a wound cleanses evils, and stripes in
the more inward parts of the belly.* That is, when we are
outwardly smitten, we are recalled, silent and afflicted, to
the memory of our sins, and we bring before our eyes all
the evil we have done, and in proportion as we suffer outwardly, the more do we grieve inwardly for our deeds.
Wherefore, it happens that together with the open wounds
of the body, the secret blow in the belly cleanses us the
more completely, in that a hidden wound of sorrow heals
the wickedness of evil-doing.

To preserve the virtue of patience, the sick are to be
admonished ever to bear in mind how great were the evils
endured constantly by our Redeemer at the hands of those
whom He had created, how many horrible insults of
reproaches He endured, how many blows in the face He
received at the hands of scoffers, while He was daily
snatching the souls of captives from the power of the
ancient Enemy; that while cleansing us with the water of
salvation, He did not screen His face from the spitting of
perfidious men, that He silently endured the scourging
to free us by His mediation from eternal torments, that He
endured buffeting to give us everlasting honours among
the choirs of angels, that while saving us from being
pierced by our sins, He did not shrink from offering His

head to thorns; that He took bitter gall in His thirst in order to inebriate us with everlasting sweetness, that when mockingly adored, He held His peace and adored in our behalf the Father, though equal to Him in the Godhead, and that He who was the life passed to death that He might prepare life for those who were dead. Why, then, is it considered hard that a man should endure stripes from God for his evil-doing, if God endured so great evil in requital for His own good deeds? Or what man is there of sane mind who is ungrateful for being himself smitten, when He who lived here without sin did not depart hence without a scourging?

CHAPTER 13

*How to admonish those who fear afflictions
and those who despise them.*

Admonition 14. Those who fear afflictions and, in consequence, live innocently, are to be admonished in one way, and those who are so hardened in evil as to be beyond correction even by afflictions, in another way. Those who fear afflictions are to be told that they should not desire temporal goods as of any great moment, since they see even wicked men in possession of them; nor should they in any way shun present evils as not to be endured, for they are not ignorant of the fact that even good men are often afflicted by them.

They are to be admonished that if they really wish to be free from evils, they should have a great horror of eternal punishments, yet not live in continual fear of them, but grow into the grace of love by cherishing charity. For it is written: *Perfect charity casteth out fear.*[83] Again it is written: *You have not received the spirit of bondage again in fear, but you have received the spirit of adoption of sons, whereby we cry, Abba (Father).*[84] Wherefore, the same teacher says again: *Where the Spirit of the Lord is, there is liberty.*[85] If, then, the fear of punishment goes on restraining a man from evil-doing, surely, no liberty of spirit pervades the soul so dominated by fear. For if it did not fear the punishment, it would doubtless do evil. The mind, therefore, that is under the slavery of fear, does not know the grace of liberty. Good should be loved for its own sake, not pursued under the compulsion of established penalties. The man who acts well from fear of the evil of torments, wishes that what he fears did not exist, so that he might boldly commit sin. Wherefore, it is clearer than daylight that innocence is thus lost before God, for in His eyes sin of desire is present.

On the other hand, those who are not restrained from iniquity by the scourges of affliction must be rebuked, and that the more severely as they have become hardened by their greater insensibility. As a rule, these should be treated with disdain, but with disdain that is not actually felt; despair should be shown, but not actually harboured. That is to say, the despair shown should strike fear and the admonition subjoined should inspire a new hope. Wherefore, divine judgment must be sternly proclaimed against them, that they may be recalled to taking stock of themselves by the consideration of eternal retribution.

Let them be told, for example, that Scripture has been fulfilled in them, when it says: *Though thou shouldst bray a fool in the mortar, as when a pestle striketh upon sodden barley, his folly would not be taken from him.*[86]

Against them the Prophet complains to the Lord, saying: *Thou hast bruised them and they have refused to receive correction.*[87] Hence it is that the Lord says: *I have killed and destroyed that people, and yet they are not returned from their ways.*[88] Hence again He says: *The people are not returned to Him who hath struck them.*[89] Hence it is that the Prophet complains by the voice of those applying the scourge of affliction: *We would have cured Babylon, but she is not healed.*[90] Babylon is cured, yet is not restored to health, when the mind in the turmoil of evil-doing hears the words of reproof and feels the scourging it brings, but yet scorns to return to the straight paths of salvation. Hence the Lord reproaches the people of Israel, captive yet not converted from their iniquity, saying: *The house of Israel is become dross to me; all these are brass, and tin, and iron, and lead, in the midst of the furnace.*[91] This is as though he said unmistakably: "I wished to purify them in the fire of tribulation, and I wanted them to become silver or gold. But they have turned from me in the furnace into brass, and tin, and iron, and lead, because even in tribulation they have rushed forward not to virtue but to vices." When brass is struck, it gives off a greater sound than do other metals. A man, therefore, who when chastised breaks forth into sounds of murmuring, has turned to brass in the midst of the furnace. Tin, however, when skilfully treated, presents the deceptive appearance of silver. He, therefore, who is not free from the vice of pretence in the midst of tribulation, has become tin in the furnace. But a man uses iron who plots against the life of the neighbour, and he is iron in the furnace when he does not put away in his tribulations the wickedness of doing harm to neighbours. Lead, again, is heavier than the other metals. He, then, is found to be lead in the furnace who is so weighed down by the burden of his sin, that even in tribulation he is not raised above earthly desires. Therefore, it is again written: *Great pains have been taken, and the great rust thereof has not gone out, not even by fire.*[92] God brings on us the fire of tribulation that He may purge out from us the rust of vices; but not even by fire do we lose the rust, when even amid scourges we are not without vices. Hence the Prophet says again: *The founder hath melted in vain, for their wicked deeds are not consumed.*[93]

We must realise, however, that sometimes when such men remain uncorrected amidst severe scourgings, they are to be soothed by loving admonition. For those whom torments do not correct, are sometimes restrained from evil-doing by gentle blandishments. As is known, frequently sick people who cannot be cured by a strong potion of drugs, have been restored to their former state of health by tepid water; and some wounds that cannot be cured by incisions, are healed by fomentations with oil. The hard diamond, too, cannot be cut at all by steel, but it is softened by the mild blood of goats.[94]

CHAPTER 14

How to admonish the taciturn and the talkative.

Admonition 15. The taciturn are to be admonished in one way, those given to much talking in another. It should be suggested to the taciturn that while shunning some vices inadvertently, they are unconsciously involved in worse. For they often bridle the tongue beyond moderation, and as a result suffer in the heart a more grievous loquacity; and so, their thoughts seethe the more in the mind, in proportion as they restrain themselves by a violent and indiscreet silence. Generally, they permit these thoughts to roam all the more as they think they are more secure for not being observed by fault-finders. Wherefore, their mind is sometimes puffed up in pride and it scorns as weaklings those whom it hears speaking. And when the mouth of its body is closed, it does not recognise how much it exposes itself by pride to vices. The man represses the tongue, but lifts up his mind, and without any regard to his bad qualities, he accuses others within his own heart, the more freely, as he does so the more secretly.

The taciturn are, therefore, to be admonished to aim carefully at knowing not only how they should appear outwardly, but also how to hold themselves inwardly, so as to fear the hidden judgment on their thoughts more than the reprehension of their speech by their neighbours. For it is written: *My son, attend to my wisdom, and incline thy ear to my prudence, that thou mayest guard thy thoughts.*[95] Truly, there is nothing in us more fugitive than the heart which deserts us as often as it slips away in evil thoughts. Wherefore, the Psalmist says: *My heart hath forsaken me.*[96] So, too, returning to himself, he says: *Thy servant hath found his heart to pray to Thee.*[97] When, therefore, thought is guarded, the heart, which was wont to flee away, is found.

Often when the taciturn suffer injustice, they come to feel keener grief from not speaking about what they are suffering. For if the tongue were to speak calmly of the annoyances inflicted, grief would fade from consciousness.

Wounds that are closed are the more painful. When, however, the suppuration that burns inwardly is driven out, the pain is opened out for healing. People, therefore, who are more silent than is expedient, should realise that they but aggravate the vehemence of their grief in withholding speech during their annoyance. For they are to be admonished that if they love their neighbours as themselves, they should most certainly not fail to speak up when they have reason to reprehend them. Thus, by the medication of speech, both parties concur in promoting mutual health, seeing that the one who administers it checks the evil act of the other, and the vehement pain of him who submits to it is relieved by opening the wound.

Indeed, those who observe evil in their neighbour and yet hold their tongue, withhold the use of salves, as it were, from wounds which they see, and thereby become the cause of death, inasmuch as they were unwilling to cure the poison when they could. The tongue, then, must be prudently curbed, but not completely tied up. For it is written: *A wise man will hold his peace till he sees an opportunity,*[98] that is to say, when he sees it opportune to speak what is fitting, he sets aside the censorship of silence, and makes it his effort to be of assistance. Again it is written: *There is a time to keep silence, and a time to speak.*[99] In other words, the various occasions are to be prudently judged: when the tongue ought to be restrained, it should not be unprofitably loosened in speech, or when it could speak with profit, it should not indolently withhold speech. The Prophet considers this matter well when he says: *Set a watch, O Lord, before my mouth, and a door round about my lips.*[100] He does not ask that a wall be set before his mouth, but a door, which, you see, can be opened and closed. Wherefore, we must take care to learn when speech should open the mouth discreetly and at the proper time, and when, on the contrary, silence should becomingly keep it closed.

But those who are addicted to much talking, are to be admonished to observe vigilantly from how great a degree of rectitude they lapse, when they fall to using a multitude of words. For the human mind behaves after the manner of water: when enclosed, it collects itself to the higher levels, because it seeks again the height from which it came down. But, when released, it loses itself, in that it scatters itself to no purpose through the lowest levels; indeed, all the superfluous words wasted when it relaxes its censorship of silence, are so many streams carrying the mind away from itself. Consequently, it does not have the power to return inwardly to self-knowledge, because, dissipated as it is by much talking, it is diverted from the secret places of inward considerations. It lays itself completely exposed to the wounds from the Enemy lying in wait for it, in that it does not encompass itself with a barrier of watchfulness. Wherefore, it is written: *As a city that lieth open and is not compassed with walls, so is a man that cannot refrain from his own spirit from speaking.*[101] For the citadel of the mind without a wall of silence is exposed to the darts of the Enemy, and when it casts itself by words out of itself, it is patently exposed to the Enemy who overcomes it with the less trouble, as the mind itself, which is overcome, fights against itself by much speaking.

Commonly, since the slothful mind is brought gradually to a downfall by our neglect to guard against idle words, we come to utter harmful ones: at first we are satisfied to talk about the affairs of others, then the tongue gnaws with detraction the lives of those of whom we speak, and finally we break out into open slanders. Hence provocations are sown, quarrels arise, the torches of hatred are lit, peace of heart is extinguished. Therefore it is well said by Solomon: *The beginning of quarrels is as when one letteth out water.*[102] For to let out water is to loose the tongue in a spate of words. On the other hand, it is again said in a good sense: *Words from the mouth of a man are as deep water.*[103] Therefore, *when one letteth out water, he is the fountainhead of quarrels*, for a man who does not curb his tongue routs concord. Wherefore, on the contrary, it is written: *He that putteth a fool to silence appeaseth anger.*[104]

Moreover, one addicted to much speaking fails entirely to keep on the straight path of righteousness, so the Prophet testifies, saying: *A man full of tongue shall not be guided on the earth.*[105] So, Solomon says again: *In the multitude of words there shall not want sin.*[106] Wherefore, Isaias says: *The service of justice shall be quietness,*[107] that is, he indicates that the righteousness of the mind is lacking where there is no restraint on immoderate speaking. Hence James says: *And if any man thinketh himself to be religious, not bridling his tongue, but deceiving his own heart, this man's religion is vain.*[108] Hence, again, he says: *Let every man be swift to hear, but slow to speak;*[109] and again, describing the power of the tongue, he adds: *An unquiet evil, full of deadly poison.*[110] That is why the Truth in person admonishes us saying: *Every idle word that men shall speak, they shall render an account for it in the day of Judgment.*[111] That is to say, a word is idle that has no justification of real necessity, or no intention of pious usefulness. If, therefore, an account is exacted for idle words, let us consider what penalty is in store for much speaking, wherein there is also the sin of harmful words.

CHAPTER 15

How to admonish the slothful and the hasty.

Admonition 16. The slothful are to be admonished in one way, the hasty in another. The former are to be persuaded not to lose the good they ought to do by deferring it. The latter are to be admonished not to spoil the merit of their good deeds by imprudent haste in anticipating the times for doing them.

The slothful should be made to realise that often when we are unwilling to do in due season what we can, soon after, when we are willing, we are not able to do it. The indolent mind, when not enkindled with timely fervour, loses completely all sense of the desire of good, as its remissness grows strongly imperceptibly. Wherefore, it is plainly said by Solomon: *Slothfulness casteth into a deep sleep.*[112] For the slothful one is, as it were, wakeful in right sentiments, but by his inactivity begins to grow remiss; and slothfulness is said to cast a man into deep slumber, because gradually even the conscientiousness in regard to right sentiments is lost, when the pursuit of good works is discontinued. In the passage cited it is rightly added: *and an idle soul shall suffer hunger.*[113] When the soul does not direct its efforts to higher things, neglecting itself, it stoops to concern itself with low desires, and when it does not restrain itself by aiming vigorously at higher things, it is wounded by the hunger of a base cupidity;

and, consequently, as it neglects the constraint of discipline, it is the more distracted in its craving for pleasure. Wherefore, it is again written by the same Solomon: *The slothful man is given utterly to desires.*[114]

Wherefore, as the Truth Himself preaches,[115] the house is said to be clean when the one spirit goes out, but when it is empty, it is taken possession of by his returning with many more. Usually, the slothful, in neglecting to do what he ought, imagines to himself certain difficulties and harbours certain unfounded fears; and when he discovers an apparent reason for having fear apparently justified, he acts as if he were quite justified in being inactive and indolent. To him it is rightly said by Solomon: *Because of the cold, the sluggard would not plough; he shall beg, therefore, in the summer and it shall not be given him.*[116] The sluggard does not plough because of the cold, when he is held back by the torpor of sloth and fails to do the good that he ought to do. The sluggard does not plough owing to the cold, when he fears trifling evils that confront him, and fails to do things of the greatest moment. And it is well said: *he shall beg in the summer and it shall not be given him.* The man who does not toil in good works now, will receive nothing in the summer, that is, when the scorching sun of Judgment shall appear, he will beg in vain to enter the Kingdom.

Again, it is well said to him by the same Solomon: *He that observeth the wind does not sow, and he that considereth the clouds does not reap.*[117] For what is symbolised by the wind, but temptation by evil spirits, and what is meant by the clouds that are driven by the wind, but adversities inflicted by evil men? That is, the clouds are driven by the winds when evil men are stirred up by the blasts of the evil spirits. He, therefore, who observes the wind does not sow, and he who considers the clouds never reaps, because anyone who fears temptations from evil spirits, anyone who fears persecutions from evil men, neither now sows the seeds of good works, nor hereafter cuts the sheaves of holy recompense.

On the other hand, when the hasty anticipate the time for doing good deeds, they destroy the merit of them, and often fall into evil from not discerning good at all. Such people never consider what to do and when to do it; and usually only when a thing has been done, do they realise that they ought not to have done it. To these, as if he intended them to be his hearers, it is appositely said by Solomon: *My son, do thou nothing without counsel, and thou shalt not repent when thou hast done.*[118] And again: *Let thy eyelids go before thy steps.*[119] The eyelids go before our steps, when right counsels go before our deeds. He who neglects to look forward by reflecting what he is doing, advances with eyes closed. He sets about accomplishing his journey, but does not go in advance of himself by looking forward, and, therefore, falls the sooner; for he simply does not consider with the eyelid of counsel where he should set his footsteps in acting.

CHAPTER 16

How to admonish the meek and the choleric.

Admonition 17. The meek are to be admonished in one way, the choleric in an another. Sometimes the meek, when in authority, suffer from inactivity, which is a neighbour, indeed, as it were, a next-door neighbour, of laziness; and commonly by their laxity of excessive gentleness they soften the vigour of severity more than they should. But on the other hand, the choleric, on assuming positions of authority, by falling headlong in their impetuous anger into a frenzy of the mind, throw into confusion the lives of their subjects by dissipating the peace of quietude. When rage drives them headlong, they do not realise what they are doing in their anger, they do not realise what suffering their anger creates for themselves. But sometimes—and this a more serious matter—they think that the goad of anger is zeal for righteousness; and when vice is thought to be virtue, guilt accumulates without apprehension.

Accordingly, the meek often grow languid in their lazy inactivity; the choleric frequently deceive themselves by what they think to be zeal for rectitude. Thus, in the former a fault is unconsciously associated with a virtue, and in the latter a fault assumes the guise of zealous virtue.

The meek are, therefore, to be admonished to flee from what is upon them; the choleric, to heed what is in themselves. The former are to discern what they do not possess, the latter, what, in fact, they do possess. The meek must deliberately strive to be solicitous, the choleric must give up their turbulence. The meek must be admonished to aim at zeal for righteousness, the choleric must be admonished to add meekness to the zeal which they think they have. It is obviously for this reason that the Holy Spirit is exhibited to us under the symbols of a dove and of fire, because all whom He fills He makes both meek with the simplicity of the dove, and glowing with the fire of zeal.

That one, then, certainly is not filled with the Holy Spirit
who either in the calmness of his meekness abandons the
fervour of his zeal, or in the fervour of his zeal loses the
virtue of meekness.

We may perhaps explain this matter better if we appeal
to the pedagogy of Paul, who recommended different kinds
of preaching aids to two of his disciples, both endowed
with a like charity. When admonishing Timothy, he says:
Reprove, entreat, rebuke, in all patience and doctrine.[120]
But when admonishing Titus, he says: *These things
speak, and exhort, and rebuke with all authority.*[121] Why
is it that, great master of the teaching art that he was, in
the present illustration of it he proposes the exercise of
authority to the one, and patience to the other? Is it not
that he sees Titus endowed with too meek a spirit, and
Timothy with a little too zealous one? He inflames the
one with zeal, the other he restrains with the gentleness
of patience. He gives to the one what is lacking, he takes
away from the other what is excessive. He aims at urging
on the one with a spur, he checks the other with a bridle.
Being the great husbandman that he is, having taken the
Church under his care, he waters some shoots that they
may grow, but prunes others, when he perceives their excessive growth. He wishes to make sure that the one set
does not fail to bear for lack of growth, and that the other
does not, owing to rank growth, lose the fruit it has put
forth.

But anger that creeps in under the guise of zeal is very
different from the anger that confounds the turbulent
heart even without pretext of just provocation. The former
grows inordinately in matters in which it should be displayed, but the latter is always set on fire where it should

not appear. For we must know that the choleric differ from the impatient in this respect, namely, that the impatient do not put up with the imposition of others, but the choleric even cause imposition that must be put up with. The choleric pursue even those who shun them, stirring up occasions of strife, rejoicing in the trouble caused by contention. It is better, however, that in correcting these people we shun them when their anger is actually seething; for when they are aroused, they do not perceive what is being said to them. But when they have been restored to their senses, they the more willingly accept words of counsel, as they blush for having been peacefully borne with. For to the mind that is intoxicated with frenzy, everything said that is right appears to be wrong. Wherefore, Abigail laudably did not speak to Nabal about his sin when he was intoxicated, and as laudably told him of it when he became sober.[122] For it was precisely because he did not hear of his fault when drunk, that he was able to recognise it.

But when the choleric so attack others that it is impossible to shun them, they should not be smitten with open rebuke, but sparingly with a certain respectful forbearance. We shall prove this better by citing the example of Abner. Scripture has it that when Asael attacked him with vehement and inconsiderate haste, Abner said to Asael: *Go off and do not follow me, lest I be obliged to stab thee to ground. . . . But he refused to hearken to him, and would not turn aside. Wherefore, Abner struck him with his spear, with a back stroke in the groin, and thrust him through, and he died.*[123] Of whom, then, did Asael serve as a type, but of those who are driven headlong in a violent access of frenzy? Such people, when under the impulse of a like frenzy, are the more cautiously to be shunned, the more carried away they are in their madness. Wherefore, too, Abner, who in our language is termed "lamp of the father," fled: that is to say, if the teacher, whose tongue symbolises the heavenly light of God, perceives the mind of a man to be carried away along the rugged path of frenzy, and refrains from bandying words with such an angered one, he is like one unwilling to strike a pursuer. But when the choleric will not restrain themselves under any consideration, and, as it were, like Asael, do not refrain from their mad pursuit, then it is necessary for those who try to check them in their frenzy, not on any account to allow their anger to be aroused, but to show all possible calmness; and let them suggest discreetly that which will, as it were, by a side stroke pierce their frenzied mind.

Wherefore, when Abner made a stand against his pursuer, he pierced him, not with a direct thrust, but with the reverse end of his spear. Of course, to smite with the sharp point is to oppose another with an attack of open rebuke, but to smite a pursuer with the reverse end of the spear is to touch the frenzied quietly and partially, and to overcome him, as it were, by sparing him. But Asael falls down dead on the spot: that is, turbulent minds, on perceiving that they are shown consideration and, on the other hand, because they are touched in their hearts in consequence of being reasoned with calmly, fall down at once from the lofty place to which they had raised themselves. Those, therefore, who withdraw from their frenzied impulse under the stroke of gentleness, die, as it were, without being struck by the head of a spear.

CHAPTER 17

How to admonish the humble and the haughty.

Admonition 18. The humble are to be admonished in one way, the haughty in another. The former should be told how genuine is that excellence which they have by hoping for it; the haughty, how worthless is the temporal glory which is not retained even when in their grasp. Let the humble be told of the eternal nature of the things which they strive after, and of the transitoriness of the things which they despise. Let the haughty be told how transitory the things are which they set themselves to acquire, how eternal the things which they forfeit. Let the humble listen to the magisterial voice of the Truth: *Everyone that humbleth himself shall be exalted.* Let the proud be told: *Everyone that exalted himself shall be humbled.*[124] Let the humble be told: *Humility goeth before glory.*[125] Let the haughty be told: *The spirit is lifted up before a fall.*[126] Let the humble be told: *To whom shall I have respect but to him that is humble and peaceful, and that trembleth at my words?*[127] Let the haughty be told: *Why is earth and ashes proud?*[128] Let the humble be told that God *looketh on the low.* Let the haughty be told: *and the high He knoweth afar off.*[129] Let the humble be told that *the Son of man is not come to be ministered unto, but to minister.*[130] Let the haughty be told that *pride is the beginning of all sin.*[131] Let the humble be told that our Redeemer *humbled Himself, becoming obedient unto death.*[132] Let the haughty be told what is written of their head: *He is king over all the children of pride.*[133]

The pride of the Devil became, therefore, the occasion of our perdition, and the humility of God proved to be the pledge of our redemption. For our Enemy, created like all other things, wished to appear superior to all, but our Redeemer, remaining great above all things, deigned to become little among all. Let the humble, therefore, be told that in abasing themselves, they rise to the likeness of God. Let the haughty be told that in exalting themselves, they debase themselves to the likeness of the rebel angel. What, then, is baser than haughtiness which, by overreaching itself, removes itself from the stature of true eminence? And what is more sublime than humility, which, in debasing itself to the lowest, joins itself to its Maker who remains above the highest?

But there is another thing in these persons that we must consider well, namely, that frequently some deceive themselves by a semblance of humility, while others are led astray through ignorance of their own haughtiness. Often, for instance, some who think themselves humble, are given to a type of fear which should not be exhibited to men, while outspokenness of speech usually characterizes the haughty. And when correction of certain faults is called for, the former are silent from fear, and yet think their silence is due to humility, but the latter speak out in impatient pride, yet believe their speech is a fearless espousal of righteousness. The former are kept from rebuking what is wrong by a faulty timidity under the guise of humility. The haughty are moved by their wild turbulence under the guise of fearlessness to rebuke what should not be rebuked, or to rebuke excessively.

Wherefore, the haughty are to be admonished not to be more outspoken than is befitting, and the humble not to be more submissive than is becoming. For the former may change a defence of righteousness into an exercise in pride, and the latter, in showing submissiveness to others more than is necessary, are driven to show respect even to vice. It is, however, to be observed that we often reprove the haughty to better effect, if with our reproofs we mingle a measure of conciliatory praise. We should introduce either some good qualities which they possess, or at least mention some such qualities that could be present, though they actually may not be; and then only should the evil in them that displeases us be cut away, when the good points which are pleasing to them have in advance rendered their mind well-disposed to listen to us. Thus, too, in the case of unbroken horses we first stroke them gently with the hand, so that afterwards we may tame them completely even by using the whip; and to the bitter draughts of drugs a portion of sweet honey is added, so that what will benefit the health may not be crude and bitter to the taste, and while the taste is beguiled by the sweetness, the deadly humours are expelled by what is bitter. So, in the very beginning reproof of the haughty must include a proportionate amount of praise, so that while they accept the approbations which they like, they may also accept the reproofs which they dislike. Again, generally we are better able to persuade the haughty to their profit, if we say that their progress is more likely to benefit us than themselves, and if we beg their amendment as a favour to us rather than to themselves. For the haughty are more easily led to good, if they believe that in turning to good they will profit others also.

Wherefore, when Moses, guided by God, was journeying through the desert, the pillar of cloud going before, and wished to deter Hobab, his kinsman, from converse with the Gentiles, and make him devoted to the dominion of Almighty God, he said: *We are going towards the place which the Lord will give us; come with us that we may do thee good, for the Lord hath promised good things to Israel.* When he answered him: *I will not go with thee, but I will return to my country wherein I was born,* he added at once: *Do not leave us, for thou knowest in what places we should encamp in the wilderness, and thou shalt be our guide.*[135] Now, ignorance of the way did not trouble Moses, whom knowledge of the Godhead had advanced to the knowledge of prophecy, who was guided outwardly by the pillar going before him, whom familiar speech and intimate converse with God were instructing inwardly about all things. No, far-seeing man that he was, talking to one who was haughty, he sought his assistance that he might give such to him, he asked the other to lead the way that he might himself lead him to life. Thus he succeeded in making the proud man listen to his words urging him to better things, and the more devoted for being thought to be necessary; and the other submitted to the exhortation, because he believed that he was serving as guide to the one exhorting him.

CHAPTER 18

How to admonish the obstinate and the fickle.

Admonition 19. The obstinate are to admonished in one way, the fickle in another. The former must be told that they deem themselves more than they actually are,

and, consequently, do not submit to the advice of others.
The latter are to be told that they treat themselves quite
beneath their own dignity and show no regard for themselves, and, therefore, in the fickleness of their thoughts
fluctuate in their judgments from one moment to another.
The former must be told that unless they esteemed themselves better than the rest of men, they would certainly
not disregard the advice of all in favour of their own judgment. The latter are to be told that if they gave the least
heed to what they are, their capricious nature would not,
like the wind, whirl them round through such a constant
flux of attitudes. To those it is said by Paul: *Be not wise
in your own conceits;* [136] but the others have this to hear:
Let us not be carried about with every wind of doctrine. [137]

Of the obstinate it is said by Solomon: *They shall eat
fruit of their own way, and shall be filled with their own
devices.* [138] Of the fickle it is again written by him: *The
heart of fools shall be inconsistent.* [139] The heart of the
wise is always consistent, because, while it remains at
peace in its upright convictions, it constantly urges itself
to good deeds. But the heart of fools is inconsistent, because, in exhibiting itself as variable and changeable,
it never remains what it was. And because certain faults
beget others, as it were spontaneously, and so, too, spring
from others, it is carefully to be noted that we then the
better cleanse these people by reproofs, when we draw
away from them the source of their bitterness. For obstinacy is begotten of pride, and fickleness of irresolution.

The obstinate, therefore, are to be admonished to realise
the pride of their thoughts, and to aim at overcoming
themselves. Otherwise, scorning to be outwardly influ-
enced by the upright counsels of others, they may he held

captive inwardly by their pride. They are to be admonished to observe with diligence that the Son of man, whose will was always one with that of the Father, giving us an example of the submission of our will, says: *I seek not my own will, but the will of Him that sent me, the Father;* [140] and that He might the more commend the agreeableness of this virtue, He declared beforehand that He would retain the same will at the Last Judgment, saying: *I cannot of myself do anything, but as I hear, so I judge.* [141] With what conscience, then, can a man despise acquiescence in the will of another, when the Son of God and of man, on coming to display the glory of His own power, testifies that He does not pass judgment as if it were His own?

But on the other hand, the fickle are to be admonished to cultivate seriousness in order to strengthen their mind. Then only will they dry up the roots of their fickleness when they first cut away from the heart the roots of levity, just as a building is strongly constructed, when a solid place is provided for its foundation. Unless, therefore, levity of mind is guarded against beforehand, fickleness of thought is not overcome at all. Paul showed that he had nothing in common with such people, when he said: *Did I use lightness? Or the things that I purpose, do I purpose according to the flesh, that there should be with me, "It is" and "It is not"?* [142] It is as though he plainly states: "For this reason I am not moved by the breeze of fickleness, because I do not yield to the fault of levity."

CHAPTER 19

*How to admonish the gluttonous
and the abstemious.*

Admonition 20. Those who are addicted to gluttony
are to be admonished in one way, those who are abstemious in another. Loquacity, levity in conduct, and impurity, accompany the former; impatience and the sin
of pride often accompany the latter. For unless gluttons
were carried away into immoderate loquacity, the rich
man who is said to have feasted sumptuously daily, would
not have been burnt so grievously in his tongue, saying
as he did: *Father Abraham, have mercy on me, and send
Lazarus that he may dip the tip of his finger in water to
cool my tongue, for I am tormented in this flame.*[143] From
these words it is evident that while feasting sumptuously
daily, he had most frequently committed sins of the
tongue, because, while burning all over, he begged to be
cooled especially in the tongue.

Furthermore, that levity of conduct follows hard on
gluttony, the Sacred Authority testifies, saying: *The
people sat down to eat and drink, and they rose up to
play.*[144] Moreover, such people are generally incited by
their gluttonous appetites to impurity, because, when the
belly is distended to satiety, the prickings of lust are
aroused. Wherefore, to the crafty Enemy who brought to
life the first man's sensuality in his concupiscence for the
apple and bound him tight in the noose of sin, the voice
of God said: *Upon thy breast and belly shalt thou*

crawl [145]—as if it had been said to him in so many words: "In thought and gluttony thou shalt dominate human hearts."

That impurity follows addiction to gluttony, the Prophet testifies who, denouncing hidden things when speaking of obvious facts, says: *The chief of the cooks broke down the walls of Jerusalem.* [146] For the chief of the cooks is the belly, to which the cooks pay respect with great care, that it may be pleasantly filled with viands. But the walls of Jerusalem are the virtues of the soul, elevated to a desire for supernal peace. The chief of the cooks, therefore, throws down the walls of Jerusalem, because, when the belly is distended through gluttony, the virtues of the soul are ruined by impurity.

On the other hand, were it not that impatience commonly shakes the minds of the abstemious from their inward tranquillity, when Peter said: *Minister in your faith, virtue, and in virtue, knowledge, and in knowledge, abstinence,* he would not at once have deliberately added: *and in abstinence, patience;* [147] for he foresaw that the abstemious lack patience, and he admonished them to have it. Again, unless the sin of pride sometimes pierced into the thoughts of the abstemious, Paul would certainly not have said: *He that eateth not, let him not judge him that eateth.* [148] And again, speaking to others, he censured the maxims of such as vaunt their virtue of abstinence, and added: *Which things have, indeed, a show of wisdom in superstition and humility, and not sparing the body, not in any honour to the filling of the flesh.* [149]

In this matter it is to be observed that the noble preacher in his discussion adds the show of humility to superstition, because when the flesh is worn by abstinence more than is necessary, humility is displayed outwardly, but inwardly there is grievous pride on account of that very humility. And unless the mind were sometimes puffed up by abstinence, the arrogant Pharisee would not have carefully enumerated this among his great merits, saying: *I fast twice in a week.*[150]

Therefore, those given up to gluttony are to be admonished not to pierce themselves with the sword of impurity by giving themselves up to the pleasure of food. They should further consider that great loquacity and levity of mind lie in wait for them, because of their eating, and how in their tender devotion to the belly they may be caught fast in the cruel snares of vices. We stray further from our Second Parent in proportion as by our hand, stretched out for food when it is used intemperately, we repeat the fall of our first parent. On the other hand, the abstemious are to be admonished to be always carefully on their guard that in fleeing from the vice of gluttony, worse vices are not generated, as it were, of virtue; that in mortifying the flesh, they do not break out in impatience of the spirit. There is no virtue in subduing the flesh, if the spirit is overcome by anger.

Sometimes, however, when the mind of the abstemious restrains itself from anger, some alien delight, as it were, corrupts it, and so destroys the virtue of abstemiousness, as the mind fails utterly to guard itself against spiritual vices. Wherefore, it is truly said by the Prophet: *In the days of your fasts your own wills are found;*[151] and shortly after: *You fast for debates and strifes, and strike with the fists.*[152] The "will" has to do with delight and the "fist" with anger. To no purpose, therefore, is the body reduced by abstinence, if the mind, abandoning itself to intem-

perate emotions, is laid waste by vices. Again, these are to
be admonished to maintain always their abstinence without abating it, but never to believe that it is a matter of
extraordinary virtue in the eyes of the hidden Judge;
otherwise, if perchance it is believed to be greatly meritorious, the hearer may be lifted up in pride. Wherefore, it is
said by the Prophet: *Is this such a fast as I have chosen?
. . . But deal thy bread to the hungry, and bring the needy
and the harbourless into thy house.*[153] In this matter we
must consider how little the virtue of abstinence is regarded, unless it deserve commendation by reason of
other virtues. So, Joel says: *Sanctify a fast.*[154] To sanctify
a fast is to show abstinence of the flesh to be worthy of
God by other good things added to it.

The abstemious are to be admonished that they should
be assured of this, namely, that they then offer a fast that
is pleasing to God, when they bestow on the poor what
they subtract from their own nourishment. For we must
diligently hearken to the reproof of the Lord by the
Prophet, who says: *When you fasted and mourned in the
fifth and the seventh month for these seventy years, did
you keep a fast unto me? And when you did eat and drink,
did you not eat for yourselves and drink for yourselves?* [155]
A man fasts not to God but to himself, if he does not give
to the poor what he denies his belly for a time, but re-
serves it to be given to his belly later.

Wherefore, lest a gluttonous appetite take the one group
off their guard, or the mortified flesh cast down the other
through pride, let the former hear from the mouth of the
Truth: *Take heed to yourselves lest perhaps your hearts
be overcharged with surfeiting and drunkenness, and the
cares of this world.* To this, fear is profitably added in the

words: *and that day come upon you suddenly. For as a snare shall it come upon you all that sit upon the face of the whole earth.*[156] Let the latter hear the words: *Not that which goeth into the mouth defileth a man, but what cometh out of the mouth, this defileth a man.*[157] Let the former hear the words: *Meat for the belly, and the belly for the meats, but God shall destroy both it and them.*[158] And again: *Not in rioting and drunkenness. . . .*[159] And again: *Meat doth not commend us to God.*[160] Let the latter be told that *all things are clean to the clean, but to them that are defiled, and to unbelievers, nothing is clean.*[161] Let the one hear the words: *Whose god is their belly, and whose glory is in their shame;* [162] and the other: *Some shall depart from the faith;* and a little farther on: *. . . forbidding to marry, to abstain from meats which God hath created to be received with thanksgiving by the faithful and by them that have known the truth.*[163] Let the one hear the words: *It is good not to eat flesh, and not to drink wine, nor anything, whereby thy brother is scandalised.*[164] Let the other hear the words: *Use a little wine for thy stomach's sake and thy frequent infirmities.*[165] Thus the former must learn not to desire inordinately the food of the flesh, and the latter, not to dare to condemm the creature of God for which they have no desire.

CHAPTER 20

*How to admonish those who give away what
is their own, and those who seize what
belongs to others.*

Admonition 21. Those who already give away what is
theirs from pity are to be admonished in one way, those
who still desire to steal, in another. Those who have compassion and give away what is their own should be warned
not to become conceited and rate themselves above those
others on whom they bestow earthly goods. They must
not esteem themselves to be better just because they see
that others are supported by them. The master of an
earthly household, in distributing the ranks and duties
to his servants, appoints some to rule, others to be ruled.
He orders the one group to supply necessaries to the rest,
and these others to take what is given. Now, it sometimes
happens that those who rule give offence, and those who
are ruled remain in favour with the father of the household. Those who are the dispensers incur anger, those
who subsist on what is dispensed continue without falling
into disfavour.

Therefore, those who in pity bestow what is theirs
must be admonished to acknowledge that they have been
appointed by the heavenly Lord to be the dispensers of
temporal means, and to display their humility the more,
inasmuch as they realise that what they dispense belongs
to others.[166] And when they consider that they are appointed for the service of others on whom they bestow

what they have received, pride must not on any account
inspire their minds with vanity, but, on the contrary, fear
should hold them down. Wherefore, it is necessary for
them to take careful thought not to distribute unworthily
what is entrusted to them: not to give to those who ought
not to be given anything, or fail to give to those who
should receive, or again, give much to whom little should
be given, or little when they should give much; not to be
in haste and bestow unprofitably, nor by being dilatory,
torment and harm those who ask. The expectation of
receiving thanks must not creep into their action, for the
desire of transitory praise will extinguish the light of
their giving, nor should accompanying moroseness in-
vest the bestowal of a gift. Nor when they have made
proper bestowal of a gift, should the mind rejoice more
than is befitting, and when they have performed their
duty aright, they should not give any credit to themselves
and so lose all they have accomplished.

Now, that they may not attribute to themselves the
virtue of liberality, let them give heed to what is written:
*If any man minister, let him do it as of the power which
God administereth.*[167] Lest they rejoice immoderately for
bestowing benefits, let them hear what is written: *When
you shall have done all these things that are commanded
you, say: We are unprofitable servants; we have done
that which we ought to do.*[168] To keep moroseness from
spoiling liberality, let them hear what Scripture says: *For
God loveth a cheerful giver.*[169] That they may not seek
transitory praise for a gift bestowed, let them heed Scripture: *Let not thy left hand know what thy right hand
doth;*[170] that is, let not the glory of this present life in-
filtrate into pious giving, but let the upright deed know

nothing of the desire of recompense. Lest they seek a return for favours bestowed, let them hear what is written: *When thou makest a dinner or a supper, call not thy friends, nor thy brethren, nor thy kinsmen, nor thy neighbours who are rich, lest perhaps they also invite thee again, and recompense be made to thee. But when thou makest a feast, call the poor, the maimed, the lame, the blind, and thou shalt be blessed, because they have not wherewith to make thee recompense.*[171]

In order that they may not bestow too late what should be bestowed sooner, let them listen to Scripture: *Say not to thy friend, Go, and come again, and tomorrow I will give to thee—when thou canst give at present.*[172] Again, lest, under the guise of liberality, they scatter uselessly what they have, let them hear what is written: *Let the alms sweat in thy hand.*[173] Again, that they may not give little when much is necessary, let them hear what is written: *He who soweth sparingly, shall also reap sparingly.*[174] That they may not bestow too much when they ought to bestow little, and afterwards not put up with want and break forth into impatience, let them heed what is written: *Not that others should be eased and you burdened, but by an equality, . . . let your abundance supply their want, that their abundance may also supply your want.*[175] For when the mind of the giver does not know how to endure want, if he withdraws much from himself, he is seeking an occasion of being impatient with himself. The soul is first to be prepared for patience, and then either much, or all, is to be bestowed; otherwise, when want overtakes him, he will not bear it with equanimity, and both the reward of former bounty is lost, and subsequent murmuring brings worse ruin on his soul.

Lest they give nothing at all to those to whom some small amount should be given, let them hear what is written: *Give to everyone that asketh thee;* [176] and lest they give something to those to whom they ought not to give anything, let them heed what Scripture says: *Give to the good and receive not a sinner. Do good to the humble, and give not to the ungodly.* [177] And again: *Lay out thy bread and thy wine upon the burial of a just man, and do not eat and drink thereof with the wicked.* [178] For he offers his bread and wine to the wicked, who gives help to the wicked because they are wicked. Some rich men there are of this world who feed stage players [179] with profuse bounty, while the poor of Christ are tortured by hunger. He, however, who gives of his bread to an indigent sinner, not because he is a sinner, but because he is a man, actually nourishes a righteous beggar, not a sinner, for he loves in him not his sin but his nature.

They, too, who compassionately bestow in alms what is their own, are to be admonished to aim carefully at being on their guard, lest, in satisfying for their past sins by almsgiving, they commit other sins which require further reparation; and lest they regard righteousness in God's sight to be something that is for sale, imagining that they can sin with impunity if only they make sure to give money for their sins. For *the life is more than the meat, and the body more than the raiment.* [180] He, therefore, who bestows food or raiment on the poor, but yet is stained with wickedness in his soul or body, offers the lesser to righteousness and the greater to sin, for to God he gives his possessions, but himself to the Devil.

On the other hand, those who aim at seizing even what belongs to others are to be admonished to hearken carefully to what the Lord says when He comes to judgment, namely: *I was hungry and you gave me not to eat; I was thirsty, and you gave me not to drink; I was a stranger, and you took me not in; naked, and you covered me not; sick and in prison, and you did not visit me.* To these He also says previously: *Depart from me, you cursed, into everlasting fire which was prepared for the Devil and his angels.*[181] Note that they are not told that they committed robberies or some other violent deeds, and yet they are consigned to the everlasting flames of hell. We must, therefore, gather how great is the damnation inflicted on those who rob others of their possessions, seeing that those who show no consideration for others and hold on to what they own, are smitten with so great a punishment. Let them, therefore, consider well how great is the imputed guilt of robbery, if failure to give alms subjects them to so great a penalty. Let them weigh well what the requital is for injustice done, observing that failure to bestow kindness is visited with so great a punishment.

When these men are set on seizing the possessions of others, let them hear what Scripture says: *Woe to him that heapeth together that which is not his own. How long doth he load himself with thick clay?*[182] Indeed, to pile up earthly gain with the load of sin, is to heap up thick clay by covetousness. When they aim at greatly enlarging their homes, let them hear what Scripture says: *Woe to you that join house to house, and lay field to field, even to the end of the place. Shall you alone dwell in the midst of the earth?*[183] It is as if it were said plainly: "How far do you extend yourselves, you who cannot bear with comrades in a common world? You keep down those adjoining you, but are forever finding someone at whose expense to expand yourselves." As they gape for an increase of their monies,[184] let them hear what Scripture says: *A covetous man shall not be satisfied with money, and he that loveth riches shall reap no fruit from them.*[185] He would, indeed, reap fruit from them, if he decided to distribute them for the purpose of doing good and without loving them; but a man who, loving them, withholds them, will surely leave them here behind him without profit.

When these people burn with the desire of being replete with all manner of wealth at once, let them hear what Scripture says: *He that maketh haste to be rich, shall not be innocent.*[186] Obviously, a man who strives to increase his resources is not interested in avoiding sin; and being caught after the way of birds, while looking greedily at the bait of earthly things, he does not perceive that he is being strangled in the noose of sin. When these long for the gains of this world and ignore the losses they will suffer in the future life, let them hear what Scripture says: *The inheritance gotten hastily in the beginning, in the end shall be without a blessing.*[187] Indeed, it is this our life from which we take our beginning, that we may come at the end to the lot of the blessed. They, therefore, who hasten to an inheritance in the beginning, cut themselves off from the lot of the blessed in the end, because, while desiring increase here through evil cupidity, they become hereafter disinherited of their everlasting patrimony. When they either aim at getting much, or are able to compass all they desired, let them hear what Scripture says: *What doth it profit a man if he gain the whole world and suffer the loss of his own soul?*[188] It is as if the Truth plainly said: "What does it profit a man if he gather together everything outside himself, if he merely damns himself?"

But commonly the cupidity of despoilers is the more quickly corrected, if they are shown in words of admonition how fleeting is the present life, and if we recall to their memory how those who endeavoured for a long time to become rich in this world, were unable to remain long in their acquired riches, how a speedy death suddenly and at once despoiled them of everything, which they in their wickedness amassed neither all at once nor suddenly, and how they not only left what they had seized here, but carried with them for judgment the arraignment of all their rapine. And so, let them hear instances of people whom they would themselves doubtless speak out to condemn; then, having thus committed themselves and examining their conscience, they will at least be ashamed to imitate persons whom they condemn.

CHAPTER 21

How to admonish those who do not, indeed, crave
the goods of others, yet withhold their own,
and those who give what they have,
yet despoil others.

Admonition 22. Those are to be admonished in one way who neither crave what belongs to others, nor yet give what they have; and in another way, those who bestow what they have, and yet do not desist from despoiling others.

Those who neither crave what belongs to others, nor

give away what they have, are to be admonished to consider seriously that the earth, out of which they were
taken, is common to all men, and therefore, too, brings
forth nourishment for all in common. In vain, therefore,
do those think themselves guiltless, who arrogate to themselves alone the common gift of God, and who, in not
giving what they have received, walk about amidst the
carnage of their neighbours, because they almost daily
destroy as many persons as are dying in poverty, the
means for whose subsistence they retain hidden away in
their own keeping. For when we administer necessities
to the needy, we give them what is their own, not what
is ours; we pay a debt of justice, rather than do a work
of mercy.

Wherefore, Truth Himself, speaking of the circumspection needed in showing mercy, says: *Take heed that
you do not your justice before men.*[189] In accordance with
this sentence, the Psalmist also says: *He hath distributed,
he hath given to the poor, his justice remaineth for ever
and ever.*[190] Here, having just mentioned bounty bestowed
on the poor, he chose to call this, not mercy but justice,
because it surely is a matter of justice that they who
receive what is bestowed by the Lord of all, should use
it for the common good. Wherefore, Solomon also says:
He that is just will give and will not cease.[191]

They are also to be admonished to give serious thought
to this, namely, that in the case of the barren fig tree the
busy husbandman complains that it also takes up the
ground.[192] For that is a barren fig tree taking up the
ground, when the soul of a niggard uselessly keeps back
what could be profitable to the many. It is a barren fig
tree taking up the ground, when the fool keeps barren

under the shade of his sloth a plot which another might have cultivated under the sun of good works. But these are sometimes wont to say: "We use what has been given to us; we do not seek what belongs to others, and if we do nothing worthy of the reward of mercy, yet we do no wrong." They think this, because they stop the ear of their heart against the language of Heaven. For instance, it is not recorded of the rich man of the Gospel, *who was clothed in purple and fine linen and feasted sumptuously every day,* that he despoiled others, but that he used what was his own unfruitfully.[193] It was after this life that avenging hell received him, not because he had done positive evil, but because he had abandoned himself immoderately to the use of what he was entitled to use.

The niggardly are to be admonished to bear in mind that they offend God in the first place, because they make no return in a sacrifice of mercy for His having given them everything. Wherefore, the Psalmist says: *He shall not give to God his ransom, nor the price of the redemption of his soul.*[194] Now, to give the price of redemption is to return a good deed for a favour which anticipated our own. Wherefore, John exclaims in these words: *Now the axe is laid to the root of the tree. Every tree that bringeth not forth good fruit shall be cut down and cast into the fire.*[195] They, therefore, who esteem themselves guiltless on the plea that they do not despoil others, should be in apprehension of the stroke of the axe close at hand, and put away the sense of their languid and improvident security, lest, in neglecting to bring forth the fruit of good works, they be completely cut off from this life, from green roots, as it were.

On the other hand, those are to be admonished who give

what they have, but also do not desist from despoiling others of their possessions, that they should not desire to appear greatly munificent, and that they become worse for the outward show of rectitude. For such persons, in giving what is theirs without discretion, do not only fall headlong into impatient murmuring, as we have said, but when want assails them, fall even into avarice. What, then, is more unhappy than the mind of those in whose case avarice is the child of bountifulness, and a harvest of sins sprouts, as it were, from the seeds of virtue? Therefore, these are to be admonished, first of all to learn how to retain their own possessions in a reasonable way, and then not to go about taking what belongs to others. For if the root of the fault is not dried out while the growth is profuse, the thorns of avarice, exuberant in the branches, will never be withered. Consequently, the occasion for despoiling others is withdrawn, if the right of ownership is first well-ordered.

Then, those who are admonished in this way must be told how to bestow in pity what they possess when, that is, they have learned not to ruin the rectitude of mercy by interposing the wickedness of rapine; otherwise, such people would violently exact as much as they mercifully give. Obviously, it is one thing to show mercy for sins committed, another to sin in order to be able to show mercy. This is mercy which certainly cannot be called mercy, for what is made bitter by the poison of a pestilent root, cannot develop into a sweet fruit. This is why the Lord, through the Prophet, rejects even sacrifices, saying: *I am the Lord that loves judgment and hates robbery in a holocaust.*[196] Hence again, He says: *The sacrifices of the wicked are abominable, because they are offered of wicked-*

ness.[197] These often go so far as to offer to God what they withdraw from the needy. But the Lord shows with what reproach He disowns them, saying through a certain wise man: *He that offereth sacrifice of the goods of the poor, is as one that sacrificeth the son in the presence of his father.*[198] What can be more unendurable than the death of a son before the eyes of his father? It is, therefore, shown with what anger such sacrifice is regarded, when it is compared with the grief of a bereaved father.

And yet, for the most part, such people carefully weigh what is the amount which they give, but neglect to consider how much they seize. They count it as a sort of requital, but refuse to consider their sins. Let them, therefore, hear what is written: *He that hath earned wages put them into a bag with holes.*[199] When a bag has holes, the money is, indeed, seen when it is put in, but it is not seen when it is being lost. They, then, who keep an eye on how much they give, but not on how much they steal, put their wages into a bag with holes because, while piling them up, they look to them in the hope that they will be secure, but lose them when they are not looking.

CHAPTER 22

How to admonish the quarrelsome and the peaceable.

Admonition 23. The quarrelsome are to be admonished in one way, the peaceable in another. The quarrelsome are to be admonished to know for certain that however great the virtues which they have, they cannot become spiritual at all, if they disregard union in concord with their neighbours, for it is written: *But the fruit of the Spirit is charity, joy, peace.*[200] He, therefore, who does not endeavour to preserve peace, refuses to bring forth the fruit of the Spirit. Wherefore, Paul says: *Whereas there is among you envying and contention, are you not carnal?* [201] Hence again, he says: *Follow peace with all men, and holiness, without which no man shall see God.*[202] Hence again, in admonition, he says: . . . *careful to keep the unity of the Spirit in the bond of peace, one body and one spirit, as you are called in one hope of your calling.*[203] The one hope of calling is, therefore, never achieved, if we do not strive for it with mind in union with our fellow men.

But it often happens that certain people, while glorying in such gifts as they have particularly, lose the gift of concord which is the greater gift; for example, if a man should perchance, by restraining his gluttony, subdue the flesh more than others do, but despise concord with those whom he surpasses in abstinence. But he who separates abstinence from concord should consider well the admonition of the Psalmist, who says: *Praise Him with timbrel and choir.*[204] For in the timbrel, the dried skin, when struck, resounds, but in the choir, voices are joined together in concord. A man, therefore, who afflicts the body but forsakes concord, praises God, indeed, on the timbrel, but not in choral harmony. Often, however, when superior knowledge exalts certain people, it separates them from the society of others, and the greater the knowledge, the less wise they are in the virtue of concord. Let them, therefore, hear what the Truth in person says: *Have salt in you, and have peace among you.*[205] For salt without

peace is not, in fact, a gift of virtue, but a cause of condemnation. For the wiser a man is, the worse his delin-
quency, and he will deserve punishment without excuse,
because, if he had prudently wished, he could have avoided
sinning. To such it is well said by James: *But if you have
bitter zeal, and there be contentions in your heart, glory
not, and be not liars against the truth. This is not wisdom
descending from above, but earthly, sensual, devilish. . . .
But the wisdom that is from above, first, indeed, is chaste,
then peaceable. . . .* [206] It is chaste, because it thinks
chastely; and it is peaceable, because it does not proudly
dissociate itself from the society of neighbours.

Those who wrangle are to be admonished to bear in
mind that they offer to God no sacrifice of a good work,
so long as they are in disaccord with the love of neighbours. For Scripture states: *If thou offer thy gift at the
altar, and there thou remember that thy brother hath
anything against thee, leave there thy offering before the
altar, and go first to be reconciled to thy brother, and then
coming, thou shalt offer thy gift.*[207] Now, by this teaching
we must realise how unendurable their fault is shown to
be when their sacrifice is rejected. Knowing that all evils
are wiped away by subsequent good deeds, let us consider
how great are the evils of discord, which allows of no
subsequent good, unless the discord is completely extinguished.

The quarrelsome are to be admonished that if they turn
away their ears from heavenly precepts, they should open
the mind to what happens in the lowest order of beings—
the fact that often birds of the same kind do not separate
from one another, but fly together in a flock, and the fact
that brute beasts feed together in herds. And if we con-

sider the case well, irrational nature evinces in its concord how great is the evil committed by rational nature through discord, when it has lost, though exercising reason, what irrational nature retains by natural instinct.

On the other hand, the peaceful are to be admonished that in loving more than is necessary the peace which they have, they may not be in a mood to achieve that peace which is everlasting. For sometimes tranquil conditions very seriously affect the bent of our mind, so that in proportion as the things which occupy them are not troublesome, the less attractive are those things which invite them, and in proportion as they are pleased with the present, the less are they concerned with the eternal. Wherefore, the Truth in person, when distinguishing earthly from supernal peace, and in order to wean His disciples from the present to that which is to come, said: *Peace I leave with you, my peace I give unto you;* [208] that is, I leave [209] a transitory peace, and give you a lasting one.

If, therefore, the heart is fixed in that peace which is left, it will never arrive at that which is to be given. Peace, therefore, as we now have it, is to be treated as something that ought to be both loved and contemned; otherwise, if it is loved immoderately, the soul of him who loves it may be caught in sin. Consequently, the peaceable are also to be admonished not to desire human peace too much and so fail entirely to reprove the evil conduct of men. By thus conniving at their perversities they will sever the bond of peace with their Creator, and in fearing to deal publicly with human quarrels, they will be punished for a breach of the law that binds their souls. Indeed, what is transitory peace but the footprint, so to speak, of the peace that is eternal? What, then, can be more insane than to love footprints made in the dust, but not to love Him by whom they were impressed?

Wherefore, when David would bind himself wholly to the covenant of peace of soul, he testifies that he maintained no concord with the wicked, saying: *Have I not hated them, O God, that hated Thee, and pined away because of Thy enemies? I have hated them with a perfect hatred, they are become enemies to me.*[210] Obviously, to hate the enemies of God with a perfect hatred is to love what they were made and to reprove what they do, to reprove the conduct of the wicked, but to be profitable to their life.

Therefore, we must consider well when we desist from chiding the wicked, how sinful it is to maintain peace with the very wicked, if so great a Prophet offered to God, as it were, in sacrifice, the fact that he had aroused the enmities of the wicked against himself in behalf of the Lord. This is the reason that the tribe of Levi, when it took up the sword and passed through the midst of the host and did not spare the sinners who were to be smitten, is said to have consecrated its hand to God.[211] Hence Phinees, spurning the favour of his fellow countrymen, smote those associated with the Madianites, and by his own wrath appeased the wrath of God.[212]

Wherefore, the Truth in person says: *Do not think that I came to send peace upon earth. I came not to send peace, but the sword.*[213] For when we imprudently associate in friendship with the wicked, we tie ourselves with the bonds of sin. Hence, too, Josaphat, who is commended by so many testimonies for his previous way of life, is rebuked for his friendship with King Achab, as if he were about to perish. To him the Lord says through the Prophet:

*Thou helpest the ungodly, and thou art joined in friend-
ship with them that hate the Lord, and, therefore, thou
didst, indeed, deserve the wrath of the Lord. But good
works are found in thee, because thou hast taken away the
groves out of the land of Juda.*[214] Evidently, our life is
already out of harmony with Him who is supremely righteous, by the very fact that it is attuned to friendships
with the wicked.

The peaceful are to be admonished not to fear disturb-
ing their temporal peace, by breaking out into words of
reproof. Further, they are to be admonished to maintain
inwardly their love unimpaired, that peace which outwardly they disturb by giving reproof. David declares
that he had prudently observed both of these, when he
says: *With them that hated peace I was peaceable: when
I spoke to them they fought against me without cause.*[215]
Note that when he spoke, he was opposed, and yet, despite
this opposition he was peaceable. He did not cease to
reprove those who were incensed against him, nor to
love those whom he reproved.

So, too, Paul says: *If it be possible, as much as is in you,
have peace with all men.*[216] When he was about to exhort
his disciples to have peace with all, he said first, *if it be
possible,* and added, *as much as is in you.* For if they reproved evil deeds, it would have been difficult for them
to have peace with all men. But when temporal peace
is disturbed in the hearts of evil men by our reproof,
peace must be kept inviolable in our own hearts. He,
therefore, rightly says: *as much as is in you,* as if he purposed to state: "Since peace consists in the agreement of
two parties, if it is expelled by those who are reproved,
let it nevertheless be maintained in the mind of you who

do the reproving." For this reason he again warns his disciples, saying: *If any man obey not our word by this epistle, note that man, and do not keep company with him, that he may be ashamed;* and he added at once: *Yet do not esteem him as an enemy, but admonish him as a brother.*[217] This is as if he said: "Break outward peace with him, but guard interior peace with him deep in your hearts, that your discord so strike the mind of the sinner, that peace depart not from your hearts even if it is rejected."

CHAPTER 23

How to admonish sowers of discord and peacemakers.

Admonition 24. Sowers of discord are to be admonished in one way, peacemakers in another. The sowers of discord are to be admonished to realise whom they follow, for it is written of the rebel angel, when tares had been sown in the good crop: *An enemy hath done this.*[218] Of a member of this class it is also said by Solomon: *A man that is an apostate, an unprofitable man, walketh with a perverse mouth. He winketh with the eyes, presseth with the foot, speaketh with the finger. With a wicked heart he deviseth evil, and at all times he soweth discord.*[219] Observe that the man whom he wished to call a sower of discord is first termed an apostate; for, unless he had first fallen away by the inward aversion of his mind from the face of his Maker, like the proud angel, he would not have come afterwards to sow discords outwardly. The man is rightly described as *winking with his eyes, speaking with his finger, pressing with his foot,* for it is inward restraint that keeps the members in order outwardly. He, therefore, who has lost the stability of his mind, afterwards slips outwardly into inconstancy of movement, and indicates by his external restlessness that he has no root within to sustain him. Let the sower of discords hear what is written: *Blessed are the peacemakers, for they shall be called the children of God.*[220]

On the other hand, let them infer that if those who make peace are called the children of God, surely those who disturb it are the children of Satan. All those who by discord cut themselves off from the sap of love, become withered branches. Even though they display in their actions fruits of well-doing, these are, in fact, no fruits at all, because they do not spring from the unity of love. Therefore, let the sowers of discords weigh well how manifold are the sins they commit. In perpetrating one single iniquity, they root out all virtues from the human heart. In one single sin of malice they work innumerable others, since by sowing discord they extinguish charity, which is, in truth, the mother of all other virtues. And since nothing is more esteemed by God than the virtue of charity, nothing is more desired by the Devil than its extinction. He, then, who sows discord and thus destroys charity in the neighbour, serves God's enemy, as if he were his familiar friend. For he takes away from the hearts he wounds that virtue by the loss of which the Devil fell, and cuts from them the path by which they rise up.

On the other hand, peacemakers are to be admonished not to deprive their great mission of its efficacy by not knowing who those are between whom they should establish peace. Thus, as it is very harmful if unity is lacking among the good, it is extremely so, if not lacking among the wicked. If, therefore, peace unites the wicked in their iniquity, the influence of their evil deeds is certainly strengthened, for the more they agree in evil, the more vigorously do they oppose the good in order to afflict them. Hence it is that the divine utterance was made to blessed Job against the preachers of that vessel of perdition, namely, Antichrist: *The members of his flesh cleave one to another.*[221] Hence, under the symbol of scales, it is said of his satellites: *One is joined to another, and not so much as any air can come between them.*[222] For inasmuch as his followers are not divided among themselves, so are they the more strongly banded together for the slaughter of the good. A man, therefore, who associates with the wicked in peace, adds strength to their iniquity, for they overwhelm the good all the worse for their unanimity in persecuting them.

Wherefore, the great preacher, overtaken by grave persecution at the hands of the Pharisees and Sadducees, seeing them firmly united against him and endeavouring to cause a division among them, exclaimed: *Men, brethren, I am a Pharisee, the son of Pharisees. Concerning the hope and resurrection of the dead, I am called in question.*[223] Whereas the Sadducees denied hope in the resurrection of the dead, while the Pharisees believed in it in accordance with the teaching of Holy Writ, their unanimity in persecuting him was ruptured, and Paul went unhurt from the divided crowd, which had previously, when united, savagely assailed him.

Such, therefore, as are engaged in the work of establishing peace are to be admonished, first to instil the love of inward peace into the minds of the wicked, so that afterwards they may be able to realise the benefits of external peace. While their hearts are still uncertain in the appreciation of the former peace, they should not on any account be hurried into wickedness by their adoption of the latter; and while they are preparing themselves for heavenly peace, they should not in any way make earthly peace an occasion of lapsing into a worse state.

But where there are perverse persons unable to harm the good, even if they desire to do so, earthly peace should, of course, be first established among them, even before they can learn what heavenly peace is. Thus they whose wicked impiety makes them embittered against the love of God, may at least become more gently disposed by loving their neighbour; and passing, as it were, from a point nearby to the best position, they may rise to the peace which as yet is far from them—the peace of their Maker.

CHAPTER 24

How to admonish those who are unlearned in sacred lore, and those who have this learning, but are not humble.

Admonition 25. Persons who have no correct understanding of the words of the Sacred Law, are to be admonished in one way, in another way, those who in fact understand them correctly, but do not preach them humbly. Those who have not a right understanding of the words of the Sacred Law, are to be admonished to observe well that they actually turn for themselves a most wholesome draught of wine into a cup of poison, and inflict a

mortal wound on themselves with the lancet which should
be curative, by destroying in themselves what was sound
and not cutting away, as they should for their health's
sake, the diseased part.

They are also to be admonished to consider well, how
Sacred Scripture is set up as a kind of lantern for us in
the night of this life, for evidently, when the words are
not rightly understood, instead of light, darkness is the
result. And obviously, their perverse mind would not
hurry them into a false understanding, unless they were
first inflated with pride. For while they think themselves
wiser than others, they scorn to follow others in matters
which these understand better. What is more, in order
that they may extort from the untutored crowd a reputation for knowledge, they make every endeavour to dis-
credit what these rightly understand, and to confirm
their own perverse views. Wherefore, it is well said by
the Prophet: *They have ripped up the women with child
of Galaad to enlarge their border.*[224] Now, Galaad is in-
terpreted as meaning "a heap of testimony"; [225] and since
the whole congregation of the Church together serves,
by its confession of it, as testimony to the truth, the
Church is not ineptly expressed as Galaad, for it witnesses to all truth concerning God by the mouth of all
the faithful.[226] But souls are said to be with child, when
they conceive an understanding of the Word by divine
love, so that when they come to full term, they will bring
forth the understanding conceived by them in showing
forth their deeds. Again, *to enlarge the border* is to extend
one's reputation. Wherefore, *they ripped up the women
with child of Galaad to extend their border*—that is to say,
heretics by their perverse preaching slay the minds of

the faithful who have already conceived some measure
of the understanding of truth; and so they extend their
reputation for knowledge. The hearts of little ones, already big with conception of the Word, they cleave with
the sword of error, and thereby make a reputation, as it
were, for their teaching. When, therefore, we endeavour
to instruct these people not to entertain perverse views,
we must first admonish them not to seek vainglory; for
if the root of pride is cut away, the branches of false
assertions become withered.

Furthermore, they are to be admonished to beware of
turning into a sacrifice to Satan, by generating error and
discord, that very law of God which He established to
prevent sacrifices to Satan. Wherefore, He complains by
the Prophet, saying: *And she did not know that I gave
to them corn and wine and oil, and multiplied their silver
and gold, which they have used in the service of Baal.*[227]
For we receive corn from the Lord when in the more
obscure passages the husk of the letter is removed, and we
perceive, through the interior force of the Spirit, the
deeper meaning of the Law. The Lord gives us His wine,
when He inebriates us with the sublime preaching of His
Scripture. He also gives us His oil, when He orders our
life with soothing gentleness by His plainer precepts. He
multiplies silver, when He supplies us with utterances
filled with the radiance of truth. He also enriches us with
gold, when He irradiates our hearts with the understanding of that splendour which is supreme.

All these things heretics offer to Baal, because they
pervert in the hearts of their hearers all these matters
by their corrupt understanding of them. They immolate
God's corn, His wine and oil, His silver and gold, in sacri-

fice to Satan, because they divert the words of peace to the error of discord. They are, therefore, to be admonished to consider this matter well, namely, that while in the perversity of their minds they produce discord from the precepts of peace, they themselves perish by the just judgment of God, dead to the words of life.

On the other hand, they who rightly understand the words of the Law, but do not utter them with humility, are to be warned that in dealing with divine utterances, they should, before setting them before others, first look to themselves lest, in following up the deeds of others, they desert themselves, and though thinking aright about all the rest contained in Sacred Scriptures, they disregard that one thing, namely, what Scripture declares against the proud. Indeed, he is a poor and unskilled physician, who aims at healing others but is ignorant of his own ailment. They, therefore, who do not speak the words of God with humility, are certainly to be admonished, when applying remedies to the sick, to look to the poison of their own infection; otherwise, while seeking to heal others, they themselves will die.

They must be admonished to take heed that their manner of saying things is not at variance with the excellence of what is said, and not to preach one thing in words, and another in their outward conduct. Hence let them hear what Scripture says: *If any man speak, let him speak as the words of God.*[228] Why, then, do men who utter words not their own, swell with pride, as if the words were their own? Let them hear what is written: *As from God, before God, in Christ, we speak.*[229] For he speaks *from God, before God,* who both understands that he has received the word of preaching from God, and by it seeks to please not men but God. Let them hear the Scripture saying: *Every proud man is an abomination to the Lord.*[230] Manifestly, while he is seeking his own glory from the word of God, he invades the right of the Giver, and does not fear at all to prefer his own praise to Him from whom he has received the very thing for which he is praised. Let them hear what is said to the preacher by Solomon: *Drink water out of thy own cistern, and the streams of thy own well. Let thy fountains be conveyed abroad, and in the streets divide the waters. Keep them to thyself alone, neither let strangers be partakers with thee.*[231] The preacher drinks the water of his own cistern when, examining his own heart, he first listens himself to what he has to say. He drinks of the streams of his own well, if he is infused with the watering of his own word. In the place cited it is fitly added: *Let thy fountains be conveyed abroad, and in the streets divide the waters.* To be sure, it is proper that he should drink first, and then give others to drink by his preaching. For to *convey the fountains abroad* is to perform the external act of instilling in others the force of his preaching; and to *divide the waters in the streets* is to dispense the divine utterances among a great multitude of hearers, adapted to each one's character. And because usually the desire of vainglory insinuates itself, while the word of God is proceeding to the knowledge of the many, the words *in the streets divide the waters* receive the apposite addition: *Keep them to thyself alone, neither let strangers be partakers with thee.* Here he calls the malignant spirits by the name of "strangers," of whom it is said by the Prophet, in the words of one who is tempted: *For strangers have risen up against me, and the mighty have sought after my soul.*[232] He, therefore, says: *Divide the waters in the streets,* and yet *keep them to thyself,* as if he were to say in so many words: "It is necessary for you to go out and perform the service of preaching, and that in such manner as not to ally yourself with the unclean spirits through pride. In the ministry of the divine word you must not take your enemies as partners." We, then, divide the waters in the streets and yet keep them to ourselves, when we diffuse our preaching far and wide, but have no intention whatever of winning the praises of men.

CHAPTER 25

How to admonish those who decline the office of preaching from excessive humility, and those who seize on it with precipitate haste.

Admonition 26. Those who can preach worthily but fear to do so from excessive humility, are to be admonished in one way, and in another, those who are debarred from it by their unfitness or age, and yet are impelled thereto by their hastiness. Men who can preach with good results, but shrink from doing so from inordinate humility, are to be admonished to infer from a consideration of what is a small matter, how greatly they are at fault in matters of greater moment. Thus, if they were to hide from their indigent neighbours money which they themselves have, they would, without doubt, show themselves to be abettors of distress. Let them, then, consider in what great guilt they are implicated, because by withholding the word of preaching from sinning brethren, they are hiding the medicine of life from souls that are dying.

Wherefore, a wise man said well: *Wisdom that is hid, and treasure that is not seen, what profit is there in them both?* [233] If a famine were wasting away the people, and these same people kept their corn hidden away, they would, undoubtedly, be the authors of death. Consequently, let them consider what punishment is to be meted out to those who do not minister the bread of grace which they themselves have received, when souls are perishing from hunger for the Word. Wherefore, too, it is well said by Solomon: *He that hideth up corn shall be cursed among the people.* [234] To hide corn is to retain with oneself the words of sacred preaching. Among the people any such man is cursed, since, for the fault of mere silence, he is condemned in the punishment of the many whom he could have corrected.

If men versed in the medical art were to observe a sore that needed lancing, and yet refused to lance it, surely they would be responsible for a brother's death by their mere failing to act. Let them see, therefore, in what great guilt they are involved who, while recognising the wounds of the soul, neglect to heal them by the lancet of words. Wherefore, again, it is well said by the Prophet: *Cursed be he that withholdeth his sword from blood,* [235] for to withhold the sword from blood is to withhold the sword of preaching from the slaying of carnal life. Of the sword it is said again: *My sword shall devour flesh.* [236]

Let those, therefore, who conceal within themselves the word of preaching, hear with terror the divine judgment against them, so that fear may expel fear from their hearts. Let them hear that he who would not lay out his

talent lost it, and condemnation was added to the loss.[237]
Let them hear how Paul believed himself clear of the blood
of his neighbour, inasmuch as he spared not the vices of
those who had to be castigated, saying: *Wherefore, I
take you to witness this day that I am clear from the blood
of all men, for I have not spared to declare unto you all
the counsel of God.*[238] Let them hear how John is admonished by the angelic voice when it is said: *He that hear-
eth, let him say: Come.*[239] That is, let him who has heard
the inner voice, raise his own voice and draw others
whither he himself is carried lest, though called, he find
the door shut if he approaches the Caller empty-handed.
Let them hear how Isaias, because in his ministry of the
word he had held his peace when illuminated by supernal
light, reproached himself in a loud cry of penitence, saying: *Woe is me, because I have held my peace.*[240] Let
them hear in the words of Solomon, how a man is promised
an increase in the knowledge of preaching, if he is not
held back by the vice of torpor in regard to the gifts that
are already his. He says: *The soul which blesseth shall
be made fat, and he that inebriateth shall be inebriated
also himself.*[241] A man who goes out and dispenses blessings by his preaching, receives the fulness of interior increase; and while he unceasingly inebriates the souls of
his hearers with the wine of eloquence, he is himself
increasingly inebriated with the draught of multiplied
grace. Let them hear how David offered this by way of
gift to God, namely that he did not hide away the gift of
preaching which he had received, saying: *Lo, I will not
restrain my lips, O Lord, Thou knowest it, I have not hid
Thy justice within my heart. I have declared Thy truth
and Thy salvation.*[242]

Let them hear what the Bridegroom says, speaking to the Bride: *Thou that dwellest in the gardens, the friends hearken, make me hear thy voice.*[243] It is the Church that dwells in the gardens, for it is she that keeps the nursery plots of virtues fresh in the hearts she cultivates. Her friends hearken to her voice, that is, all the elect desire the words of her preaching. The Bridegroom also desires to hear her voice, for He yearns for her preaching through the souls of His elect.

Let them hear how Moses, on perceiving that God was angered with the people and commanded swords to be taken up to execute vengeance, declared those to be on God's side who should without hesitation smite the crimes of the wicked, saying: *If any man be on the Lord's side, let him join with me. . . . Put every man his sword upon his thigh; go, and return from gate to gate through the midst of the camp, and let every man kill his brother, and friend, and neighbour.*[244] To put the sword on the thigh is to prefer the zeal for preaching to the pleasures of the flesh, so that when one is zealous for speaking of holy matters, he must be careful to overcome forbidden temptations. To go from gate to gate is to hasten with rebuke from vice to vice, whereby death enters the soul. To pass through the midst of the host is to live with such perfect impartiality within the Church, as to rebuke the faults of sinners, and not to turn aside to favour anyone. Wherefore, too, it is properly added: *Let every man kill his brother, and friend, and neighbour;* that is, a man kills brother, and friend, and neighbour, when, discovering what should be punished, he does not refrain from using the sword of reproof, even in the case of those whom he loves for his kinship with them. Wherefore, if a man is said to belong to God when in his zeal for divine love he is moved to smite vice, then he surely denies his fellowship with God who declines to reprove sufficiently the lives of the carnal.

But, on the other hand, those who, being debarred from the office of preaching owing to incapacity or age, are yet impelled by precipitancy to undertake it, are to be admonished not to cut themselves off from the way to future progress by hastily arrogating to themselves the burden of so great an office.[245] They must not, by unseasonably attempting what they cannot do, lose in addition the opportunity of doing it when the proper time comes; and they should beware of offering the spectacle of having rightly lost their knowledge, for their unbecoming efforts to display it.

They should be admonished to bear in mind that when fledglings attempt to fly upwards before their wings are fully developed, they fall down from where they tried to soar. We should admonish them to bear in mind that if in a new building the frame has not been sufficiently strengthened and heavy timbers are placed on it, the result is not a dwelling but a ruin. Let them be admonished to bear in mind that if women give birth to offspring not fully developed, they are filling not a home but a sepulchre. This is the reason that the Truth in person, who could have strengthened in a moment those whom He wished to strengthen, but who desired to set an example to His followers, that they should not presume to preach before they were competent to do so, instructed His disciples on the power of preaching and immediately added: *But stay you in the city till you be endued with power from on high.*[246] We stay in the city, if we so confine ourselves within the enclosure of our souls so as not to wander about talking; only when we are completely invested with divine power, do we, as it were, depart from ourselves and go abroad also to instruct others. Wherefore, through a certain wise man it is said: *Young man, scarely speak in thy own cause. If thou be asked twice, let thy answer be short.*[247] Hence it is that our Redeemer Himself, though He, the Creator, is in Heaven and is always the Teacher of the angels by the manifestation of His power, did not wish to become a teacher of men on earth before His thirtieth year. Obviously, He wished to instil into the hasty a most salutary fear, seeing that He Himself who could not fall, did not preach the grace of a perfect life until He had reached a perfect age. Scripture states: *When He was twelve years old, . . . the Child Jesus remained in Jerusalem.*[248] Concerning Him, whom His parents had sought, it is presently added: *They found Him in the Temple, sitting in the midst of the doctors, hearing them and asking them questions.*[249]

We must, therefore, ponder well and carefully consider how Jesus, being twelve years of age, is recorded as sitting in the midst of the doctors, and was discovered, not teaching, but asking questions. The example shows that no one who is unfitted should dare to teach, seeing that the Boy who by His divine power administered the word of knowledge to the very men who were His teachers, wished to be taught by asking questions. But when it is said by Paul to his disciple: *These things command and teach, let no man despise thy adolescence,*[250] we must know that in Sacred Scripture youth is sometimes called adolescence. This is the more evident when the words of Solomon are cited, who says: *Rejoice, therefore, O young man, in thy adolescence.*[251] Unless he had meant the same by both words, he would not have called him a "youth," whom he was admonishing in his "adolescence."

CHAPTER 26

How to admonish those who succeed in everything according to their wishes, and those who succeed in nothing.

Admonition 27. Those who prosper in their pursuit of temporal things are to admonished in one way, but in another, those who desire, indeed, the things of the world, but yet are wearied out by the toils of adversity. Those who prosper in all their temporal wishes are to admonished that when everything accords with their wishes, they should not neglect to seek out the Giver and not fix their hearts solely on what is given. They must not love their pilgrimage instead of their country, nor turn the supplies they receive for their journey into hindrances to their safe arrival, nor become so exhilarated by the moon shining in the night as to shrink from beholding the bright radiance of the sun.

They should, therefore, be admonished that whatsoever they achieve in this world, is to be taken as a solace in calamity, not as reward and recompense. On the contrary, they must lift up their minds against the favours of this world, lest their heart be completely absorbed in enjoying them and they succumb in the midst of them. For whosoever does not by his own heart's discernment depreciate the prosperity which he enjoys, in favour of the love for the better life, transforms the gift of this life into an occasion of everlasting doom. Thus it was that under the figure of the Idumeans, who allowed themselves to be the victims of their own prosperity, those who rejoice in worldly prosperity are rebuked, when it is said: *They have given my land to themselves for an inheritance with joy, and with all the heart, and with the mind.*[252] Weighing these words carefully, we see that they were smitten with severe rebuke, not because they merely rejoiced, but because they rejoiced with the whole heart and mind.

Wherefore, Solomon says: *The turning away of little ones shall kill them, and the prosperity of fools shall destroy them.*[253] Hence Paul admonishes, saying: *They that buy shall be as though they possessed not, and they that use this world, as if they used it not;*[254] that is, the things which suffice us should so serve us outwardly as not to take away our minds from the pursuit of supernal delight, and the things that merely support us in our exile, must not abate the mourning of our soul's pilgrimage. We who see ourselves miserable in our present state of separation from the eternal, must not rejoice as though we were happy in the possession of what is transitory.

Hence it is that the Church says by the voice of the elect: *His left hand is under my head, and his right hand shall embrace me.*[255] She has put under her head, as it were, the left hand of God, that is, the prosperity of the present life, and presses it down in the rapture of supreme love; but the right hand of God embraces her, because in her complete devotion, she is enfolded with His eternal happiness. Wherefore, it is said again by Solomon: *Length of days is in her right hand, and in her left hand,*

riches and glory.[256] He showed, then, how riches and
glory are to be regarded, inasmuch as he recorded them
as placed in the left hand. Wherefore, the Psalmist says:
Save me with Thy right hand.[257] He does not say, "with
the hand," but "with the right hand," to indicate by using
the words, "right hand," that he was seeking eternal salvation. For this reason it is written again: *Thy right hand,
O Lord, hath destroyed the enemy.*[258] For the enemies of
God, though prosperous in His left hand, are destroyed
by His right hand, because very often the present life
raises up the wicked, but the coming of eternal bliss condemns them.

Those who prosper in this world are to be admonished
to consider wisely, that prosperity in this life is sometimes
granted to incite men to the better life, but sometimes,
to result in their greater eternal damnation. It was for
this reason that we see the land of Canaan promised to
the people of Israel, namely, to urge them finally to hope
for the eternal. For that uncultured people would not
have trusted in God's promises for a distant future, unless
they had received something ready to their hand from God
who had made the promises. Therefore, that they might
the more surely be strengthened to hope for eternal things,
they were drawn not merely by the hope of material
things, but by material things drawing them to hope.
The Psalmist clearly testifies to this, saying: *He gave
them the lands of the Gentiles, and they possessed the
labours of the people, that they might observe His justifi-
cations and seek after His law.*[259]

But when the human mind does not respond to the
bountiful favours of God by the requital of good deeds,
it is the more justly condemned in the measure in which

it was cherished with kindness. Therefore, it is again said by the Psalmist: *When they were lifted up, Thou hast cast them down;* [260] that is, because the reprobate do not requite divine favours by good works, when here on earth they neglect themselves entirely and give themselves up to their great prosperity, their progress in the world brings on the ruin of their souls. So, it is said to the rich man, tortured in hell: *Thou didst receive good things in thy lifetime.* [261] For, though he was bad, he received good things here that he might receive a fuller measure of evil things there, inasmuch as he did not change his ways, despite the benefits which he had received.

On the other hand, those who crave for the things of this world, yet are wearied out by the toils of adversity, are to be admonished to take profound and solicitous notice of the great favour it is, that the Creator and Dispenser of all things watches over those whom He does not abandon to their own desires. When a physician gives up hope for a patient, he allows him to have whatever he fancies; but a person whose cure he deems possible, is forbidden much that he desires. [262] We take money away from our children, yet at the same time reserve for them, as our heirs, the whole patrimony. Therefore, let those who are humbled by temporal adversity, take joy from the expectation of an eternal inheritance, because God in His Providence would not curb them in order to school them by discipline, unless it were His decree that they should be saved forever. [263]

They, therefore, who in their temporal desires are exhausted by the toils of adversity, are to be admonished to consider carefully that, for the most part, even the righteous when elevated to temporal power are, so to speak, caught in the net of sin. David, for instance, as we have stated in a previous part of this work,[264] beloved of God, was more upright in his subjection than when he came to the throne. For when he was a servant, he loved righteousness and feared to smite his captive enemy, but when he was king, being impelled to lechery, he even resorted to fraud to destroy the life of a loyal soldier. Who, then, can seek wealth, who can seek power, who glory, and remain blameless, if these proved harmful even to one who possessed them unsought? Who in possession of these things will be saved without a great and valiant fight, seeing that he who had been prepared for them by the choice of God, was overwhelmed by them when sin intervened?

They are to be admonished to consider that Solomon, who is recorded to have fallen even into idolatry after having possessed such great wisdom, is not recorded to have suffered any adversity in this world before his fall. The wisdom granted to him deserted his heart completely, for it was not guarded by even the smallest discipline of tribulation.[265]

CHAPTER 27

How to admonish the married and the celibate.

Admonition 28. Those bound in wedlock are to be admonished in one way, those free from the ties of wedlock in another. Those bound in wedlock are to be admonished that while mutually taking thought for each other, they should study to please their consorts without offence to their Maker. They must so act in the affairs of this world, as not to fail to desire the things that are God's. They should rejoice in present good, but fear earnestly and with solicitude eternal evil. They should so grieve over temporal evils, as to fix their hope with every reassurance on everlasting good, to the end that they remain conscious that what they are engaged on now is transitory, but what they hope for is permanent. The evils of this world must not destroy the courage of their heart, and they should let the hope of celestial things give it strength. Nor must the good things of this life deceive them, when the dread of the evil of the Judgment casts them into sadness.

Now, then, the mind of married Christians is both weak and steadfast, inasmuch as it cannot altogether disregard temporal matters, and yet is able in desire to unite itself with the eternal. Though the mind is now debased in fleshly delights, it must grow strong with the refreshment which supernal hope affords; and though it possesses worldly things for use on the way, it should hope for the enjoyment of divine things at the end. It should not give itself entirely to the things it is now engaged in, lest it wholly fall from what it should steadfastly hope for. St. Paul expresses this well and succinctly when he says: *They who have wives, should be as if they had none, and they that weep, as though they wept not, and they that rejoice, as if they rejoiced not.*[266] Now, that man has a wife as though he had not, who so enjoys carnal solace by her means, that for love of her he is never deflected from the rectitude of better purposes to evil deeds. He has a wife as though he had not, who views all things as transitory and endures the cares of the flesh as a necessity, but looks forward in his desires to everlasting spiritual joys. That man weeps as though not weeping,

who laments outward adversities in such a way, as yet
to know how to rejoice in the consolations of eternal hope.
And again, to rejoice as though not rejoicing, is so to
uplift the mind from things below, as never to cease to
be concerned regarding the things that are above. Paul
aptly adds at once to the aforesaid passage: *For the fashion of this world passeth away* [267]—as if he plainly said:
"Love not the world constantly, since the world which
you love cannot itself remain constant." It is in vain that
you fix your heart, as though you were yourself abiding,
whilst that which you love passes away.

The married are to be admonished to bear with mutual
patience the things in which they sometimes displease
each other, and to assist each other to salvation by mutual
encouragement; for Scripture says: *Bear ye one another's
burdens, and so you shall fulfil the law of Christ.*[268] Indeed, the law of Christ is love, for it was this that
prompted Him to bestow bountifully His blessings on us
and to bear our evils in patience. Then, therefore, do we
fulfil the law of Christ by our imitation of it, when we,
too, are generous in bestowing our own good things, and
lovingly endure the evil things of our fellow men. They
are also to be admonished to consider not so much what
each has to endure from the other, as what the other is
made to endure. For if one considers what is endured
from oneself, that which is endured from another is the
more easily borne.

The married must be admonished to bear in mind that
they are united in wedlock for the purpose of procreation,
and when they abandon themselves to immoderate intercourse, they transfer the occasion of procreation to the
service of pleasure. Let them realise that though they do

not then pass beyond the bounds of wedlock, yet in wedlock they exceed its rights. Wherefore, it is necessary that they should efface by frequent prayer what they befoul in the fair form of intercourse by the admixture of pleasure.[269] Hence it is that the Apostle, versed in celestial medicine, did not so much prescribe for the hale, as point out the remedies for the weak, when he said: *Concerning the things whereof you wrote to me, it is good for a man not to touch a woman, but for fear of fornication, let every man have his own wife, and let every woman have her own husband.*[270] For in setting out beforehand the fear of fornication, he surely did not give a precept to those who stood on their feet, but pointed out the bed to such as were falling, lest perhaps they should collapse to the ground. Wherefore, he further added for the weak: *Let the husband render the debt to his wife, and the wife also in like manner to the husband.*[271] So, for the sake of those in whose case he made a certain concession to pleasure in the most honourable estate of wedlock, he added: *But I speak this by indulgence, not by commandment.*[272]

Now, the mention of indulgence suggests the presence of sin, but sin which is the more readily forgiven, in so far as the sinfulness does not consist in what is done, but in what is done lawfully, indeed, but is not kept under control. This truth is well expressed by Lot in his own case when he fled from burning Sodom, and yet on coming to Segor, he did not at once go up into the mountains.[273] To flee from burning Sodom is to shun the sinful fires of the flesh, and the mountain height is the purity of those who are continent; and those are at least, as it were, on a mountain, who beyond exercising carnal intercourse as far as is required for the procreation of offspring, do not indulge in fleshly pleasure. To stand on the mountain is to seek nothing in the flesh but the fruits of offspring. To stand on the mountain is to avoid cleaving to the flesh in a fleshly way.

But as there are many who, though abandoning the sins of the flesh, yet in the state of wedlock do not restrict themselves to the practice of intercourse as is due, this is the case of Lot abandoning Sodom, but not proceeding as far as the mountains: these people do relinquish a reprehensible life, but still they do not really attain to perfection in conjugal continence. There is the midway city of Segor for saving the weak fugitive: that is to say, when the married are incontinent in having intercourse, but shun falling into grievous sins,[274] they are nevertheless pardoned and saved.

They find, as it were, a little city in which to be protected from the fire, for the conjugal life as they practice it is not, indeed, conspicuously virtuous, yet it is secure from punishment. Wherefore, the same Lot says to the angel: *There is a city here at hand to which I may flee; it is a little one, and I shall be saved in it. Is it not a little one, and my soul shall live?* [275] The city is said to be near, and yet is represented as a refuge of safety, because conjugal life is neither greatly separated from worldly life, nor yet is it alien from the joy of salvation. But then only do the married in this manner of conduct save their lives, so to say, in a little city, when they intercede for one another by assiduous supplications. Wherefore, the angel rightly said to the same Lot: *Behold, also in this I have heard thy prayers, not to destroy the city for which thou hast spoken.*[276] For it is evident that when supplication is made to God, such manner of conjugal life is by no means condemned. In regard to such supplication, Paul also admonishes, saying: *Defraud not one another except, perhaps by consent for a time, that you may give yourselves to prayer.*[277]

On the other hand, those who are not bound in wedlock are to be admonished to observe heavenly precepts the more strictly, in that the yoke of carnal union does not make them prone to worldly concerns. Since the lawful burden of wedlock does not press them down, so the unlawful burden of earthly cares should not weigh them down. Indeed, the Last Day should find them the more prepared for it; otherwise, because they are disengaged and the more able to do the better things, and yet neglect them, they will deserve to be punished the more severely. Let them hear what the Apostle said when he desired to instruct certain people on the grace of celibacy. He did not depreciate wedlock, but condemned the cares of the world that issue from wedlock: *This I speak for your profit, not to cast a snare upon you, but for that which is decent, and which may give you power to attend upon the Lord, without impediment.*[278] Earthly cares arise from wedlock, and, therefore, the Teacher of the Gentiles urged his hearers to better things, lest they should be tied up in earthly cares. The unmarried man for whom earthly cares have proved to be an impediment, though he is not bound in wedlock, has yet not escaped the burden of it. The unmarried are to be admonished that they must not think that they may have intercourse with unmarried women, without incurring the sentence of damnation. For when Paul included the vice of fornication in the number of so many execrable crimes, he pointed out their guilt by saying: *Neither fornicators, nor idolaters, nor adulterers, nor the effeminate, nor liers with mankind, nor thieves, nor covetous, nor drunkards, nor railers, nor extortioners, shall possess the kingdom of God.*[279] And again: *For fornicators and adulterers God will judge.*[280]

They are, therefore, to be admonished that if they suffer from the storms of temptations with risk to their salvation, they should seek the harbour of wedlock, for Scripture says: *It is better to marry than to be burnt.*[281] These come to marriage, indeed, without blame, provided they have not yet vowed what is better; for one who has determined to submit himself to a greater good, makes the lesser good, which would otherwise have been lawful for him, unlawful. Scripture states: *No man putting his hand to the plough and looking back is fit for the kingdom of God.*[282] A man, therefore, who had been determined on a more valiant aim, is convicted of looking back, when, relinquishing the greater good, he turns to the good which is less.

CHAPTER 28

*How to admonish those who have had experience of
sins of the flesh, and how those who have not.*

Admonition 29. Those conscious of carnal sins are to be admonished in one way, those who are free from them, in another. Those who have had experience of sins of the flesh are to be admonished to be in dread of the sea, at least after having suffered shipwreck, and to fear the risk of perdition when apprised of it, lest they who have

been mercifully preserved after evil done, die after repeating it. Wherefore, it is said to the soul that sins and
never ceases from sinning: *Thou hadst a harlot's forehead, thou wouldst not blush.*[283]

They must, therefore, be admonished to see to it that
if they have been unwilling to preserve intact the natural
goodness they have received, they should at least repair
it when violated. These people must, indeed, bear in mind
how many there are in the great multitude of the faithful
who both keep themselves undefiled, and lead others back
from their aberrations. What, then, will these be able to
say, if they do not amend even after doing evil, when
others remain steadfast in innocence? What can they say
if, while many bring others besides themselves into the
Kingdom, they do not bring back even themselves to the
Lord who awaits them?

They are to be admonished to think of their past transgressions and to shun others which threaten to overtake
them. For this reason, under the figure of Judea, the Lord
by the Prophet recalls their past sins to the memory of
souls corrupted in this world, that they may blush at the
thought of defilement by future sins. He says: *They
committed fornication in Egypt, in their youth they committed fornication. There were their breasts pressed
down, and the teats of their virginity were bruised.*[284]
The breasts are pressed down in Egypt, when the wish
of the mind is prostituted to the evil desire of this world.
The teats of virginity are bruised in Egypt, when the
natural senses, still uncorrupted, are vitiated by the corrupting onslaughts of concupiscence.

Those who have had experience of the sins of the flesh
are to be admonished to consider with watchful care the

great benevolence with which God opens the bosom of His loving-kindness to us if we return to Him after sinning, for He says by the Prophet: *If a man put away his wife, and she go from him and marry another man, shall he return to her any more? Shall not that woman be polluted and defiled? But thou hast prostituted thyself to many lovers; nevertheless return to me, saith the Lord.*[285] Note how the plea of justice is proposed in regard to the wife who commits fornication and is deserted, and yet, for us who return after our fall, it is not justice but loving-kindness that is shown. The inference is obvious, namely, that if our sins are spared with such great love, how great would be our wickedness if we sinned, but failed to return after our sin, and what pardon can the wicked expect from Him who does not cease to call them after they have sinned! This mercy of God in calling us after our sin is well expressed by the Prophet, when it is said to him who turns away from Him: *And thy eyes shall see thy teacher, and thy ears shall hear the word of one admonishing thee behind thy back.*[286]

The Lord did, indeed, admonish the human race to its face when man, being created in paradise and having free will, was told by Him what he ought to do, and what he ought not to do. But man turned his back on the face of God, when in his pride he spurned His commands. Yet God did not desert him in his pride, for He gave man His law for the purpose of recalling him, sent His angels to exhort him, and He appeared Himself in our mortal flesh. He, therefore, stood behind our back and admonished us, in that He recalled us to the recovery of grace, even though we despised Him. Hence, what can be stated of all men in general must be understood of the individual. For each one of us, as if he stood in the presence of God, perceives the words of His admonition when, before we sin, the precepts of His will are known to us. To remain standing before His face is not as yet to despise Him by sinning. When, however, a man forsakes the blessing of innocence and chooses and desires iniquity, then he turns his back on His face. But you see that God follows him even after he has turned his back, and warns him, inviting him to return even after having committed sin. He calls man back when he turns his face away from Him, He regards not his sins, He opens His heart to him with loving compassion when he returns. Therefore, if at least after sinning we return to the Lord calling us, we are hearkening to the voice of Him who warns us behind our back. We should, then, if we will not fear His justice, feel shame in view of that loving-kindness inviting us to return, for our contempt for Him is the more wicked, in that in spite of this contempt He does not disdain to call us still.

On the other hand, those who are innocent of the sins of the flesh are to be admonished to dread all the more anxiously headlong ruin, the loftier the eminence on which they stand. We should admonish them to realise that the more conspicuous their position, the more numerous are the arrows hurled against them by him who lies in wait for us. The more stoutly he sees himself worsted, the more energetically does he bestir himself. The more intolerable to him is his shame of being conquered, the more clearly he perceives that he is opposed by an unbroken barrier of weak flesh.

They are to be admonished to look unceasingly to their rewards, and then, without doubt, they will gladly spurn the toils of temptation which they suffer. For if we regard

the happiness which we attain and which does not pass
away, then the toil which passes becomes light. Let them
hear what is said by the Prophet: *Thus saith the Lord
to the eunuchs: They that shall keep my Sabbaths, and
shall choose the things that please me, and shall hold
fast my covenant, I will give to them in my house and
within my walls a place and a name better than sons and
daughters.*[287] This means: eunuchs are those who by re-
sisting the passions of the flesh, cut away their inclination
to evil. What esteem they enjoy with their Father is indicated: in the house of the Father, that is, in their eternal
home, they are preferred even to sons. Let them hear what
is said by John: *These are they who were not defiled by
women, for they are virgins, and follow the Lamb whither-
soever He goeth.*[288] And let them hear how they sing a
song which no one can utter, except those one hundred
and forty-four thousand.[289] To sing a special song to the
Lamb means to rejoice with Him forever, and before all
the faithful, also in the incorruption of the flesh.[290] The
rest of the elect can hear this song, but they may not utter
it. Though by their love they rejoice in the exaltation of
those others, they do not rise to the height of their reward.

Let those who are innocent of sins of the flesh hear
what the Truth in person says about that integrity:
All men take not this word.[291] And He indicated this as
the highest, in that He spoke of it as not belonging to all,
and if He states by way of preface that it is difficult to
take, He signifies to His hearers the care with which it
should be guarded when taken. Therefore, those who are
innocent of sins of the flesh should be admonished to
realise that the state of virginity is superior to the state
of wedlock; but at the same time they must not extol

themselves above those who are married. They should esteem virginity in the first place, but put themselves last. Thus they will the better keep what they prize, and so guard themselves from vainly extolling themselves.

They are to be admonished to consider that the life of the continent is often put to shame by the conduct of worldly persons, when they, too, undertake works beyond their position, while the former do not bestir their hearts in accord with what is properly the condition of their life. Wherefore, it is well said by the Prophet: *Be thou ashamed, O Sidon, saith the sea.*[292] Sidon is brought to shame, as it were, by the voice of the sea, when the life of one who is fortified and supposedly steadfast, is reprobated in comparison with the lives of those who are worldly and are being tossed about in this world. For often there are those who, returning to the Lord after their sins of the flesh, evince themselves the more zealous in doing good works, as they realise they were worthy of condemnation for their evil deeds. And often certain people who persevere in preserving the integrity of the flesh, on perceiving that they have less to deplore, think to themselves that the innocency of their lives is sufficient, and do not arouse themselves by zealously striving to be fervent in spirit.[293]

And so it often comes about that the life of one burning with love after having sinned is more pleasing to God than a life of innocence that grows languid in its sense of security. Wherefore, it is said by the voice of the Judge: *Many sins are forgiven her because she hath loved much.*[294] And again: *There shall be joy in Heaven upon one sinner that doth penance, more than upon ninety-nine just who need not penance.*[295] The truth of this we gather the more readily from our own experience, if we consider the judgments which our own mind makes: for example, we love land that produces abundant fruit when its thorns are ploughed in, more than land that had no thorns but which, though cultivated, yields a barren harvest.

They who are innocent of sins of the flesh are to be admonished not to prefer themselves in the eminence of their loftier estate, seeing that they do not know how many better things are done by those of inferior estate in these matters. For on the assessment of the righteous Judge, the character of our conduct reverses the merit due to our rank. Indeed, who, taking the more outward appearances of objects, does not know that in the realm of gems the garnet is preferred to the jacinth, yet the blue jacinth is preferred to the pale garnet, because what the order of nature has denied to the former, is added to it by the phase of its beauty, and though the latter is superior in the order of nature, it is depreciated by the quality of its colour? So, then, in the case of man there are some who, though of higher rank, are inferior, and others who are in a lower estate, are better, because the latter by their good way of life transcend the character of the lower estate, while the former fall short of the merit of their higher estate by not living up to it.

CHAPTER 29

*How to admonish those who have evil deeds to
grieve for, and those who have
only sins of thought.*

Admonition 30. Those who grieve for evil deeds are to
be admonished in one way, those who grieve only for sins
of thought, in another. Those who grieve for evil deeds
are to be admonished to cleanse the evil they have done
by a perfect sorrow, lest they be the more involved in the
debt of evil done, because of the inadequate satisfaction
they make by their tears of reparation. Scripture says:
He gave us for our drink tears in measure.[296] That is to
say, the soul of each should in its penitence drink the
tears of compunction in proportion as it remembers how
because of its sins it has turned from God and withered.

They are to be admonished never to stop recalling their
sins to mind and to make it their life's work, that their
sins may not be taken into account by the strict Judge.
Wherefore, when David made the petition: *Turn away
Thy eyes from my sins,*[297] he had said shortly before:
My sin is always before me,[298] as if he had said: "I beseech
Thee not to regard my sin, for I cease not from regarding
it." Wherefore, through the Prophet the Lord says: *I will
not remember thy sins, but do thou remember them.*[299]

They should be admonished to consider their every
sin, and while they deplore the defilement of their way-
wardness in each and every sin, they must cleanse themselves through and through by their tears. Wherefore, it

is well said by Jeremias, when the several transgressions of Judea were considered: *My eye hath run down with streams of water.*[300] We shed streams of water from our eyes when we weep for each sin separately, for the mind does not grieve for all sins equally at one and the same moment, but, while memory stings more sharply now for this sin, now for that, the soul is cleansed from all by its pangs of sorrow for each.

They are, however, to be admonished to rely confidently on the mercy they ask for, lest they perish through the violence of immoderate affliction. Obviously, the Lord would not with loving-kindness confront the sinner's gaze with sins to be lamented, if He had wished only to punish them severely. For it is manifest that He then wished to screen from His condemnation those whom in His prevenient mercy He made their own judges. Wherefore, it is written: *Let us come before the face of the Lord in confession.*[301] Therefore, it is said by Paul: *If we would judge ourselves, we should not be judged.*[302]

On the other hand, they are to be admonished to have only such a degree of confidence in hope, that they will not grow remiss in the sense of a false security. For often when the crafty Enemy observes the soul afflicted because of its fall, he seduces it with the blandishments of a baneful reassurance, in order to trip it up in sin. This is expressed figuratively by the history of Dina. For Scripture says: *Dina went out to see the women of that country. And when Sichem, the son of Hemor, the Hevite, the prince of that land, saw her, he was in love with her, and took her away, and lay with her, ravishing the virgin. And his soul was fast knit unto her, and whereas she was sad, he comforted her with sweet words.*[303] Dina goes out to see the women of a foreign land, when a soul, neglecting its own concerns and giving heed to the doings of others, wanders about outside its own condition and state. And Sichem, the prince of the country, overpowers it, that is, the Devil corrupts it, when it is preoccupied with external things. *And his soul was fast knit unto her,* because he saw it was united with him in iniquity. And when the soul, converted from sin, condemns itself and would weep for its trangressions, the seducer dazzles it with false hopes and grounds for security, in order to withdraw from it the benefits of its grief. So, it is rightly added: *He comforted her with sweet words,* for he speaks at one time of the graver deeds of others, at another time that the ill done was of no account, then of the mercy of God, and gives assurance that there is time for repentance later on. He wants the soul to deceive itself by such considerations and to defer its purpose of penitence, to the end that, feeling no compunction for the evils it does now, it may receive no blessings hereafter. Thus it will be the more completely overwhelmed with punishments, as it now experiences even joy in its sins.

On the other hand, those who grieve for sins of thought are to be admonished to consider carefully deep down in their minds, whether it was by pleasure only that they sinned, or by consent also. For, as a rule, the heart is tempted and feels pleasure in the sinfulness of the flesh, and yet opposes a rational resistance to the sinfulness, so that in its innermost thought it is saddened by what pleases it, and pleased by what saddens it.[304] Sometimes, however, the mind is so engulfed in temptation, that it offers no resistance at all, but deliberately consents to what thrills it with delight; and if external opportunity offered, it would at once execute in effect its inward wishes. But when this matter is regarded and truly measured by the strict Judge, the sin is not only one in thought, but one of deed also, for if lack of opportunity defers the external sin, the will has consummated the sin by its act of consent.

We have learned in the case of our first parent that a sin is committed in three stages,[305] namely, the suggestion of it, the pleasure experienced, and the consent. The first is the act of the Enemy, the second that of the flesh, the third that of the spirit. For he who lies in wait for us suggests the evil, the flesh submits to the pleasure, and at last, the spirit, overcome by the pleasure, consents. Wherefore, the serpent suggested evil, Eve, the flesh, as it were, gave herself up to the pleasure, but Adam, the spirit, so to say, overcome by the suggestion and the pleasure, gave consent. We, then, become aware of sin by suggestion, we are overcome by pleasure, and by consenting we are also put in bonds.

Those, therefore, who grieve for the evil of thoughts only, are to be admonished to consider carefully the degree of sin into which they have fallen, to the end that they may raise themselves to a degree of sorrow in proportion to the known degree of their fall, lest, if they do not feel horror at evil thoughts, these may lead them to evil deeds. Still, while they are to be stricken with fear in these circumstances, they should not become despondent. For often the merciful God absolves sins of thought the more readily, in that He does not allow them to issue in deed, and wickedness that is merely conceived is the more readily absolved, because it has not been brought under the stronger bondage of the consummated deed. Wherefore, it is rightly said by the Psalmist: *I said, I will confess*

*against myself my injustices to the Lord; and Thou hast
forgiven the wickedness of my heart.*[306] He used the term
"wickedness of the heart" because he indicated that he
wished to confess sins of thought; and when he said: *I
said, I will confess . . . ,* and at once added, *Thou hast
forgiven . . . ,* he showed how readily these are pardoned.
For while he is still uttering a promise that he would ask,
he obtained what he was promising to ask for. Inasmuch
as his sin had not gone so far as act, his penitence was
not to go so far as self-torment, and the affliction which
he entertained was to cleanse his mind, for it was only
an iniquity that was thought of which had defiled him.

CHAPTER 30

*How to admonish those who weep for their sins but
do not desist from them, and those who, though
desisting from them, do not weep for them.*

Admonition 31. Those who grieve for their sins yet do
not abandon them, are to be admonished in one way, and
those who abandon their sins yet do not grieve for them,
in another.[307] As for those who lament their sins but do
not give them up, these are to be admonished to realise
and observe carefully, that, though bewailing their sins,
their attempts to cleanse themselves are vain if they continue defiling themselves with evil in their way of life.
They bathe themselves in tears, only to return, when
cleansed, to their filth. Wherefore, Scripture, says: *The
dog is returned to his vomit, and the sow that was washed*

to her wallowing in the mire.[308] When a dog vomits, it obviously casts forth the food that lay heavily on its stomach, but when it returns to its vomit, it again loads itself with what it had been relieved of. So, too, those who bewail their sins, by confessing them, do, indeed, cast forth their wickedness with which they had been evilly satiated, and wherewith the soul's inmost was weighed down, but by repeating their wickedness after confession, they return to it again. When the sow takes a bath in its muddy wallow, it makes itself even filthier. So, too, he who bewails his sins but does not abandon them, subjects himself to punishment for a more grievous sin. For he despises the pardon which he could have obtained by his tears, and, as it were, wallows in muddy waters, because when he excludes cleanliness of life from his weeping, he renders even his tears filthy in God's sight. Wherefore, it is again written: *Repeat not the word in thy prayer.*[309] For to repeat the word in prayer is to commit, after weeping, what must be wept for again. Wherefore, it is said by Isaias: *Wash yourselves; be clean.*[310] He who does not keep innocence of life after weeping, neglects to be clean after washing; and those are not clean after washing who, though not ceasing to weep for their sins, yet commit again what has to be wept for. Wherefore, it is said by a man of wisdom: *He that washeth himself after touching the dead, if he toucheth him again, what does his washing avail?* [311] Now, that man washes himself after touching the dead, who cleanses himself from his sins by weeping, but he who repeats his sin after weeping for them, touches the dead after his washing.

They who bewail their sins but do not abandon them are to be admonished to realise that in the eyes of the

strict Judge they are like those who, when coming into
the presence of certain men, fawn upon them with great
obsequiousness, but on leaving them, cruelly bring upon
them all the hatred and harm they can. For what is it
to weep for sin but to display to God the humility of one's
devotion? What else is it to do evil after weeping but
to evince proud enmity against Him to whom entreaty
had been made? James attests this, saying: *Whosoever
will be a friend of this world, becometh an enemy of
God.*[312]

They who lament their sins but do not abandon them
are to be admonished to consider carefully that, for the
most part, evil men are moved in vain by compunction
to righteousness, just as, for the most part, the good are
tempted to sin without harm. Thus there comes about a
remarkable showing of what interior disposition is present,
corresponding to the merits present: those who do some
part of a good deed without completing it are proudly
confident in the midst of all the evil which they bring
to most complete consummation; while the other class,
though tempted to evil to which they give no consent at
all, do the more truly set the steps of the heart on the
road to righteousness by their humility, for the very
reason of their faltering from infirmity. Thus Balaam,
looking on the tents of the righteous, says: *Let my
soul die the death of the just, and my last end be like to
them.*[313] But when the time of compunction had passed,
he gave counsel against the life of those whose like he
had prayed to be in death, and when he found an occasion
of avarice, he promptly forgot all that he had desired in
the way of innocence.[314]

Wherefore, Paul, the teacher and preacher of the Gentiles, says: *I see another law in my members, fighting against the law of my mind, and leading me captive in the law of sin that is in my members.*[315] He is, in fact, tempted that he may be the more strongly rooted in good through the knowledge of his own weakness. Why is it, then, that the one is full of compunction, and yet does not come to righteousness, and the other is tempted, and yet does not defile himself with sin, except that it is obvious that the good that is not completed does not help the bad, and evil that is not actualised does not serve as condemnation of the good?

On the other hand, those who desist from sinning but do not lament their sins are to be admonished not to suppose that their sins are forgiven on the mere plea that they have not been repeated, if they have not been cleansed by tears. A writer, for instance, who has given up writing, has not deleted what he has written, just because he has not added anything. So, too, one does not make reparation for insults offered, merely by holding one's peace, for, in truth, it is necessary that he abjure the words of his former pride by expressions of subsequent humility. Nor, again, is a debtor discharged, merely because he incurs no further debts, if he has not paid the debts already incurred. So, too, when we sin against God, we certainly do not make reparation merely by ceasing from evil, unless those sinful pleasures we have indulged in are succeeded by sorrow abjuring them.[316] Indeed, even if no sin of deed had stained us in this life, our innocence would not, by any means, suffice to save us so long as we live here, for there would still be much that is unlawful to knock at our hearts. With what assurance, then, does he feel secure who, after having committed evil, is a witness against himself that he is not innocent?

It is not that God is regaled by our tortures; no, He heals the diseases of our sins by their contrary antidotes, so that we who have departed from Him by the delight of pleasures, may return to Him in tearful grief, and after having fallen by losing ourselves amid sinful things, we may rise up by restraining ourselves even in what is lawful. The heart which had been flooded with insane delight, He wants made clean by a saving sorrow, and wounds inflicted by the elation of pride, He wants healed by the lowliness of a humble life. Wherefore, Scripture says: *I said to the wicked, do not act wickedly, and to the sinners, lift not up the horn.*[317] Sinners lift up the horn, if they fail to acknowledge their wickedness and to do humble penance. Wherefore, it is said again: *A contrite and humbled heart God does not despise.*[318] For anyone who bewails his sins, but does not desist from them, has a contrite heart, indeed, but scorns to humble it; whereas he who desists from sin, but does not bewail it, does, indeed, humble himself, but fails to have a contrite heart.

Wherefore, Paul says: *And such some of you were; but you are washed, but you are sanctified.*[319] Obviously, those are sanctified by their amended life, who are washed in penitence by the cleansing affliction of tears. Hence, Peter, on seeing some who were terrified by the consideration of their evil deeds, admonished them saying: *Do penance, and be baptized every one of you.*[320] Here, when he was about to speak of baptism, he spoke first of the grief of penitence, that is, they were first to bathe themselves in the waters of their sorrow, and afterwards wash themselves in the sacrament of baptism. With what conscience, then, can those who neglect to weep for their past sins, live with a secure sense of pardon, when the supreme pastor of the Church himself believed that penitence was to be added even to that sacrament, whose principal function it is to wipe away sins? [321]

CHAPTER 31

How to admonish those who praise the wrongs of which they are conscious, and those who, while condemning such things, do not in any way guard against them.

Admonition 32. Those who even approve of their misdeeds are to be admonished in one way, in another, those who confess their sins yet do not avoid them. Those who even uphold their misdeeds are to be admonished to consider that often they offend more by their mouth than by deed. For the evil that they do is, in fact, only personal, but by their evil words they make themselves responsible for wickedness in as many persons as there are individuals who hear them and are instructed in wickedness by their extolling it. They are, therefore, to be admonished that if they fail to eradicate their own evil, they should, at least, dread the sowing of it. They are to be warned to be content with their individual damnation.

Again, they are to be admonished that if they are not afraid of being wicked, they should at least be ashamed of being seen for what they are. Often a sin that is concealed is avoided, because a mind that is ashamed to be taken for what it does not fear to be in fact, is sometimes ashamed to be in fact what it avoids appearing to be. On the other hand, when a man is shamelessly and notoriously wicked, then, the more freely he commits every kind of evil, the more he thinks it lawful, and in imagining it lawful, he is thereby undoubtedly immersed in it all the more. Wherefore, it is written: *They have proclaimed abroad their sin as Sodom, and they have not hid it.*[322] For if Sodom had concealed its sin, she would still have sinned, but in fear. But she had completely lost the curb of fear, in that she did not seek even darkness in her sinning. Wherefore, it is said again: *The cry of Sodom and Gomorrha is multiplied.*[323] For sin in words is sin in act, but sin that is cried out is sin committed with deliberation.

On the other hand, those who confess their evil deeds, but do not avoid them, must be admonished to weigh betimes what they will say to excuse themselves when confronted with the strict judgment of God, seeing that they cannot excuse themselves from the guilt of their grave sins even when they are their own judges. What else, then, are these men but their own accusers? They prefer charges against their sins, and drag themselves to judgment as guilty of misdeeds.

They are, therefore, to be admonished to understand that it is already indicative of the hidden retribution of judgment that their mind is enlightened to perceive the evil which it does, while not striving to overcome it. Thus, the more clear its vision, the worse will be its end, because it both perceives the light of understanding, and does not abandon the darkness of evil-doing. For when these reject the insight given to help them, they convert it into a testimony against themselves; and because the light of understanding had, in fact, been given to them that they might be able to blot out their sins, they do but augment their punishments. Indeed, their wickedness in doing the evil which their understanding condemns, is a foretaste here of the judgment to come. And so, while being reserved for eternal punishment, the soul is not absolved here on earth by scrutinising itself, and it shall thereafter experience the greater torments, the more it fails to abandon evil which even itself condemns.

Wherefore, the Truth says: *A servant who knew the will of his Lord and prepared not himself, and did not according to His will, shall be beaten with many stripes.*[324] Wherefore, the Psalmist says: *Let them go down alive to hell.*[325] It is evident that those who are alive know and feel what is done to them, but the dead feel nothing. Men would be dead in going down to hell, if they did evil out of ignorance; but if they have knowledge of evil and yet commit it, they go down alive—wretched and conscious—to the hell of iniquity.

CHAPTER 32

How to admonish those who sin in sudden impulse, and those who sin wilfully.

Admonition 33. Those who are overcome by sudden concupiscence are to be admonished in one way, those in another, who deliberately put on the fetters of sin. Those whom sudden concupiscence overcomes are to be admonished to consider that they are daily engaged in the warfare of this life,[326] and to protect the heart unable to foresee wounds, with the shield of anxious fear. They are to have a horror of the hidden darts of the Enemy lurking in ambush. They must fortify themselves within the mind's fortress with unceasing vigilance in so darksome a conflict. For if the heart lacks anxious circumspection, it exposes itself to wounds, for the crafty Enemy smites the breast the more freely, as he catches it unprotected by the breastplate of forethought.

Those who are overcome by sudden concupiscence are to be admonished to cease being over-attached to earthly things, because, when they are immoderately taken up with transitory things, they are not aware of the darts of sins that may pierce them. Wherefore, the utterance of one who is stricken and still sleeps is expressed by Solomon, when he says: *They have beaten me, but I was not sensible of pain: they drew me, and I felt not. When shall I awake and find wine again?* [327] A mind sleeps with no care to worry it, and is beaten and feels no pain, when it does not forsee impending evils and so, too, is unaware of those which it has committed. It is drawn and feels not, that is, it is attracted by the allurements of vices, and yet does not arouse itself to its self-defence. But at the same time it wishes to be awake in order to find wine, that is, though it is so weighed down in its languid sleep as not to keep watch over itself, nevertheless, it still tries to be awake to the cares of the world, so as ever to inebriate itself with pleasures. And when it is asleep to that whereto it should be vigilantly awake, it wishes to be awake to something else, in regard to which it might have been laudably asleep. Wherefore, it was written previously: *And thou shalt be as one sleeping in the midst of the sea, and as a pilot fast asleep when the stern is lost.* [328] A man sleeps in the midst of the sea who in the temptations of this world neglects to provide against the attacks of vices that beset him, like waves threatening mountain-high. And the pilot loses the rudder, as it were, when the mind loses all anxious solicitude for guiding the ship of the body. To lose the rudder at sea is to fail to keep attentive forethought amidst the storms of this world. But if a pilot carefully holds fast the rudder, he steers the ship, now against advancing billows, now by cleaving the impetuous winds aslant. So, when the mind vigilantly rules the soul, it now surmounts and treads down some things with forethought, turns aside from others. It thus overcomes the present dangers with great toil, and by looking forward, gathers strength to face future conflicts.

Wherefore, it is said again of the valiant warriors of the heavenly country: *Every man's sword upon his thigh, because of the fears of the night.*[329] The sword is put upon the thigh when an evil suggestion of the flesh is subdued by the sharp blade of holy preaching. The term "night" expresses the blindness of our infirmity, because attacks that threaten by night are not perceived. Therefore, *every man's sword* is put *upon the thigh, because of the fears of the night,* that is to say, holy men, being in fear of what they do not see, are always ready to engage in a struggle. Wherefore, it is said again to the bride: *Thy nose is as the tower of Libanus.*[330] Evidently, we often anticipate by smell what we do not perceive by sight, and it is with the nose that we discriminate between perfumes and stenches. What else is, then, indicated by the nose of the Church, but the foreseeing discernment of the saints? This is also compared to the tower of Libanus, because that discerning foresight is so set on high, as to perceive the attacks of temptations even before they come, and to stand fortified against them when they do come. For things to come that are foreseen are of less force when they come to pass, because when one is more prepared for a blow, the Enemy, thinking himself to be unexpected, is weakened by the very fact of having been anticipated.

On the other hand, those who are in the bonds of wilful sin, must be admonished to consider betimes that in doing evil deliberately, they provoke a severer judgment against themselves. The sentence will smite them the harder, as the bonds of deliberate sin are the more firmly shackled on them. Perhaps they would the more quickly wash away their transgressions by penitence, if they had fallen into them only by their precipitancy, for the bond of sin is more tardily loosened, if deliberation was also present to fasten it. If it were not for the fact that the soul despises the eternal, if would not of its own choice die in sin. The difference, then, between those who perish through deliberate sin and those others who fall by their precipitancy, consists in this that when the former fall from the state of righteousness by sin, they frequently also fall into the snare of despair. For this reason the Lord through the Prophet does not so greatly reprehend evil done precipitately, as that done wilfully, when He says: . . . *lest my indignation come forth like fire, and burn, and there be none that can quench it, because of the wickedness of your doings.*[331] And so, being angered, He says again: *I will visit upon you for the evil of your doings.*[332] Therefore, as sins deliberately committed are different from other sins, the Lord does not censure wicked deeds so much as wicked purposes. For in deeds the sin is often due to infirmity or negligence, but in evil purposes it is always due to a malicious intent.

The opposite case is well stated by the Prophet, describing the blessed man: *And he sat not in the chair of pestilence.*[333] Now, a chair is usually the seat of a judge or of one who presides. To sit in the chair of pestilence is to commit evil deeds with deliberation. To sit in the chair of pestilence is to discern what is evil by the use of reason, and yet commit it deliberately. He sits, as it were, in the chair of perverse counsel: he is lifted up with so great an elation of iniquity, as to aim at accomplishing evil after deliberation. And as those who are upheld by the dignity of being seated in the chair, are set above the crowd that stands by, sins that are deliberately sought out, surpass in guilt the sins of those who fall through precipitancy. They, therefore, who go so far as to bind themselves in wilful sin, are to be admonished to infer what kind of retribution will smite them some day, inasmuch as they now become, not the companions, but the princes of, evil-doers.

CHAPTER 33

How to admonish those who commit only small sins
but commit them frequently, and those who
avoid small sins, but sometimes
sink into grave ones.

Admonition 34. Those who commit only small sins but commit them frequently, are to be admonished in one way; in another, those who guard themselves against small sins, but occasionally sink into grave ones. Those who transgress in small matters only, but do so frequently, are to be admonished to consider, not what kind of sins they commit, but how many. For if they despise all fear when they consider their evil actions, they should be alarmed when they number them. Indeed, it is small raindrops, but countless ones, that make up the towering torrents of streams; and bilge water rising imperceptibly produces the same effect on a ship as a hurricane raging over the main. Small, too, are the sores which erupt on the bodily members in pimples, but when a countless number of these invade the body, they destroy life as effectually as a single serious wound inflicted on the breast. Wherefore, it is written: *He that contemneth small things falls by little and little.*[334] For he who neglects to lament and avoid small sins does not, indeed, fall suddenly from the state of righteousness, but falling away little by little, falls completely.

Those who transgress frequently by small sins are to be admonished to consider well that sometimes a worse sin is committed in a small matter than in one of greater moment. For a greater sin is more quickly recognised to be such and is the more speedily amended, whereas the lighter sin, being believed to be practically no sin at all, is fostered with worse result, in that it is committed with less concern. And thus it commonly happens that the mind, by becoming inured to slight sins, does not dread even great ones; and, being emboldened in sinning, it comes to a kind of justification of evil, and disdains fear in the case of the greater sins, in proportion as it has learned to sin without fear in the case of lesser sins.

On the contrary, those who preserve themselves from

small sins, but are plunged now and then into grave ones, are to be admonished to take anxious heed to their state, for when their heart is elated for having avoided small sins, they become swallowed up in the pit of their pride. While mastering small sins outwardly, but inwardly becoming conceited with vainglory, they ruin their soul, overcome within by the lethargy of pride, also outwardly by committing grave sins.

Those, therefore, who preserve themselves from slight sins, but occasionally plunge into grave ones, are to be warned against inward lapses when they think they are outwardly upright, and lest, as a retribution by the strict Judge, the pride they display in their lesser righteousness becomes a path to a pitfall into graver sins. For they who in their vain elation attribute to their own strength their maintaining even the smallest good, when justly left to themselves are overcome by greater sins; and by their fall they learn that it was not due to themselves that they stood upright, seeing that immense evils may humble a heart that is puffed up by its very meagre amount of virtue. They are to be admonished to reflect that, though in their more serious sins they bind themselves in fetters of profound guilt, nevertheless, for the most part, they sin worse in the little sins which they conceal, because, though in the former sins they, indeed, do evil, yet in the smaller ones they hide from men the fact that they are wicked.

Thus it happens that when they do grave evil in God's sight, their wickedness is manifest, and when they maintain what is a trifling good before men, their holiness is simulated. For this reason it was said to the Pharisees: . . . *straining out a gnat and swallowing a camel,*[335] as if it were said in so many words: "You discern the trifling evils, but swallow the greater." Wherefore, they are again chidden by the voice of Truth, when they are made to hear: *You tithe mint, and anise, and cummin, and have left the weightier things of the law, judgment, and mercy, and faith.*[336] Here we must carefully note that when He said that the smallest things were tithed and chose to mention the lowest of herbs, they were yet such as are sweet-smelling. Surely, He wished to show that when hypocrites observe trifling matters, they are actually seeking to spread for themselves the odour of a holy reputation; and though they neglect to fulfil the weightier matters, yet they observe such of the smallest as will spread the perfume of human opinion far and wide.

CHAPTER 34

*How to admonish those who do not even begin to
do good, and those who begin to do
good but do not finish it.*

Admonition 35. Those who do not even begin to do good are to be admonished in one way, those who begin but do not finish, in another. In the case of those who do not even begin to do good, these should not begin with building up what they may very well love, but with demolishing those things in which they occupy themselves evilly. These people will not adopt the untried matters which they hear of, until they have discovered how pernicious are those things with which they are familiar. A man who is not aware that he has fallen, simply has no desire to be lifted up, and one who does not feel the pain of a wound, will not seek any healing remedy.

Therefore, these must first be shown how vain are the things they love, and then only should they be carefully taught how salutary are the things they disregard. Let them first see that what they love must be shunned, and then afterwards come to perceive without any difficulty that what they are shunning must be loved. They will the sooner accept what they have not tried, if they recognise the truth about what they have tried. They will learn with entire willingness to seek the true good, once they realise how vainly they held to what was false.

Let them, then, be told that while the present good will soon pass away from their enjoyment, the account that they must render will, for their retribution, persist and not pass away. What pleases them at present is withdrawn from them against their will, and the pains that are reserved for them hereafter in requital will also be against their will. Therefore, let them be filled with a salutary fear by those same things in which they take harmful delight. Thus, when the mind is smitten and perceives how very seriously it has harmed itself by its fall, and observes that it has brought itself to the precipice, it should retrace its steps, and dreading profoundly what it loved, it should learn to love what it once despised.

Wherefore, it is said to Jeremias, when he was sent to preach: *Lo, I have set thee this day over the nations and over kingdoms, to root up, and to pull down, and to waste, and to destroy, and to build, and to plant.*[337] Obviously, unless he first destroyed the wrong, he could not profitably build up the right. Unless he plucked from the hearts of his hearers the thorns of vain love, he would fruitlessly try to plant in them the words of holy preaching. Hence, Peter first pulls down, so that he may afterwards build up, when he did not admonish the Jews as to what they were to do, but reproved them for what they had done, saying: *Jesus of Nazareth, a man approved of God among you by miracles, and wonders, and signs, which God did by Him in the midst of you, as you also know, this same, being delivered up by the determinate counsel and foreknowledge of God, you, by the hands of wicked men, have crucified and slain. Whom God hath raised up, having loosed the sorrows of hell.*[338] Being overcome by the recognition of their cruelty, they were to seek the more earnestly the edification of holy preaching [339] and then hear it with all the greater profit.

Therefore, they replied at once: *What, then, shall we do, men and brethren?* To whom Peter replied immediately: *Do penance, and be baptised every one of you.*[340] Now, they surely would have despised these words spoken for their upbuilding, had they not realised first, for their own good, their fall and destruction. It was for this reason that when the bright light from Heaven burst on Saul, he did not hear at once what he ought rightly to do, but what he had done wrongly. When, after falling to the ground, he asked: *Who art Thou, O Lord?* he at once received the answer: *I am Jesus, whom thou persecutest.* And when he immediately added: *Lord, what wilt Thou have me do?* it was at once added: *Arise, and go into the city, and there it shall be told thee what thou must do.*[341] Note that the Lord, though speaking from Heaven, reproved the deeds of His persecutor, but did not at once indicate what had to be done. Observe how the whole structure of his pride had already collapsed and how then, after his fall, he humbly sought to be built up. And when his pride had been destroyed, the words of his up-building were yet withheld: the cruel persecutor was to remain prostrate long after his overthrow, and afterwards arise the more firmly built up in good, in proportion as he had previously become an utterly changed man and broken completely with his former error.

Wherefore, people who have not yet begun to do any good, are to be first overthrown from the obstinacy of their wickedness by the hand of correction, that they may be raised up afterwards to a state of correct conduct. For this reason, too, we cut down the lofty timber of the forest, that we may raise it up to the roof of the building. It is not, however, put at once into the structure. Its greenness, which is a defect, must first be dried out; and the more thoroughly the moisture is dried out as it lies flat, the more firmly can it be set up.

On the other hand, those who do not complete the good they have begun, are to be admonished to consider with careful regard that when they do not accomplish what they purposed to do, they also shatter to pieces what they had begun. For if that which evidently must be done is not advanced with assiduous application, even what had been done well deteriorates. For in this world the human soul is like a ship going upstream: it is not allowed to stay still in one place, because it will drop away to the lower reaches unless it strives to gain the upper. If, then, the strong hand of the worker does not carry to completion the good works begun, the very fact of this slackness in working contends against what is already accomplished. This is the reason why Solomon says: *He that is loose and slack in his work is the brother of him that wasteth his own works.*[342] One who does not vigorously complete the good works which he has begun, imitates in his careless slackness the hand of a destroyer. Hence it is said by the angel to the Church of Sardis: *Be watchful and strengthen the things that remain, which are ready to die. For I find not thy works full before my God.*[343] Therefore, because her works were not found full before God, the angel foretold that those which remained, even such as had been done, were ready to die. For if that which is dead in us is not kindled unto life, that which is retained, as though still living, also perishes.

They are to be admonished to ponder well that it might have been more tolerable for them not to start in the way of rectitude, than to turn back after having begun. For unless they had looked back, they would not have become torpidly remiss in their projected purpose. Let them, therefore, hear what Scripture says: *It had been better for them not to have known the way of justice, than after they have known it, to turn back.*[344] Let them hear Scripture: *I would thou wert cold or hot, but because thou art lukewarm, and neither cold nor hot, I will begin to vomit thee out of my mouth.*[345] A person is hot who both undertakes and completes good enterprises. He is cold who does not even begin anything to be completed. And as lukewarmness forms the transition from cold to heat, so the return from heat to cold lies through lukewarmness. Whosoever, then, has left the cold of unbelief so as to live, but makes no effort at all to pass beyond lukewarmness so as to be hot, he, giving up heat and lingering in the state of harmful lukewarmness, doubtless is on the way to become cold. But as before the lukewarmness there is hope in cold, so when cold comes on, the hope in lukewarmness is gone. For he who is still in his sins does not lose the hope of conversion, whereas he who has become lukewarm after conversion has removed what hope was possible for a sinner. It is required, therefore, that a man should be either hot or cold, lest being lukewarm, he be vomited out: that is, he should either in the state of non-conversion give hope of conversion, or, being already converted, he should be kindled with virtues; otherwise, he will be vomited out as lukewarm, in that he goes back from the heat for which he set out, to the deadly cold.

CHAPTER 35

How to admonish those who do evil secretly and good openly, and those who act contrariwise.

Admonition 36. Those who do evil secretly and good openly are to be admonished in one way, those in another, who hide the good they do, and yet allow evil to be thought of them because of some things they do in public.

Those who do evil secretly and good openly are to be admonished to consider how swiftly human judgments pass away, but how permanent and lasting are divine judgments. They are to be admonished to fix the vision of their mind on the end of things, when the testimony of human praise passes away, but the sentence of Heaven, which penetrates even to what is hidden, will be in force for everlasting requital. When, therefore, they set their secret misdeeds before the divine judgment, and the good they do before the eyes of men, the good they do openly is without a witness, but their secret evil is not without one, namely, the Eternal Witness. Thus, by concealing their sins from men and displaying their virtues to them, they both reveal what they should be punished for through concealing it, and hide away, by disclosing it, what they might have been rewarded for. The Truth rightly calls these men *whited sepulchres, outwardly beautiful, but full of dead men's bones:* [346] that is, they cover up the evil of interior vices, whereas, by displaying certain of their works to human eyes, they flatter themselves only for the outward show of righteousness.

These, therefore, should be admonished not, indeed, to despise what they do aright, but yet to believe that it deserves higher recognition; that is to say, those greatly misjudge their good deeds who think that human approval is a sufficient reward. Actually, when transitory praise is sought for a good deed, then what is worthy of an eternal reward is sold for a trifling price. And as to the price received, the Truth says: *Amen, I say to you, they have received their reward.* [347] They are to be admonished to consider that when they prove themselves to be wicked in hidden matters, and yet offer themselves as examples publicly for their good deeds, they are showing that what they avoid ought to be adopted, they proclaim that what they hate is to be loved; in fine, they live to others but die to themselves.

On the contrary, those who do good in secret, yet allow themselves to be thought ill of openly for some of their deeds, are to be admonished that while they keep themselves alive thanks to the good they perform, they must not use themselves to slay others by the example of their evil repute, and should not love their neighbours less than themselves. If they themselves take a wholesome draught of wine, they should not pour out a draught of poison for minds that make a point of observing them. Indeed, these men not only contribute little to the lives of their neighbours, but prove to be a great burden, when they aim at acting aright in secret, while in certain of their actions they sow the seeds of evil by example. A man, for example, who is able to tread underfoot the desire for praise, is guilty of withholding edification if he conceals the good which he does. When a man does not come forth with a work that should be imitated, this is like sowing seed and then, as it were, removing the germinating roots.

Wherefore, the Truth states in the Gospel: *Let them see your good works, and glorify your Father who is in Heaven.*[348] But here that other statement is uttered also, which apparently enjoined something entirely different: *Take heed that you do not your justice before men, to be seen by them.*[349] Now, what else is meant by being ordered to perform our deeds as not to be seen, and yet that they should be seen, except that what we do is to be hidden lest we be praised, and yet to be displayed, that we may increase the glory of our Heavenly Father? For in forbidding us to do our righteous deeds before men, He at once added: *that you may be seen by them.* And when again He ordered that our good works should be seen by men, He forthwith added: *that they may glorify your Father who is in Heaven.* How, then, they are to be seen and how not to be seen, He showed from the motive of the injunction, namely, that the mind of the doer should not seek the work to be seen on his own account, and yet that on account of the glory of the Heavenly Father it should not be concealed.

Therefore, it commonly happens that a good deed is both secret when it is done publicly, and again it is public when it is done secretly. For when one seeks in a good deed done openly, not one's own glory, but that of the Father on high, one conceals what is done: the only witness he has is He whom he wished to please. But when one desires to be observed and praised for a good work done in secret, and when, perhaps, no one has observed what was done, still it was before men that he did it, because he has brought as many witnesses to his good work as the number of human praises sought in his heart. But when evil repute, in so far as it prevails without sin committed, is not eliminated from the minds of observers, the cup of sin is proffered by way of example to all who think that evil is present. Thus it often happens that they who carelessly allow evil to be attributed to them, do not, indeed, commit evil personally, yet in the persons of those who imitate them they do commit a multiple sin. Consequently, Paul says to those who ate certain unclean food without polluting themselves, but in doing so became the occasion of scandal and temptation to the weak: *Take heed lest perhaps this your liberty become a stumbling-block to the weak.*[350] And again: *And through thy knowledge shall the weak brother perish, for whom Christ hath died? Now when you sin thus against the brethren, and wound their weak consciences, you sin against Christ.*[351] Wherefore, it is that Moses, when he said: *Thou shalt not speak evil of the deaf,* at once added: *nor put a stumbling-block before the blind.*[352]

To speak evil of the deaf is to disparage one who is absent and does not hear. To put a stumbling-block before the blind is to do a thing that is proper of itself but which affords an occasion of scandal to one who fails to understand the propriety of it.

CHAPTER 36

The exhortation intended for delivery to a general audience, in which the virtues are fostered in each without encouraging the growth of vices opposed to such virtues.

These are the things that a director of souls should observe in the various phases of his preaching, so that he may carefully propose the remedies indicated by the wound in each given case. But whereas in exhorting individuals great exertion is required to be of service to each individual's particular needs, whereas it is very laborious to instruct each one in what applies to him in particular by urging appropriate considerations, the task is a far more laborious one when on one and the same occasion one has to deal with a numerous audience subject to different passions. In this case the address must be formulated with such skill that, notwithstanding the diversity of failings in the audience as a whole, it carries a proper message to each individual, without involving itself in self-contradictions. Thus, in one direct stroke it should pass straight through the passions. Yet, this should be as with a double-edged sword, so as to lance the tumours of carnal thoughts on both sides:

humility is to be preached to the proud in a way not to increase fear in the timorous, and confidence infused into the timorous, as not to encourage the unbridled impetuosity in the proud. The idle and the remiss are to be exhorted to zeal for good deeds, but in a way not to increase the unrestraint of intemperate action in the impetuous. Moderation is to be imposed on the impetuous without producing a sense of listless security in the idle. Anger is to be banished from the impatient, but so as not to add to the carelessness of the remiss and easy-going. The remiss should be fired with zeal in such a manner as not to set the wrathful ablaze. Bountiful almsgiving should be urged on the niggardly without slackening the rein on prodigality. Frugality is to be indoctrinated in the prodigal, but not so as to intensify in the niggardly their tenacity of things doomed to perish. Wedlock is to be preached to the incontinent, but not so as to recall to lust those who have become continent. Physical virginity is to be commended to the continent, yet so as not to make the married despise the fecundity of the body. Good things are so to be preached as not to give incidental help to what is bad. The highest good is to be so praised, that the good in little things is not discarded. Attention should be called to the little things, but not in such a way that they are deemed sufficient and there is no striving for the highest.

CHAPTER 37

*The exhortation addressed to an individual who
labours under contrary passions.*

It is, indeed, difficult for a preacher in speaking to a
congregation to pay regard to the hidden emotions and
motives of individuals, and after the manner of the
wrestlers to turn skilfully from side to side. But the
burden of his task is much heavier, when he has to
preach to an individual who is a slave to contrary vices.
Take the common case of one of a quite too gay temperament becoming extremely depressed when sadness suddenly comes upon him. Here the preacher must take care
to dispel the temporary sadness, without permitting his
gay temperament to assert itself too much; at the same
time he must so moderate his gay nature as not to aggravate the temporary sadness. Here is a man burdened with
the habit of inordinate hastiness, but now and then, when
something should be done quickly, he is thwarted by
fear gripping him suddenly. Another man is burdened
with the habit of immoderate fear, yet occasionally is
impelled by rash precipitancy to fulfil some desire or
other. Consequently, in the one the sudden fear must
be repressed, but so that his persistent precipitancy does
not increase; in the other his sudden hastiness must be
checked, but so that his temperamental fear does not
revive. Indeed, is it a matter of wonder that the physicians
of souls should be on their guard in such cases, seeing
that those who heal, not hearts, but bodies, regulate their

treatment with such skilful discrimination? Often, for instance, a violent illness assails the weak body, and such illness should really be treated with the antidote of drastic remedies, and yet a weak body cannot endure a strong remedy. The doctor, therefore, makes it his business to draw out the present malady in such a way, that the existing weakness of the body is not increased, lest perchance the illness ends with life itself. He, therefore, compounds the remedy with such great refinement, that at one and the same time he counteracts both the malady and the infirmity. If, then, medicine for the body can be so compounded and administered as to serve separate ends—for it is then truly medicine when it serves as a remedy for an existing disease, while at the same time meeting the needs of the prevailing constitution—why should medicine for the soul, administered by one and the same preaching, fail to be able to combat moral evils of different kinds, seeing that it is a more delicate art, in that it deals with what is unseen?

CHAPTER 38

Sometimes lesser vices must be disregarded so that greater ones may be removed.

But since, usually, when the infirmities of two vices assail a man, one oppresses him more lightly, the other perhaps more severely, it is best to hasten help in the case of the vice that tends to a more speedy death. If the one cannot be checked from causing imminent death unless the other develops and increases what is contrary, the preacher must be content by the skilful moderation of his monitions to allow one of them to increase, if so he can prevent the other from causing immediate death. Following this procedure, he is not aggravating disease, but he is actually saving the life of his patient in administering medicine to him, hoping to find the given occasion to restore him to complete health. Often, for example, a man who does nothing at all to moderate his gluttony, is hard pressed by temptations to impurity and is on the point of yielding to them. Thoroughly frightened by his struggles, he tries to check himself by abstinence, with the result that he is now harassed by temptations to vainglory. In his case, it is quite impossible to extinguish the one vice unless the other is fostered. Which, then, of the two plagues should be attacked more vigorously? Surely that one which presses with greater danger. It is simply [353] to be tolerated that by the virtue of abstinence arrogance should, for the time being, gather strength in the case of one who is alive; otherwise, by his gluttony impurity would cut him off from life utterly.

Wherefore, Paul, considering that his weak hearer would still wish to go on committing evil, or take complacency in the reward of human praise for his well-doing, says: *Wilt thou not be afraid of the power? Do that which is good, and thou shalt have praise from the same.*[354] For it is not that good is to be done so that no power of the world is to be feared, or that the glory of transitory praise may be won. But when he considered that the weak soul could not rise to the strength required to avoid at the same time both sin and praise, the great preacher in his admonition offered something and took away some-

thing: but overlooking what was mildly wrong, he took
from him what mattered seriously. Thus, since the soul
could not so assert itself as to relinquish, once and for
all, all its vices, it could be detached without difficulty
from one, if it were left to occupy itself with the other.

CHAPTER 39

*In preaching to weak souls, deep subjects should
certainly not be dealt with.*

Now, the preacher should realise that he must not
overtax the mind of his hearer, lest, so to speak, the
string of the soul be strained too much and snap. All
deep matters should be veiled from the multitude of
hearers, and scarcely disclosed to a few.[355] Wherefore,
the Truth in person says: *Who, thinkest thou, is the
faithful and wise steward, whom his lord setteth over his
family, to give them their measure of wheat in due season?* [356] What is expressed here by a measure of wheat
is the properly measured word, that it may not be wasted
on a heart too limited in its capacity to hold it. Wherefore,
Paul says: *I could not speak to you as unto spiritual, but
as unto carnal. As unto little ones in Christ, I gave you
milk to drink, not meat.*[357] Hence, when Moses comes forth
from the sanctuary of God, he veils his shining countenance when in presence of the people, because he is not
going to reveal to the multitude the secrets received in
profound enlightenment.[358] Hence God speaking through
him enjoined, that if anyone dug a pit and neglected to

cover it over, then if an ox or an ass fell into it, he should pay the price of the animal.[359] So, when a man who has arrived at the deep streams of knowledge, does not cover them up before the unlearned hearts of his hearers, he is judged liable to punishment if by his words a soul, whether clean or unclean, takes scandal. Hence it is said to blessed Job: *Who gave the cock understanding?* [360] Indeed, when a holy preacher cries aloud in this time of darkness, he is as a cock crowing in the night and says: *It is now the hour for us to rise from sleep,*[361] and again: *Awake, ye just, and sin not.*[362] The cock has the custom of crowing loud in the darkest hours of the night, but when morning is near, he reduces the length and volume of his notes. So, the true preacher proclaims aloud plain truths to hearts still in the dark, showing them no hidden mysteries. Then only are they to learn all the profounder things of Heaven, when they approach the light of truth.

CHAPTER 40

Preaching in word and deed.

But at this juncture we are brought back in the zeal of our charity to what we have already said, namely, that every preacher should make himself heard rather by deeds than by words, and that by his righteous way of life should imprint footsteps for men to tread in, rather than show them by word the way to go. For that cock,[363] too, which the Lord in His figure of speech took as a symbol of the good preacher, when he is preparing to crow, first shakes his wings, and beating himself with them, makes himself more alert. So, it is obviously necessary that they who give utterance to words of holy preaching, should first be awake in the earnest practice of good deeds, lest, being themselves slack in performing them, they stir up others by words only. Let them first rouse themselves up by lofty deeds, and then make others solicitous to live good lives. Let them first smite themselves with the wings of their thoughts. Let them carefully examine themselves and discover in what respects they are idling and lagging, and make amends by severe penance. Then, and only then, let them set in order the lives of others by their words. They should first take heed to punish their own sins by tears, and then declare what deserves punishment in others; and before they utter words of exhortation, they should proclaim in their deeds all that they are about to say.

PART FOUR

How the Preacher When He Has Done Everything as Required, Should Return to Himself,
to Prevent His Life or Preaching
From Making Him Proud.

Now, seeing that often when a sermon is delivered
with due propriety and with a fruitful message, the mind
of the speaker is exalted by joy all his own over his performance, he must needs take care to torment himself
with painful misgivings: in restoring others to health
by healing their wounds, he must not disregard his own
health and develop tumours of pride. Let him not, while
helping his neighbours, neglect himself, let him not,
while lifting up others, fall himself. In many instances,
indeed, the greatness of certain men's virtues has been
an occasion of their perdition, in that they have felt inordinately secure in the assurance of their strength, and
they died suddenly because of their negligence. For as
virtue struggles against vice, the mind, as it were, exhilarated by this virtue, flatters itself; and it comes to pass
that the soul of one actually engaged upon doing good
casts aside all anxiety and cicumspection, and rests secure
in its self-confidence. In this its state of inertia the cun-
ning Seducer enumerates all that the man has done well,
and aggrandizes him with conceited thoughts about his
pre-eminence over all others.

Whence it happens that in the eyes of the just Judge the consciousness of virtue is a pitfall for the soul. In calling to mind what it has done, in exalting itself before itself, it falls in the presence of the Author of humility. Wherefore, it is said to the soul that is proud: *Whom dost thou excel in beauty? Go down and sleep with the uncircumcised;* [1] which means in plain words: "Since you exalt yourself because of the beauty of your virtues, it is this your beauty that is hurrying you on to your ruin." Hence, under the figure of Jerusalem, the soul which vaunts its virtue is reproved, when it is said: *Thou wast perfect through my beauty, which I had put upon thee, saith the Lord, but trusting in thy beauty, thou playedst the harlot because of thy renown.* [2] The mind is lifted up in the confidence of its beauty, when with blithe self-assurance it glories over its virtues. But through this same confidence it is led on to play the harlot: that is, when by its thoughts the mind robs and deceives itself, evil spirits seduce and corrupt it with numerous vices. Note, too, that it is said: *Thou playedst the harlot because of thy renown*—meaning that when the soul has no regard for the Supernal Ruler, it at once seeks its own praise and begins to arrogate to itself all the good it has received for its mission as a herald of the Giver. Its desire is to spread the glory of its esteem, and its one concern is to impress all with its admirable qualities. Therefore, it plays the harlot because of its renown, when, forsaking the wedlock of its lawful bed, it prostitutes itself to the corrupting spirit in its lust for praise. Hence David says: *He delivered their strength into captivity, and their beauty into the hands of the enemy.* [3] Virtue is, indeed, delivered into captivity, and beauty into the hands of the foe, when the ancient Enemy lords it over the deceived soul for its elation in well-doing.

Often this elation in virtue in a measure tempts the minds even of the elect, though it does not quite overcome them. In this case when the mind is lifted up, it is deserted, and deserted, it is recalled to fear. It is for this reason that David says again: *In my abundance I said: I shall never be moved.* But because in the assurance of his virtue he became conceited, he presently added what he had endured: *Thou turnedst away Thy face from me, and I became troubled;* [4] which is as if he were saying plainly: "I believed myself strong in my virtues, but when I was deserted, I came to realise how great my weakness was." Wherefore, he says again: *I have sworn and am determined to keep the judgments of Thy justice.* But because it was beyond his power to continue to observe his oath, he at once, on being troubled, discovered his weakness. Therefore, he betook himself at once to the help of prayer, saying: *I have been humbled, O Lord, exceedingly. Quicken thou me according to Thy word.* [5]

Sometimes, too, divine guidance recalls to the mind the recollection of its infirmity before advancing it by gifts, lest it pride itself on the virtues it has received. Wherefore, the Prophet Ezechiel, as often as he is led to the contemplation of heavenly things, is first called *son of man,* [6] as though the Lord plainly admonished him, saying: "That you may not proudly lift up your heart because of what you are to see, consider carefully what you are. When you penetrate the sublimest things, remember that you are a man; for when you are enraptured above yourself, you will be recalled in anxiety to yourself by the curb of your infirmity."

Hence, it is necessary that when a wealth of virtues flatters us, the eye of the soul should turn its gaze on its infirmities, and for its own good it should prostrate itself. It should look to the good not that it has done, but that which it has neglected to do, so that while the heart becomes contrite in recalling its weakness, it may be the more solidly established in the eyes of the Author of humility. For Almighty God perfects in great measure the minds of those who rule, but leaves them partially imperfect, for this reason, that when they are resplendent with extraordinary attainments, they may grieve with disgust for their imperfections, and, least of all, exalt themselves for great things, when they have to labour and struggle against very small matters. And as they are not able to overcome the very little things, they should not presume to pride themselves on the great things they accomplish.

See, my good friend, compelled by the urgency of your remonstrances with me, I have tried to show what a pastor should be like. I, miserable painter that I am, have painted the portrait of an ideal man; and here I have been directing others to the shore of perfection, I, who am still tossed about on the waves of sin.[7] But in the shipwreck of this life, sustain me, I beseech you, with the plank of your prayers, so that, as my weight is sinking me down, you may uplift me with your meritorious hand.

NOTES

INTRODUCTION

[1] Gregory, *Regist.* 1. 41a (1. 58 Ewald-Hartmann); trans. by J. L. Stoddard in his version of P. Batiffol's work, *Saint Grégoire le Grand: Saint Gregory the Great* (New York 1929) 111.

[2] *Regist.* 5. 53 (1. 352 E.-H.).

[3] Cf. *ibid.* 1. 3, 5, 6, 20, etc., excerpted at length by F. H. Dudden, *Gregory the Great. His Place in History and Thought* (London 1905) 1. 225-8.

[4] Cf. *ibid.* 1. 24a (1. 37 E.-H.). Isidore of Seville, *De vir. ill.* 39. 51, 40. 53, and Ildefonsus of Toledo, *De vir. ill.* 1, identify this John as John the Faster, patriarch of Constantinople. The earliest extant biography of Gregory, composed by an English monk of Whitby about the year 713, is the first source which refers to the archbishop of Ravenna as the one to whom the *Pastoral Care* was dedicated. Paul the Deacon, *Vita* 14, and John the Deacon, *Vita* 4. 73, followed this English tradition, and this seems to be the correct one. At the beginning of Gregory's pontificate John of Ravenna was a rather close friend of Gregory and was, like the Pope himself, Roman-born: cf. Dudden, *op. cit.* 1. 436-40. For the English biography, see F. A. Gasquet, *A Life of Pope St. Gregory the Great* (Westminster 1904); C. W. Jones, *Saints' Lives and Chronicles in Early England, together with First English Translations of the Oldest Life of Pope St. Gregory the Great by a Monk of Whitby* (Ithaca 1947).

[5] The plan of the *Regula Pastoralis* is given by Gregory in *Moralia* 30.3. 12 f. (ML 76. 530 f.); there he adds: 'Auctore Deo in alio opere id explere appetit animus, si tamen laboriosae huius vitae adhuc aliquantulum restaverit.' The *Regula Pastoralis* itself was, on the other hand, condensed or abstracted in the so-called Synodical Letter which Gregory sent to the patriarchs of the East in 591, very soon after he had composed the work. Such letters were sent by recently consecrated bishops to their fellow bishops and conveyed to them a profession of the orthodox faith. For Gregory's *Synodica*, see *Regist.* 1. 24 (1.38-42 E.-H.) and the notes there added; also Dudden, *op. cit.* 1. 240 f.

[6] See Gregory, *Regist.* 5. 53 (1. 352 E.-H.): *'Librum Regulae Pastoralis, quem in episcopatus mei exordio scripsi.'*

[7] Cf. D. M. Wertz, *The Influence of the Regula Pastoralis to the Year 900* (typescr. diss. dep. in Cornell Univ. Library, Ithaca 1936) 28-31; L. Weber, *Hauptfragen der Moraltheologie Gregors des Grossen* (Paradosis 1, Freiburg i. Swit. 1947) 44 f. For the history and content of the Benedictine *Regula,* see I. Herwegen, *Sinn und Geist der Benediktinerregel* (Einsiedeln 1944).

[8] Cf. Dudden, *op. cit.* 107-109; P. de Labriolle, in Fliche-Martin, *Histoire de l'Eglise* 4 (Paris 1948) 595 f.

[9] Alcuin, *Epist.* 116.

[10] See the edition by H. Sweet, *King Alfred's West-Saxon Version of Gregory's Pastoral Care* (Early English Text Society, London 1871); cf. Wertz, *op. cit.* 114-22.

[11] Cf. Wertz, *op. cit.* 126-205.

[12] Hincmar, *Opusc. praef.* (ML 126. 292 C); cf. Dudden, *op. cit.* 2. 239.

[13] Dudden, *loc. cit.*

[14] Gregory of Nazianzus, *Orat.* 2. 30.

[15] These passages are listed and arranged in parallel columns by Wertz, *op. cit.* 44-47.

[16] Cf. *Regist.* 7. 29 (1. 476 E.-H.), 11. 55 (2. 330 E.-H.), and elsewhere; see Dudden, *op. cit.* 153 f.

[17] Rufinus of Aquileia in 399 or 400 made a hurried translation of nine of Gregory's *Orations,* including the apology. For the text, cf. A. Engelbrecht, *Tyrannii Rufini Orationum Gregorii Nazianzeni novem interpretatio* (Corp. script. eccles. lat. 46, Vienna 1910).

PART ONE

[1] The art of arts is the government of souls. St. Gregory of Nazianzus had expressed the same thought when he wrote, *Orat.* 2. 16: 'It seems to me that to rule men is the art of arts, and the science of sciences, for man is a being of diverse and manifold character.'

[2] The comparison between the physician and the pastor is treated at considerable length by St. Gregory of Nazianzus, *ibid.* 2. 16-34; cf. the Introd. 14.

[3] See Matt. 23. 6 f.

[4] Osee 8. 4.

[5] Luke 13.27; also Matt. 7. 23.

[6] Isa. 56. 11.

[7] Jer. 2. 8.

[8] 1 Cor. 14. 38.

[9] Matt. 15. 14; also Luke 6. 39.

[10] Ps. 68. 24. The Psalmist wishes that the backs of his foes should be bent under the weight of burdens put upon them. The sinner is bowed down beneath the burden of his sins, when those who ought to lead them have lost the light of true knowledge.

[11] Ezech. 34. 18 f. Pastors of evil life corrupt their subjects, and are like shepherds who muddy clear waters by walking in them.

[12] A conflation of Osee 5. 1 and 9. 8.

[13] Ezech. 44. 12.

[14] In the *Decretum* of Gratian, D. 83, c. 2: *Nemo quippe* (293 Friedberg), the compiler assigned these last two sentences to St. Augustine, with the following addition: 'Episcopus itaque qui talium crimina non corrigit, magis dicendus est canis inpudicus quam episcopus.' Also in C. 2. q. 7. c. 32: *Qui nec regiminis* (493 Friedberg), he repeats the ascription to St. Augustine of the term *canis inpudicus*.

[15] Matt. 18. 6. See Luke 17. 1 f.

[16] James 3. 1. Our Lord had said, Matt. 23. 8, 10: *But be not you called Rabbi. For one is your master and all you are brethren;* ... *neither be you called masters, for one is your master, Christ.*

[17] John 6. 15.

[18] Cf. 1 Kings 10. 21-23; 15. 17, 30.

[19] Cf. *ibid.* 15. 30, 35. Samuel had anointed Saul (1 Kings 10. 1).

[20] Cf. 2 Kings 11. 2 ff.

[21] Cf. *ibid.* 11. 15.

[22] Ecclus. 11. 10. The wise man who wrote *Ecclesiasticus* (between 175 and 170 B. C.) was Jesus, son of Sirach.

[23] Cf. 4 Kings 20. 12-18; Isa. 39. 1-7.

[24] Cf. Dan. 4. 21-24.

[25] *Ibid.* 3. 95-100.

[26] *Ibid.* 4. 27.

[27] Matt. 5. 14 f. In the present and the two following chapters (see also 3. 5 and 7) Gregory takes notice of the two ways of Christian life, the contemplative and the active, and sets forth how the

former must frequently yield to the latter. Gregory had made this sacrifice, but he never lost or forgot the mystical experiences and satisfactions that were his during his monastic days at St. Andrew's. In fact, during the early Middle Ages he was recognised and followed as a master of mystical theology. Cf. Dom Cuthbert Butler, *Western Mysticism. The Teaching of SS. Augustine, Gregory, and Bernard on Contemplation and the Contemplative Life* (London 1922) 89-133.

28 John 21. 17.

29 *Loc. cit.* Gregory has added: 'Si diligis me.'

30 2 Cor. 5. 14 f. The Vulgate has: *Si unus pro omnibus mortuus est, ergo omnes mortui sunt: et pro omnibus mortuus est Christus.*

31 Cf. Deut. 25. 5-10. The levirate (from the Latin *levir* = 'husband's brother') law obliged the brother of a dead man to marry the latter's widow, and raise up children to his brother's name. Cf. the story of Noemi and Booz: Ruth 4. 1. 11.

32 Matt. 28. 10.

33 Eph. 6. 15.

34 Isa. 6. 8.

35 Jer. 1. 6.

36 Cf. Isa. 6. 6.

37 1 Tim. 3. 1.

38 *Ibid.* 3. 2.

39 Probably in reference to the servant in the parable—Matt. 25. 18—who had received one talent and hid it instead of investing it.

40 Cf. Matt. 23. 13.

41 Isa. 58. 9. Gregory here quotes the Vulgate freely, or from an older Latin version. It has been rightly said that 'certainly Gregory is second to none in his knowledge of and enthusiasm for Holy Writ.' Cf. F. H. Dudden's review of Gregory's knowledge and application of Scripture: *Gregory the Great. His Place in History and Thought* (London 1905) 2. 299 ff. D. M. Wertz, *The Influence of the Regula Pastoralis to the Year 900* (diss. Cornell Univ.: Ithaca 1936) 18, has counted no less than 485 Biblical references in the present treatise!

42 Cf. Gratian, *Decretum*, D. 49 *init.*, and c. 1 (175-7 Friedberg), where a lengthy passage from Gregory is cited, recounting the blemishes that would preclude a sacred minister from offering sacrifice.

43 Lev. 21. 17-20. A 'pearl' in the eye (Lat. *albugo*) is a white

spot or film—a cataract. For being afflicted with a 'rupture' the
Vulgate has *herniosus* = 'afflicted with intestinal hernia'; Gregory
uses the old version *ponderosus* (cf. Du Cange, *Gloss. med. et inf.
Lat.* 6. 403, *s. v.*).

[44] 1 Kings 2. 9. The canticle of Anna from which this verse is
taken, has a striking similarity with the *Magnificat* of Our Lady,
recorded by St. Luke, 1. 46-55. A few instances may be mentioned:
(2. 1) *My heart hath rejoiced in the Lord;* (2. 4) *The bow of the
mighty is overcome;* (2. 5) *The hungry are filled;* (2. 8) *The Lord
raiseth up the needy from the dust.*

[45] Heb. 12. 12 f., with quotations from Isa. 35. 3 and Prov. 4. 26.
The Westminster version expresses the meaning thus: *Therefore,
'brace up the hands that have grown helpless, and the knees that
totter,' and 'make straight paths for your feet,' so that that which is
lame may not be put out of joint, but rather be cured.*

[46] Cant. 7. 4. As is seen from the following, Gregory interprets
the 'Bride' of the Canticle of Canticles as the Church.

[47] Ps. 37. 9. The Vulgate has: *afflictus sum,* for Gregory's *incur-
vatus,* the Old Latin version.

[48] Luke 8. 14.

[49] Apoc. 3. 18.

[50] Rom. 1. 22. They became fools, as St. Paul explains regarding
pagan philosophers, because professing themselves wise, they closed
their minds to obvious truths.

[51] 1 Cor. 10. 13. This was a wish expressed by St. Paul, that the
Corinthians might suffer no temptation which they could not overcome. The Greek version reads: *No temptation has taken hold of
you, but such as is human.* This means that St. Paul encourages
and consoles the Corinthians, in that they had not been too sorely
tried; and for the future, continues Paul, *God is faithful, who will
not suffer you to be tempted above that which you are able.*

[52] 1 Tim. 6. 10, which has *cupiditas* for the Greek φιλαργυρία,
'love of money.'

PART TWO

[1] Isa. 52. 11.

[2] *Rationale iudicii*—cf. Exod. 28. 15, where the sacred vestments of Aaron and his sons are described in detail. The *rationale,* bearing twelve gems for the tribes of Israel, appears to have been used in connection with an ancient Jewish practice of consulting the divine will, known as Urim and Thummim (cf. also Exod. 28. 30). In the Middle Ages the *rationale* was an ornamental garment, resembling the pallium, and worn over the shoulders by bishops in certain dioceses of the West. It is still used today at Pontifical High Mass in the dioceses of Eichstätt, Paderborn, Toul-Nancy, and Cracow. Cf. H. Leclercq, 'Rational,' *Dict. d'archéol. chrét. et de lit.* 14. 2 (1948) 2066 f.; also the briefer, but illustrated, note by A. Manser: 'Rationale,' *Lex. f. Theol. u. Kirche* 8 (1936) 644 f.

[3] *Ibid.* 28. 30.

[4] Isa. 40. 9.

[5] Cf. Exod. 29. 22.

[6] *Ibid.* 29. 28.

[7] Reading *ad sublimia armo* (for *arma*) *operis.*

[8] The ornamental dress of the Jewish high priest known as the 'ephod'—cf. Exod. 29. 5.

[9] 2 Cor. 6. 7. Gregory applies the metaphor of St. Paul to the priest who must safeguard himself in both prosperity and adversity. The armour is both offensive and defensive.

[10] Cf. Exod. 28. 8.

[11] 1 Peter 2. 9. The verse brings together titles first applied to the chosen people in Exodus 19. 5 f. (see also the Septuagint version of the same).

[12] John 1. 12.

[13] Ps. 139. 17.

[14] John 10. 12 f.

[15] Isa. 56. 10.

[16] Ezech. 13. 5.

[17] Lam. 2. 14.

[18] Titus 1. 9. St. Paul is here speaking of the duties of the bishop. He enumerates some of the gainsayers (*ibid.* 10 f.): the disobedient, vain talkers, perverters of the faith.

[19] Mal. 2. 7.

[20] Isa. 58. 1.

[21] Acts 2. 3.

[22] Cf. Exod. 28. 33 f.

[23] *Ibid.* 28. 35.

[24] Ps. 131. 9.

[25] Mark 9. 49.

[26] Rom. 12. 3.

[27] Cf. Exod. 28. 34.

[28] Lev. 15. 2.

[29] *Seminiverbius,* the Vulgate rendering of σπερμολόγος , a term of contempt given by the Epicureans and Stoics of St. Paul as he preached at Athens; cf. Acts 17. 18. The word is descriptive of a crow or other bird picking up seeds or grains where it finds them. The philosophers implied that Paul was a 'babbler,' or, perhaps, less unkindly, that he was a 'dabbler in thought'—retailing scraps of knowledge and doctrine he had 'picked up' from various sources.

[30] 2 Tim. 4. 1 f.

[31] Cf. 2 Cor. 12. 1-6.

[32] 1 Cor. 7. 2 f.

[33] *Ibid.* 7. 5.

[34] 2 Cor. 11. 29.

[35] 1 Cor. 9. 20. That is, Paul lived as a Jew to win over the Jews.

[36] 2 Cor. 5. 13. All that the shepherd of souls does he must do for God or his neighbour. St. Paul's adversaries accused him of madness when he spoke of the special graces which he had received from God. But he spoke and acted as he did, for the glory of God and the welfare of his people—here the Corinthians.

[37] Cf. Gen. 28. 11-18.

[38] Cf. Luke 6. 12: 'And it came to pass in those days, that *He went out into a mountain to pray, and He passed the whole night in the prayer of God';* and some verses later (17 f.): *'And coming down . . . , He stood in a plane place . . . and a very great multitude of people . . . who were come to hear Him and to be healed of their diseases. And they that were troubled with unclean spirits, were cured.'*

[38a] Regarding this sentence and other statements in the remainder of the present chapter, Bishop J. C. Hedley, *Lex Levitarum* (Westminster 1905) 55, writes: 'St. Gregory, in this fifth chapter, seems undoubtedly to refer to the sacrament of penance,

and to confession'; cf. *ibid.* 58 f.; Dudden, *op. cit.* 2. 422-5. For the very difficult problems of public and private penance, of sacramental confession and absolution, during the time of Gregory, see the excellent study by E. Göller, *Papsttum und Bussgewalt in spätrömischer und frühmittelalterlicher Zeit* (Freiburg i. Br. 1933) 125-97 (192 f., consideration of the present chapter in the *Regula;* Göller is in substantial agreement with Hedley). In these pages Göller also mentions and appraises the important studies of other scholars on the subject, especially Lagarde, Tixeront, and Poschmann. Cf. also P. Galtier, *L'Eglise et la rémission des péchés aux premiers siècles* (3rd ed. Paris 1932) 100-140; 421-30.

[39] Cf. 3 Kings 7. 23 ff.

[40] 1 Cor. 9. 9 and 1 Tim. 5. 18, taken from Deut. 25. 4.

[41] *Mor.* 21. 15. 22 (ML 76. 203 BC).

[42] Here there is an evident reminiscence of St. Benedict's Rule, which states in Ch. 64: 'sciatque (abbas) sibi oportere *prodesse magis quam praeesse!*' Gregory, born three years before the death of Benedict, was a warm admirer of Benedictine monasticism. The monastery which he had established in his father's palace at Rome and which he himself entered *ca.* 575, probably was governed by the Rule of St. Benedict or by a modified version of it. See Gregory's tribute to the Rule in *Dial.* 2. 36 (ML 66. 200 CD). Cf. Bishop Hedley's chapter on 'The Monasticism of St. Gregory the Great,' *op. cit.* xxxviii—lvi.

[43] Gen. 9. 1 f.

[44] Job 41. 25, where the Leviathan is spoken of.

[45] Isa. 14. 13 f., loosely quoted. Lucifer is referred to.

[46] 1 Kings 15. 17.

[47] Acts 10. 26. Gregory adds: 'Do not act so.'

[48] Cf. Acts 5. 3-5.

[49] 2 Cor. 1. 23. The pastor is not superior to his subjects in faith. As St. Paul did not lord it over the Corinthians in regard to their faith, so the pastor may not lord it over subjects when they act aright.

[50] 1 Thess. 2. 7.

[51] 2 Cor. 4. 5.

[52] 1 Cor. 4. 21. St. Paul rebuked the Corinthians for certain failings, their tolerance, for instance, of the incestuous adulterer (*ibid.* Ch. 5). The pastor must correct the faults of his subjects fearlessly.

[53] Ecclus. 32. 1.

[54] 1 Peter 5. 3.

[55] Matt. 20. 25-28.

[56] *Ibid.* 24. 48-51.

[57] 1 Kings 2. 29. The priest Heli honoured his sons Ophni and Phinees more than God, in that he did not punish them for their sacrilegious knaveries.

[58] Ezech. 34. 4.

[59] *Mor.* 20. 5. 14 (ML 76. 143-5).

[60] 'Sed erga subditos suos inesse rectoribus debet et iuste consulens misericordia et pie saeviens disciplina.'

[61] Cf. Luke 10. 33 ff.

[62] Cf. Heb. 9. 4.

[63] Ps. 22. 4.

[64] Luke 21. 34 f.

[65] *Ibid.* 16. 13.

[66] 2 Tim. 2. 4.

[67] 1 Cor. 6. 4. *The most despised*, that is—in Gregory's understanding of the difficult passage—persons who are of little consequence in the Church are to deal with secular affairs.

[68] Cf. Exod. 18. 17 ff.

[69] Osee 4. 9.

[70] Lam. 4. 1.

[71] Πλάτος = 'breadth.' The adjective πλατύς = 'broad,' 'wide,' taken in the feminine form, πλατεῖα (supply ὁδός) = 'wide way' = 'street,' was transliterated into the Latin *platea*.

[72] Matt. 7. 13. The Vulgate has: '*Wide is the gate and broad the way. . . .*'

[73] 1 Peter 5. 1 f.

[74] *Ibid.*

[75] 1 Tim. 5. 8.

[76] Ezech. 44. 20. The priests are to poll the head only, that is, cutting short the hair, neither shaving it, nor allowing it to grow long. To shave the head was a sign of mourning, to grow the hair long was a sign of luxury or barbarity, both unbecoming in a priest. See also St. Jerome, *Comm. in Ezech.* 13. 44 (ML 25. 437 A).

[77] Gregory's wordplay *sacerdotes* (= 'the givers of sacred things,' the 'priest') and *sacrum ducatum* (= 'sacred guidance, leadership') is quite inimitable in: '*sacerdotes* namque iure vocati sunt, qui ut *sacrum ducatum* praebeant, fidelibus praesunt.'

⁷⁸ *Ibid.* 13. 18. The passage refers to pseudo-prophets, men and women, who delude the people through sorcery and divination. Gregory applies it to bishops who allow subjects to go unchecked in their evil ways.

⁷⁹ *Ibid.* 34. 4.

⁸⁰ Cf. Gal. 2. 11. The action of Peter afforded a specious support to the Judaizers, who wished the converted Gentiles to conform to the Jewish law. St. Paul regarded this policy to be opposed to the liberty of the Gentiles on their conversion.

⁸¹ Cf. 2 Kings 12. 7 ff. Nathan rebuked David for having caused Urias to be killed in battle and for taking his wife to be his own wife.

⁸² 1 Cor. 10. 33.

⁸³ Gal. 1. 10.

⁸⁴ Isa. 57. 11.

⁸⁵ Ps. 128. 3. 'Wrought,' rendering the Vulgate *fabricaverunt.* The oppressors of Israel, from Pharao down to the Exile, had, as it were, ploughed her back like a field, leaving no part untouched by the cruel ploughshare. Gregory applies the text to the case of heavy burdens being put upon the back.

⁸⁶ Ezech. 8. 8-10. The passage cited by Gregory is an account of idolatrous practices which were shown in vision to the Prophet. Gregory applies the words to the disclosure to subjects of their faults.

⁸⁷ Col. 3. 5.

⁸⁸ Gal. 6. 1.

⁸⁹ Ezech. 4. 1-3. The passage is a prophecy of the siege and destruction of Jerusalem by the Babylonians in 587 B. C. Gregory applies it to the duty of the ruler to explain to his subjects virtues, vices, and temptations.

⁹⁰ 2 Cor. 11. 29.

⁹¹ Deut. 19. 5 f., with slight divergences.

⁹² 1 Tim. 4. 13.

⁹³ Ps. 118. 97.

⁹⁴ Exod. 25. 12-15.

⁹⁵ 1 Peter 3. 15. 'To satisfy,' that is, to give answer.

PART THREE

¹ Cf. *Orat.* 2. 15. Gregory of Nazianzus works out (*ibid.* 2. 16-34) at great length the treatment which physicians of souls must apply. But our author enumerates many more classes of people than does the former, and goes into great detail.

² 1 Tim. 5. 1.

³ Isa. 54. 4.

⁴ *Ibid.* 54.11.

⁵ *Ibid.* 48. 10. *Furnace of poverty:* Israel is represented as impure silver refined in the furnace, but not wholly purified.

⁶ 1 Tim. 6. 17. *High-minded,* that is, haughty. Gregory's *superbe sapere* is the Vulgate's *sublime sapere.*

⁷ Luke 6. 24.

⁸ Cf. 1 Kings 16. 23; 18. 10.

⁹ Cf. 2 Kings 12. 1 ff., where is recorded Nathan's story of the poor man's ewe lamb being stolen and slaughtered by the rich man. When David heard the story, he condemned himself by angrily denouncing the rich man in the Prophet's tale. His crime had been the death of Urias, and taking the man's wife as his own. David was punished by the death of the child of this union.

¹⁰ Luke 6. 25.

¹¹ John 16. 22.

¹² Col. 3. 21 f.

¹³ This stricture on superiors is cited by Gratian, *Decretum,* C. 11, q. 3, c. 3 (634 Friedberg).

¹⁴ Prov. 6. 6.

¹⁵ *Ibid.* 6. 1 f.

¹⁶ *Ibid.* 6. 3 f.

¹⁷ Cf. Ezech. 1. 18; 10. 12; Apoc. 4. 6.

¹⁸ Cf. 1 Kings 24. 4 ff.

¹⁹ *Ibid.* 24. 6.

²⁰ Exod. 16. 8.

²¹ Cf. Col. 3. 22.

²² 1 Tim. 6. 1.

²³ Eph. 6. 9. In the time of Gregory the Great slaves still constituted the backbone of the economic structure, agricultural and

industrial, of the Roman world. These also worked the lands of the Church's patrimony. Gregory's correspondence attests his deference to the contemporary civil legislation governing slavery as a juridical institution. At the same time this correspondence furnishes ample testimony of his vigilant efforts to protect and foster the legitimate liberation of slaves. His espousal of the Christian principle that all men, masters and slaves, were created equal (*aequaliter conditi, aequales per naturae consortium*, as he states in the present chapter), is most emphatic. We may quote the celebrated preamble of a document by which he manumitted two Roman slaves, Montana and Thomas (*Regist.* 6. 12 [1. 390 f. Ewald-Hartmann]): 'Since our Redeemer, the Creator of every creature, in His loving-kindness vouchsafed to assume human flesh for this purpose, that by the grace of His divinity He might break the bonds of the slavery in which we were formerly held, and restore us to freedom, it is a salutary deed to restore by the benefaction of manumission to the state of liberty in which they were born, men whom nature originally begot free but whom the law of nations subjected to the state of slavery. Wherefore, in view of our love and the consideration of this matter, we make you, Montana and Thomas, servants of the Holy Roman Church, whose servant we are by God's authority, free as from this day, and make you Roman citizens, and we release to you all your savings.' Gregory was particularly active in promoting the manumission of slaves who became sincere converts to Christianity or who were genuinely desirous of giving themselves to the practice of the monastic life; cf. *Regist.* 5. 57a. 6 (1. 365 E.-H.); 6. 10 (1. 388 f. E.-H.). Though he defended the legal rights of the Jews, he insisted on their observing the prohibition aganist their having Christian slaves; cf. *Regist.* 9. 213 and 215 (2. 199, 203 E.-H.); etc. Cf. J. Dutilleul, 'Esclavage,' *Dict. de théol. cat.* 5. 1 (1913) 457-519 (478 f., Gregory); R. Aigrain, in Fliche-Martin, *Histoire de l'Eglise* 5 (1947) 550-52; Dudden, *op. cit.* 1. 263; 393 f.; 2. 156-58; 181. For the history of slavery during the first Christian centuries, cf. P. Allard, *Les esclaves chrétiens depuis les premiers temps de l'Eglise jusqu'à la fin de la domination romaine en occident* (6th ed. Paris 1914).

[24] *Ut amittant scire quae sciunt*—so the majority of manuscripts. The meaning seems to be that the wise must not show themselves aware or conscious—that is, proud—of the knowledge they have.

The German translator Funk renders: 'The wise are to be reminded that one day they will lose their present knowledge.'

[25] 1 Cor. 3. 18.

[26] *Ibid.* 1. 26.

[27] *Ibid.* 1. 27.

[28] Rom. 1. 14.

[29] Heb. 8. 13, referring to the Old Covenant made obsolete by the New.

[30] *Ibid.* 11. 36 f.

[31] *Ibid.* 13. 7.

[32] Jer. 3. 3. The Prophet explains that the Jews persisted in their evil ways with the shameless arrogance of a harlot.

[33] Isa. 54. 4 f.

[34] Gal. 3. 1 and 3.

[35] Phil. 4. 10.

[36] Cf. 1 Cor. 1. 12; 3. 4.

[37] *Ibid.* 5. 1 f.

[38] 2 Thess. 1. 3 f.

[39] *Ibid.* 2. 1 f.

[40] 1 Cor. 13. 4.

[41] Prov. 19. 11.

[42] Eccles. 7. 9.

[43] Cf. Ezech. 43. 13.

[44] *Ibid.* 43. 14. Gregory attaches significance to the width of the trench, that of a standard unit of measurement among the Hebrews—one cubit, *'ammāh* (as one foot or one metre are standard units in modern systems of measurement). As the cubit is the unifying standard of the various measurements, so patience is the standard and unifying element of all other virtues.

[45] Gal. 6. 2.

[46] Prov. 16. 32.

[47] Luke 21. 19.

[48] Prov. 29. 11.

[49] 1 Cor. 13. 4.

[50] Eph. 4. 31.

[51] Matt. 5. 44; cf. Luke 6. 27 f.

[52] Matt. 7. 3.

[53] *Ibid.* 7. 5.

[54] Wisd. 2. 24.

[55] The thought that the Devil aggravates his own guilt and

punishment by his seductions of man, is also shared by St. Ambrose, *Comm. in Lucam* 7. 149. Cf. also John Chrysostom, *In Epist. ad Col. hom.* 2. 5.

[56] Gen. 4. 4 f.

[57] Prov. 14. 30. That is, the mental outlook of a man has an effect on the physical disposition of the body.

[58] John 16. 12.

[59] Rom. 16. 19.

[60] Matt. 10. 16.

[61] Ps. 139. 10. The mischief created by their own speech shall prove to be their destruction.

[62] Jer. 9. 5.

[63] Isa. 34. 14. Isaias mentions the hedgehog as one among the animals that will infest ruined Assyria, doomed to be depopulated and become the habitat of animals (cf. also *ibid.* 14. 23). Gregory takes the animal as a symbol of successful deceit and evasion. The present section, containing the comparison of the actions of the hedgehog and the behaviour of the insincere person, is taken by the author from his earlier work, *Mor.* 23. 29. 53 (ML 76. 707 D-708 B).

[64] Prov. 10. 9.

[65] Wisd. 1. 5.

[66] Prov. 3. 32.

[67] Soph. 1. 14-16. Gregory omits some expressions that would have made the warnings of the Prophet still more terrible. The present passage, incidentally, gave to Thomas of Celano the first line and keynote of his immortal sequence: *Dies irae, dies illa.*

[68] 2 Cor. 6. 2.

[69] Prov. 1. 24-26.

[70] *Ibid.* 1. 28.

[71] *Ibid.* 5. 9-11. That is, avoid the occasions of sin, especially of lust, which entails grave consequences to both soul and body.

[72] Ps. 77. 34.

[73] Apoc. 3. 19.

[74] Heb. 12. 5 f.; cf. Prov. 3. 12. The sorrows of the life of the just are proofs of God's love.

[75] Ps. 33. 20.

[76] Job 10. 15.

[77] Cf. 3 Kings 6. 7.

[78] Heb. 12. 9 f.

[79] Cf. Num. 22. 23 ff.—the episode of Balaam and the ass.

[80] 2 Peter 2. 16.

[81] Prov. 20. 30. Calamities and chastisements restore the order of justice, deter evil men from wrong-doing, and urge them to amendment. For the application of the present verse, see also Gregory, *Mor.* 23. 21. 40 (ML 76. 275 C).

[82] *Ibid.* 20. 27.

[83] 1 John 4. 18.

[84] Rom. 8. 15.

[85] 2 Cor. 3. 17. Gregory distinguishes very clearly between servile fear and filial fear. The latter is, of course, consistent with perfect love of God. Cf. Augustine, *In Ioan. Ev. tract.* 43. 7.

[86] Prov. 27. 22.

[87] Jer. 5. 3.

[88] *Ibid.* 15. 7.

[89] Isa. 9. 13.

[90] Jer. 51. 9.

[91] Ezech. 22. 18.

[92] *Ibid.* 24. 12.

[93] Jer. 6. 29.

[94] This strange belief is also found with other Fathers: cf. Augustine, *De civ. Dei* 21. 4; Isidore of Seville, *Etym.* 12. 1. 14; 16. 13. 2. All these authors seem to be dependent, directly or indirectly, on Pliny, *Nat. hist.* 20, *prooem.*; 37. 55. This polyhistor finds the invention so unusual that only gods can have devised it. For the history of the diamond in antiquity, see H. Blümner, 'Diamant,' Pauly-Wissowa, RE 5. 1 (1903) 322-4.

[95] Prov. 5. 1.

[96] Ps. 39. 13.

[97] 2 Kings 7. 27.

[98] Ecclus. 20. 7.

[99] Eccles. 3. 7.

[100] Ps. 140. 3.

[101] Prov. 25. 28.

[102] *Ibid.* 17. 14. *Letteth out water,* that is, acting like men who break open a dam and let the water flow out.

[103] *Ibid.* 18. 4.

[104] *Ibid.* 26. 10.

[105] Ps. 139. 12.

[106] Prov. 10. 19.

107 Isa. 32. 17.

108 James 1. 26.

109 *Ibid.* 1. 19.

110 *Ibid.* 3. 8.

111 Matt. 12. 36.

112 Prov. 19. 15.

113 *Ibid.*

114 Cf. *ibid.* 21. 26. The Vulgate has: *Tota die concupiscit et desiderat.*

115 Cf. Matt. 12. 44 f.

116 Prov. 20. 4.

117 Eccles. 11. 4. The sower must often disregard the weather, else he will never sow or reap. Those who fear temptations and do not act, will never have a reward. Cf. Gregory, *Mor.* 27. 9. 15 (ML 76. 406 D).

118 Ecclus. 32. 24.

119 Prov. 4. 25.

120 2 Tim. 4. 2.

121 Titus 2. 15.

122 1 Kings 25. 37. Nabal had greatly offended David by his churlish behaviour to David's servants. Abigail, the wife of Nabal, interceded for her husband and appeased the wrath of David. When Nabal died ten days later, Abigail became David's wife.

123 2 Kings 2. 22 f. After a battle in which Abner and his men of Israel were routed, Asael pursued Abner and was slain by him. The killing was done *adversa hasta,* probably not by a backward stroke of the spear, but with the butt-end of the weapon thrust by Abner facing Asael. This extremity of the lance was also pointed or spiked so that it could be set upright in the ground (cf. 1 Kings 26. 7). See Theodoret, *Quaest. in II Reg. interr.* 9.

124 Luke 18. 14.

125 Prov. 15. 33.

126 *Ibid.* 16. 18.

127 Isa. 66. 2, from a pre-Vulgate text, corresponding precisely to the Septuagint version. The Vulgate has: *To whom shall I have respect but to him that is poor and little, and of a contrite spirit, and that trembleth at my words?*

128 Ecclus. 10. 9.

129 Ps. 137. 6.

130 Matt. 20. 28.

131 Ecclus. 10. 15.

132 Phil. 2. 8.

133 Job. 41. 25. The Leviathan is referred to.

134 For an acute discussion of pride and of true and false humility, see John Chrysostom, *In Epist. ad Phil. hom.* 6. 3.

135 Num. 10. 29-31.

136 Rom. 12. 16.

137 Eph. 4. 14.

138 Prov. 1. 31.

139 *Ibid.* 15. 7. The fool is contrasted with the wise man. The latter dispenses knowledge, that is, truth, but the mind of the fool dispenses folly and falsehood.

140 A conflation of John 5. 30 and 6. 38 f.

141 *Ibid.* 5. 30.

142 2 Cor. 1. 17. St. Paul repels the charge of insincerity, levity, and fickleness.

143 Luke 16. 24.

144 Exod. 32. 6.

145 Gen. 3. 14, following a pre-Vulgate text.

146 4 Kings 25. 10; Jer. 52. 12. The *princeps cocorum* of Gregory is the Vulgate *princeps militum* ('commander of the troops') of 4 Kings, and *magister militum* ('general of the army') of Jeremias. The Septuagint gives in both places ἀρχιμάγειρος which appears in several manuscripts of the Old Latin version as *princeps coquorum* ('the chief cook'): cf. P. Sabatier, *Bibliorum Sacrorum latinae versiones antiquae* (Paris 1751) 2. 2. 720 f.

147 2 Peter 1. 5 f. That is, furnish your faith with virtue, your virtue with knowledge, etc.

148 Rom. 14. 3.

149 Col. 2. 23. A proud exaggerated austerity is merely inflated sensuality. Cf. also St. Augustine, *De Serm. Dom. in Monte* 2. 12. 40 f.

150 Luke 18. 12.

151 Isa. 58. 3 f. The Prophet complains that the Jews on their fast days do as they please, with no regard for God's will in the matter.

152 *Ibid.* 58. 4. The Jews do not profit spiritually from their fastings, but add new sins to their old ones.

153 *Ibid.* 58. 5, 7.

154 Joel 2. 15. The Prophet exhorts the people to come together

to worship God, and beseech Him to lay aside His wrath.

155 Zach. 7. 5 f.

156 Luke 21. 34 f.

157 Matt. 15. 11.

158 1 Cor. 6. 13.

159 Rom. 13. 13.

160 1 Cor. 8. 8.

161 Titus 1. 15. The legal distinction between clean and unclean is no longer binding. All things are clean to the pure in mind. St. Paul's statement—*All things are clean to the clean*—has a sententious or axiomatic ring and has, therefore, lways been quoted, and sometimes misquoted: see the study by J. C. Plumpe, 'Omnia munda mundis,' *Theol. Stud.* 6 (1945) 509-523.

162 Phil. 3. 19.

163 1 Tim. 4. 1, 3. Continence was enjoined in some pagan rites. St. Paul warns the Corinthians against being seduced by pagan errors in regard to marriage and other matters. Every creature of God is good. *He that giveth his virgin* (daughter) *in marriage doth well* (1 Cor. 7. 38).

164 Rom. 14. 21.

165 1 Tim. 5. 23.

166 God has entrusted, not given, wealth to certain people, that they be wise custodians and dispensers of it to the actual owners, the poor and needy—a thought recurring frequently in the patristic writings: cf. Basil, *Hom. de avar.* 6. 2, 7; *Hom. in div.* 3; John Chrysostom, *In Matt. hom.* 77. 4; Augustine, *Enarr. in Ps.* 147. 12 ('res alienae possidentur, cum superflua possidentur').

167 1 Peter 4. 11.

168 Luke 17. 10.

169 2 Cor. 9. 7.

170 Matt. 6. 3.

171 Luke 14. 12-14.

172 Prov. 3. 28.

173 Very strangely, this apothegm, repeatedly quoted by the Fathers as in the Bible, is not found there. It is adduced as Biblical in the *Didache* 1. 6 (cf. J. A. Kleist's note, ACW 6. 155), and by Augustine, *Enarr. in Ps.* 102. 12: '*Desudet eleemosyna in manu tua*, donec invenias iustum, cui eam tradas.' The thought that one should not give rashly, but investigate a case in hand with prudence, is found in Ecclus. 12. 1: *If thou do good, know to whom*

thou dost it.
174 2 Cor. 9. 6.
175 *Ibid.* 8. 13 f.
176 Luke 6. 30.
177 Ecclus. 12. 5, 6.
178 Tob. 4. 18.

179 Gregory's example of 'the wicked'—actors—is characteristic of the ancient Roman contempt for people practising the histrionic art. In the present series, see especially Arnobius's trenchant criticism, *Adv. nat.* 4. 35 f., 7. 33; also the very informative notes by G. E. McCracken, ACW 8. 564 n. 226 and 613 n. 113. For the oldest canonical legislation against actors, see J. Quasten, *Musik und Gesang in den Kulten der heidnischen Antike und christlichen Frühzeit* (Liturgiegeschichtl. Quellen u. Forsch. 5, Münster i. W. 1930) 166-72.

180 Luke 12. 23; Matt. 6. 25.
181 Ibid. 25. 41-43.
182 Hab. 2. 6.
183 Isa. 5. 8.

184 It is, indeed, difficult to find indications in Gregory's writings that he had any acquaintance with the ancient classical authors; cf. F. H. Dudden, *op. cit.* 1. 284. But this description of the greedy rich panting for additional wealth—cum augendis *pecuniis inhiant* —may very well be indebted to Horace's description of the rich miser falling asleep as he regards his moneybags with open-mouthed affection (*Sat.* 1. 1. 70 f.): congestis undique saccis indormis *inhians.*

185 Eccles. 5. 9. Love of God and love of money do not harmonize —see St. Augustine, *In Ioan. Ev. tract.* 40. 10.

186 Prov. 28. 20.
187 *Ibid.* 20. 21.
188 Matt. 16. 26.

189 Ibid. 6. 1. Though we are to do good works that we may be seen by men, and that God may be glorified, we are forbidden to do our good works merely that we may be seen by men. No reward can be given for such ostentation.

190 Ps. 111. 9.

191 Prov. 21. 26. The just man will not cease giving alms; or, the just man who gives alms will be rewarded and enriched by God, and will always be able to give alms.

[192] Cf. Luke 13. 7.

[193] Cf. Luke 16. 19 ff.

[194] Ps. 48. 8 f. No man can give a bond to God, nor a ransom for himself. Riches cannot ransom us from death.

[195] Luke 3. 9, words of St. John the Baptist recorded by St. Luke.

[196] Isa. 61. 8.

[197] Prov. 21. 27. The sacrifices of the wicked are offered in wickedness, that is, with evil intention, or are offerings of what is stolen.

[198] Ecclus. 34. 24.

[199] Agg. 1. 6. Your wages profit you nothing when you squander them to no purpose.

[200] Gal. 5. 22.

[201] 1 Cor. 3. 3.

[202] Heb. 12. 14.

[203] Eph. 4. 3 f.

[204] Ps. 150. 4.

[205] Mark 9. 49. As salt preserves from corruption, the pastor must have in himself that which will keep him and his subjects from the corruption of sin, and make them a pleasing sacrifice.

[206] James 3. 14 f., 17.

[207] Matt. 5. 23 f.

[208] John 14. 27.

[209] Gregory interprets 'leave' (Vulg. *relinquo*) in the sense of 'abandon,' 'disclaim.' Elsewhere, *Mor.* 6. 34. 53 (ML 75. 758 B), he explains that the peace 'left' by the Saviour is 'initial' peace, consisting of man's terrestrial longing for his Creator; while the peace 'given' is 'perfect' peace, the peace of beatific vision in Heaven.

[210] Ps. 138. 21 f.

[211] Cf. Exod. 32. 27 ff.

[212] Cf. Num. 25. 7. Phinees, in his indignation, killed an Israelite with his dagger for going in to a prostitute.

[213] Matt. 10. 34.

[214] 2 Par. 19. 2 f. The prophet was Jehu. The 'groves' removed were the seats of idolatrous worship.

[215] Ps. 119. 7.

[216] Rom. 12. 18.

[217] 2 Thess. 3. 14 f.

[218] Matt. 13. 28.

[219] Prov. 6. 12-14.

²²⁰ Matt. 5. 9.

²²¹ Job 41. 14. The whole body is firm and compact and bound together.

²²² *Ibid.* 41. 7.

²²³ Acts 23. 6.

²²⁴ Amos 1. 13. The Ammonites wished to secure for themselves the fertile land of Galaad, and exterminated its inhabitants, even to the slaughter of infants in the womb.

²²⁵ Cf. Gen. 31. 47 f.

²²⁶ See St. Augustine's interpretation of *meus est Galaad* (Ps. 59. 9), *Enarr. in Ps.* 59. 9. He applies the signification 'heap of testimony' to the martyrs.

²²⁷ Osee 2. 8.

²²⁸ 1 Peter 4. 11—that is, if any man speak, let it be as delivering the words of God.

²²⁹ 2 Cor. 2. 17.

²³⁰ Prov. 16. 5.

²³¹ *Ibid.* 5. 15-17. The metaphor of the cistern and the fountains is used to signify the relations of husband to wife. Gregory applies the passage to the pastor's preaching.

²³² Ps. 53. 5.

²³³ Ecclus. 20. 32.

²³⁴ Prov. 11. 26.

²³⁵ Jer. 48. 10. He was cursed who, being ordered by God to lay waste the land of the Moabites, did not fulfil the divine purpose. So, too, is any man cursed who does the work of God negligently.

²³⁶ Deut. 32. 42.

²³⁷ Cf. Matt. 25. 24-30.

²³⁸ Acts 20. 26 f.

²³⁹ Apoc. 22. 17.

²⁴⁰ Isa. 6. 5. On the serious consequences to the minister who because of fear or diffidence fails to preach to his charges and to reprimand them, cf. especially Julianus Pomerius, *Vita contempl.* 1. 20. 2 f. (ACW 4. 42 f.); also St. Augustine, *Serm.* 46. 20.

²⁴¹ Prov. 11. 25. He that comes to the assistance of others in their need will be more than rewarded for his efforts and sacrifices.

²⁴² Ps. 39. 10.

²⁴³ Cant. 8. 13. In the following Gregory applies the traditional interpretation of the bridegroom and bride of the Canticle of Canticles as the divine Bridegroom Christ and His Bride, the Church.

For the material in the patristic literature, cf. S. Tromp, 'Ecclesia Sponsa Virgo Mater,' *Gregorianum* 28 (1937) 3-29; cf. C. Chavasse, *The Bride of Christ. An Enquiry into the Nuptial Element in Early Christianity* (London 1940), *passim*.

[244] Exod. 32. 26 f. The killing of these sinners at the behest of Moses was merely a fulfilment of a divine command.

[245] See Gregory Nazianzen's animated description, *Orat.* 1. 49, of men with little preparation rushing to be ordained and presuming to instruct the faithful. Rashness in seeking, or imparting, ordination to the sacerdotal office is also dwelt on by John Chrysostom. *De sac.* 4. 1 f.

[246] Luke 24. 49.

[247] Ecclus. 32. 10 f.

[248] Luke 2. 42 f.

[249] *Ibid.* 2. 46.

[250] 1 Tim. 4. 11 f.

[251] Eccles. 11. 9. The Romans usually distinguished five stages or ages in human life: 1) *pueritia,* childhood, boyhood, up to the 15th (17th) year; 2) *adolescentia,* (earlier) youth, approaching manhood, up to the 20th or even 30th year; 3) *iuventus,* youth, young manhood, from the 20(30)th to the 40(45)th year; 4) *aetas seniorum,* manhood, fully matured and in its best years, from the 40(45)th to the 60th year; 5) *senectus,* old age, beginning with the 61st year. In the present passage Gregory suggests that the Vulgate does not always distinguish sharply between *adolescentia* and *iuventus,* but actually uses the terms interchangeably; and that, therefore, Paul's reference—in Jerome's version—to Timothy's age as *adolescentia* does not prove that Timothy was told to *command and teach* when he was still of immature age.

[252] Ezech. 36. 5.

[253] Prov. 1. 32. Those who in their smallness turn away from wisdom shall be destroyed, and the prosperity of fools which engenders an arrogant sense of security and urges them to despise wisdom, shall be their ruin.

[254] Cf. 1 Cor. 7. 29. Gregory applies the passage to the shortness of the span of human life.

[255] Cant. 2. 6.

[256] Prov. 3. 16.

[257] Ps. 107. 7.

[258] Exod. 15. 6.

259 Ps. 104. 44 f.

260 *Ibid.* 72. 18.

261 Luke 16. 25 ff.

262 For the same simile of God the Physician refusing many of our pleas because He wishes to preserve our spiritual health, or to restore it, see St. Augustine, *Serm.* 237. 6. 5. Sometimes this divine Physician also resorts to a more radical means of restoring health— spiritual surgery, for instance, the excision of concupiscence. And this Surgeon is a master of His art: no patient ever dies under His hands through His fault, for He who has made *(creavit)* body and soul of every patient, also knows how to restore *(recreet)* the health of each; cf. the beautiful exposition in Augustine, *Enarr. in Ps.* 102. 5. On Christ the Physician, see the remarks by J. C. Plumpe, ACW 5. 190 f.

263 'Hinc ergo de spe aeternae haereditatis gaudium sumant, quos adversitas vitae temporalis humiliat; quia *nisi salvandos in perpetuum cerneret, erudiendos sub disciplinae regimine divina dispensatio non frenaret.* As in other problems of theology, Gregory's views on predestination are predominantly Augustinian. This is also evident from passages in his greater work, the *Moralia:* 16.25. 30 (ML 75. 1134-6); 18. 63-5 (ML 76. 73-5). Cf. R. Garrigou—Lagrange, 'Prédestination III,' *Dict. de la théol. cat.* 12. 2 (1935) 2901; Dudden, *op. cit.* 2. 400-402.

264 1. 3; but see also 3. 2 and n. 9.

265 Cf. 3 Kings 11. 4 ff.

266 1 Cor. 7. 29 f.

267 *Ibid.* 7. 31.

268 Gal. 6. 2.

269 Gregory here appears to state that married people pass beyond the bounds of wedlock, when they seek pleasure in marital intercourse. Such was the strict view of some ancient writers. It is, indeed, true that if the married make pleasure the sole purpose of their act, and indulge in it for pleasure alone, to the exclusion of every rational purpose, then undoubtedly they are hedonists. Their act then becomes irrational and sinful. But that is not to say that married people are not allowed to take pleasure in the exercise of a natural function, and even to be induced to exercise the act, moved thereto by the anticipation of pleasure, provided that they do not exclude every rational purpose of their activity. St. Augustine, in his *Faith, Hope, and Charity (Enchiridion)* 21. 78, wrote

(trans. by L. A. Arand, ACW 3. 77 f.): 'Thus we see that for some sins allowance was made even by the Apostles. Such was the case, for instance, when the venerable Paul said to married people: *Defraud not one another, except by consent for a time, that you may give yourselves to prayer; and return together again, lest Satan tempt you for your incontinency.* Here this could possibly be considered as being no sin, that is, for married people to have intercourse, not for the sake of procreating offspring—which is the purpose of marriage—but also for the sake of carnal pleasure, thus providing an escape for the incontinent weak from the deadly sin of fornication, or adultery, or any other form of uncleanness which it is shameful even to mention, but to which they might be seduced by lust through the temptation of Satan. It is possible, I said, that this should not be thought a sin, had Paul not added: *But I speak this by way of concession, not by commandment.* And now, who will deny this to be a sin, when admittedly those who do this have only a concession made on apostolic authority to excuse them?'

St. Augustine stated that view in several passages of his writings. Most of the earlier Christian writers shared this view, but not St. John Chrysostom, *De virg.* 19. 29. The strict interpretation of the words of St. Paul is incorrect. The concession mentioned by St. Paul is the concession to do what is less perfect, but not sinful, since sin cannot be conceded or permitted; cf. Dr. Arand's remarks, *op. cit.* 135 f. For Gregory's views on Christian marriage, cf. L. Godefroy, 'Mariage dans les Pères: après Saint-Augustin,' *Dict. de théol. cat.* 9. 2 (1927) 2116 f.

[270] 1 Cor. 7. 1 f.

[271] *Ibid.* 7. 3.

[272] *Ibid.* 7. 6.

[273] Cf. Gen. 19 f.

[274] The word *scelus* is used, which, along with *crimen*, is employed by Gregory to express 'extreme modes of *peccatum*'; cf. Dudden, *op. cit.* 2. 385. For the early Christian concept of grievous or 'mortal' sin, cf. P. Galtier, *op. cit.* 259-63, 303-320 (Augustine); J. Mausbach, *Die Ethik des hl. Augustinus* (2nd ed. Freiburg i. Br. 1929) 1. 230-35.

[275] Gen. 19. 20.

[276] *Ibid.* 19. 21.

[277] 1 Cor. 7. 5.

[278] *Ibid.* 7. 35.

[279] *Ibid.* 6. 9 f.

[280] Heb. 13. 4.

[281] 1 Cor. 7. 9. It is better to marry than to abandon oneself to ravaging concupiscence; cf. also St. Paul's advice (1 Tim. 5. 14) to young widows that they remarry.

[282] Luke 9. 62.

[283] Jer. 3. 3; cf. above, n. 32 to Part 3.

[284] Ezech. 23. 3. The Prophet describes the many misdeeds of the people of Samaria and Jerusalem, both descended from Abraham and Sara, under the figure of two sisters who have become harlots. Gregory applies the passage to admonitions to be given by the pastor to those who have been unchaste.

[285] Jer. 3. 1. The Jews deserved to be described by God as a wife who had committed fornication. She deserves to be deserted by her husband. But God does not, like other husbands, divorce her, but He invites the Jews to return to Him, though they had prostituted themselves, as it were, to many lovers. On the faithful love of God Yahweh for His spouse, ever-unfaithful Israel, see the study by J. Ziegler, *Die Liebe Gottes bei den Propheten* (Alttest. Abh. 11. 3, Münster i. W. 1930) 49-85: 'Das Bild der Ehe.'

[286] Isa. 30. 20 f.

[287] *Ibid.* 56. 4 f.

[288] Apoc. 14. 4.

[289] Cf. *ibid.* 14. 3.

[290] This incorruption *(incorruptio carnis)* is the final state of imperishableness, or immortality, of soul and body as a reward for our faithfulness when we were in our perishable, mortal bodies—the state of corruption; for *incorruptio* (ἀφθαρσία) as a designation for the reward of immortality in Heaven, cf. Rom. 2. 7; Eph. 6. 24; 2 Tim. 1. 10; 1 Cor. 15. 43: 'Seminatur in corruptione, surget in incorruptione.'

[291] Matt. 19. 11.

[292] Isa. 23. 4.

[293] Elsewhere, *Mor.* 1. 37. 55 (ML 75. 554), Gregory states that the good we do avails us nothing, if we relax and do not continue doing good to the end.

[294] Luke 7. 47.

[295] *Ibid.* 15. 7.

[296] Ps. 79. 6. By its humiliation through Assyria, God had given the Jewish people the drink and bread of tears in full measure. Cf.

also Ps. 41. 4: *My tears have been my bread day and night.*

²⁹⁷ *Ibid.* 50. 11.

²⁹⁸ *Ibid.* 50. 5.

²⁹⁹ Isa. 43. 25 f. Gregory here quotes from a Latin version of the Septuagint. The Vulgate reads: *I will not remember thy sins. Put me in remembrance.*

³⁰⁰ Lam. 3. 48.

³⁰¹ Ps. 94. 2.

³⁰² 1 Cor. 11. 31.

³⁰³ Gen. 34. 1-3.

³⁰⁴ Gregory here states the doctrine of concupiscence and indicates the stages in sins of concupiscence. The sensitive faculty is first moved to concupiscence, the rational faculty apprehends the pleasure; if the will accepts irrational pleasure, sin is committed. This is set forth in detail in *Mor.* 4. 26. 49-28. 54 (ML 75. 661-5). See also *Hom. in Ev.* 16. 1 (ML 76. 1135). Cf. Dudden, *op. cit.* 2. 385 f.

³⁰⁵ There are three stages in the progress of sin, namely, the temptation of the Devil, the concupiscence of the flesh, and the consent of the will. See also Gregory, *Regist.* 11. 56a. 9 (343 Ewald-Hartmann). Cf. Rom. 7. 23: *But I see another law in my members, fighting against the law of my mind, and captivating me in the law of sin, that is in my members.* Gregory adds a fourth element in sin, namely a proud contumacy by which a man seeks to justify his sinful act: *audacia defensionis per elationem;* cf. *Mor.* 4. 49 (ML 75. 661).

³⁰⁶ Ps. 31. 5.

³⁰⁷ From the first part of the present chapter, in which St. Gregory discusses recidivism, or the reversion to sin, four passages were extracted by Gratian, *Decretum, De penitentia,* D. 3, cc. 13-16 (1213 f. Friedberg).

³⁰⁸ 2 Peter 2. 22; cf. also Prov. 20. 11. This metaphor of the dog or sow, introduced by St. Peter as a 'true proverb,' was frequently quoted by the Fathers in discussing relapses into sin: cf. John Chrysostom, *In Gen. hom.* 6. 1; Augustine, *Enarr. in Ps.* 83. 3; Jerome, *Epist.* 54. 4.

³⁰⁹ Ecclus. 7. 15. Do not commit again the sin you have deplored.

³¹⁰ Isa. 1. 16.

³¹¹ Ecclus. 34. 30.

³¹² James 4. 4.

313 Num. 23. 10.

314 *Ibid.* 24. 14.

315 Rom. 7. 23.

316 Gregory anticipated the reply given to heretics of later days, who maintain that mere cessation from sinning, or a change of mind, that is, a determination not to sin again, is sufficient, and no formal sorrow is needed for forgiveness. In one of his earliest sermons, *Serm.* 351. 5. 12, St. Augustine had already made this clear statement: 'Non enim sufficit mores in melius commutare, et a factis malis recedere, nisi etiam de his quae facta sunt, satisfiat Deo per poenitentiae dolorem, per humilitatis gemitum, per contriti cordis sacrificium, cooperantibus eleemosynis.'

317 Ps. 74. 5.

318 *Ibid.* 50. 19. The Vulgate reads: *A contrite and humbled heart, O God, Thou wilt not despise.*

319 1 Cor. 6. 11.

320 Acts 2. 38.

321 Regarding Gregory's insistence on penance to be performed prior to the reception of baptism, cf. Galtier, *op. cit.* 125. In this Gregory was, of course, only upholding ancient Christian tradition: for instance, on fasting as a prerequisite for baptism, see the *Didache* 7. 4; Justin, *Apol.* 1. 61. 2; Tertullian, *De bapt.* 20. 1; *Peregr. Aetheriae* 46. 1; etc.

322 Isa. 3. 9.

323 Gen. 18. 20.

324 Luke 12. 47.

325 Ps. 54. 16. The word 'alive' implies the suddenness of their damnation; cf. Num. 16. 33: *And they went down alive into hell.*

326 That our life here on earth is a constant warfare for Christ against the forces of hell, is a thought that pervades all patristic writings from the beginning (cf. the previous volumes in the series— ACW 2. 148 n. 339; 5. 190 n. 140; 7. 304 n. 22). But the thought had received its classical formulation earlier, in the Old Testament; cf. Job 7. 1: *Militia est vita hominis super terram.*

327 Prov. 23. 35. The man steeped in sin who wishes to sin again is compared to the drunken man who is insensible to pain when intoxicated, but on waking, wishes for wine again.

328 *Ibid.* 23. 34. 'Stern' = 'helm,' 'tiller,' 'rudder.' The metaphor of life as a voyage over tempestuous seas, or of the life of the Christian as a voyage into eternity on the ship of the Church, always

appealed to the imagination of the Fathers. Frequently such comparisons contain reminiscences of the wanderings and adventures of the ancient rover of the seas, Odysseus. See the very interesting discussion and collection of materials by H. Rahner, *Griechische Mythen in christlicher Deutung* (Zurich 1945) 430 ff.: 'Die Seefahrt des Lebens.'

[329] Cant. 3. 8.

[330] *Ibid.* 7. 4. The outstanding feature of the face, namely, the nose, is compared to a tower standing out over the plain.

[331] Jer. 4. 4. The Vulgate has *cogitationum* for *studiorum*.

[332] *Ibid.* 23. 2.

[333] Ps. 1. 1.

[334] Ecclus. 19. 1.

[335] Matt. 23. 24.

[336] *Ibid.* 23. 23.

[337] Jer. 1. 10.

[338] Acts 2. 22-24. The verses are from the second part of St. Peter's address to the Jews after the descent of the Holy Spirit on Pentecost.

[339] *Aedificationem sanctae praedicationis. Aedificatio* (οἰκοδομή, οἰκοδομία) is an important concept in the New Testament, especially in the Pauline epistles (Rom. 15. 2, 1 Cor. 14. 26, Eph. 4. 29, etc.), whence it found its way into many passages of the Fathers (cf. esp. Hermas). *Aedificatio* designates the act of 'building,' 'building up,' usually taken in the spiritual sense of 'causing (promoting) or making advancement or progress' within the Christian community or in the individual Christian. This comes about through preaching, example, etc.—hence our English 'edification.' Cf. H. M. Scott, 'The Place of οἰκοδομή in the New Testament,' *Princeton Theol. Rev.* 2 (1904) 402-424; O. Michel, 'οἰκοδομέω, οἰκοδομή,' *Theol. Wörterb. z. Neuen Test.* 5 (1949) 139-50.

[340] Acts 2. 37 f.

[341] *Ibid.* 9. 5-7.

[342] Prov. 18. 9.

[343] Apoc. 3. 2.

[344] 2 Peter 2. 21.

[345] Apoc. 3. 15.

[346] Matt. 23. 27.

[347] *Ibid.* 6. 2.

[348] *Ibid.* 5. 16.

349 *Ibid.* 6. 1.

350 1 Cor. 8. 9. The Corinthians had proposed the following problem to St. Paul: much of the meat served in their pagan surroundings, both on public occasions and at private meals, was actually sacrificial meat, that is, it had been previously offered in idolatrous sacrifice. Meats sold in the shops and markets had also been consecrated in a special manner to the gods. Hence it was quite difficult, if not impossible, for Christians to obtain meat that was not somehow contaminated by pagan religious custom. Paul observes that some Christians (the 'strong') with advanced—and correct—ideas, had no scruples against buying and using such meats: there was only one God, the meat 'consecrated' to the 'gods' was still an indifferent article—plain meat. The Apostle indicates that some of these better instructed Christians, to show their disdain of pagan ritual, or to put into practice their new enlightenment, might even go so far as to eat 'plain meat' by taking part in the pagan religious services or banquets. He warns such 'liberals' against going too far and that they must not, by their proud exhibitionism, cause scandal to the 'weak'; that is, those who do not as yet realise that, ordinarily, and apart from actual participation in pagan religious rites, it is not sinful for Christians to partake of such meats, but who, nevertheless, following the example of their enlightened brethren, eat of them in bad faith and, consequently, sin. See J. Sickenberger, *Die Briefe des hl. Paulus an die Korinther und Römer* (4th ed. Bonn 1932) 38-40; C. Lattey, *Readings in First Corinthians* (St. Louis—London 1928) 149-55.

351 *Ibid.* 8. 11 f.

352 Lev. 19. 14.

353 Here the Migne edition, followed by Hurter and Hedley, reads '*nunquam*,' obviously a misprint for '*namque*' (so in the older editions—Galliccioli, Dillinger, etc.).

354 Rom. 13. 3.

355 Gregory obviously refers especially to difficult and obscure passages in Holy Writ. On this subject Augustine, *De doct. Christ* 4. 9. 23, has this to say: 'There are certain passages whose import is not understood, or scarcely understood, however thoroughly, however much, and however clearly they may be treated by the speaker's oratory. Such matters should never be brought before a popular audience, or but rarely, when there is some need for it.'

356 Luke 12. 42; cf. Matt. 24. 45.

[357] 1 Cor. 3. 1 f.; cf. Lattey, *op. cit.* 68-70.
[358] Cf. Exod. 34. 33.
[359] *Ibid.* 21. 33 f.
[360] Job 38. 36. The instinct of the cock is compared to intelligence.
[361] Rom. 13. 11.
[362] 1 Cor. 15. 34.
[363] *Gallus iste,* apparently referring back to the text in Job 38. 36 —cf. above, n. 360.

PART FOUR

[1] Ezech. 32. 19. The Prophet warns the people of Egypt of the abominable doom that awaits them. Neither beauty, nor pride, nor power will avail them anything. The uncircumcised were loathed by the Jews. The same attitude is here implied for the Egyptians, who also practiced circumcision. In effect, the latter are told by the Prophet: The greater your overweening pride, the greater will be your fall, the more detestable your lot.
[2] *Ibid.* 16. 14 f.
[3] Ps. 77. 61.
[4] *Ibid.* 29. 7 f.
[5] *Ibid.* 118. 107.
[6] Ezech. 2. 1, 3, 6, 8; 3. 1, 3, 4, 6; etc.
[7] As at the conclusion Gregory again turns to his addressee, Bishop John of Ravenna, so, too, in concluding he practises what he has preached in this last part and throughout the treatise— return to self, self-examination.

INDEX

INDEX

ANCIENT CHRISTIAN WRITERS

The Works of the Fathers in Translation

Edited by

J. QUASTEN, S. T. D., and J. C. PLUMPE, Ph. D.